Man and Woman, *Alone and Together*

*Gender Roles, Identity,
and Intimacy in a Changing Culture*

A
BRIDGEPOINT
BOOK

BridgePoint,
the academic
imprint of
Victor Books, is
your connection
for the best in
serious reading
that integrates
the passion of
the heart with
the scholarship
of the mind.

MAN & WOMAN
ALONE & TOGETHE[R]

KAYE COOK & LANCE LEE

A
BRIDGEPOINT
BOOK

Unless otherwise noted, Scripture quotations are from the *New American Standard Bible,* © the Lockman Foundation 1960, 1962, 1963, 1968, 1971, 1972, 1973, 1975, 1977. Other quotations are from the *Holy Bible, New International Version* (NIV), © 1973, 1978, 1984, International Bible Society. Used by permission of Zondervan Bible Publishers; the *Revised Standard Version of the Bible* (RSV), © 1946, 1952, 1971, 1973; and the *New Revised Standard Version of the Bible* (NRSV), © 1989 by the Directors of Christian Education of the National Council of the Churches of Christ in the United States of America.

Copyediting: Robert N. Hosack
Cover Design: Mardelle Ayres
Manuscript Coordinator: Howard Frost

Library of Congress Cataloging-in-Publication Data

Cook, Kaye V.
　　Man and woman : alone and together / by Kaye V. Cook and Lance Lee.
　　　　p.　　cm.
　　Includes bibliographical references and index.
　　ISBN 0-89693-181-1
　　1. Sex role — Religious aspects — Christianity. 2. Sex role — Biblical teaching. 3. Sexism — Religious aspects — Christianity. 4. Men (Christian theology) 5. Women (Christian theology) 6. Interpersonal relations — Religious aspects — Christianity.
　　I. Lee, Lance (Lance L.) II. Title.
　　BT708.C66　　1992
　　261.8'343–dc20　　　　　　　　　　　　　　　　92-7909
　　　　　　　　　　　　　　　　　　　　　　　　　　　　CIP

BridgePoint is the academic imprint of Victor Books.

1 2 3 4 5 6 7 8 9 10 Printing/Year 96 95 94 93 92

Contents

Preface   7

Gender Roles in Transition:
A Model of Adaptation

1   *Gender Roles: A Contemporary Crisis*   13
2   *Identity and Interdependence: In Quest of a Biblical Model*   29
3   *A Developmental Model of Gender-Mature Spirituality*   49

Gender Roles:
Their Problems and Possibilities

4   *Becoming Male and Female: Myths and Realities*   67
5   *The Total (and Totaled) Woman*   87
6   *Modern Masculinity: In Transition from Macho to Sensitive*   115
7   *The New Male and Female: Great Expectations and Their Stresses*   136

Responding to Our Calling

8   *Relationships: Avoiding Stereotypes and Being a Friend*   161
9   *Singleness: Living in a Couples' World*   182
10   *Successfully Negotiating the Dating Game*   203
11   *Marriage: Old Dance, New Steps*   226
12   *Toward the Future: Redeeming Man and Woman in Community and the Church*   250

Index   285

Dedication:

for Kaye: To Chuck, who continually challenges me to gender-role flexibility, and to Jennie and Caleb, who teach me daily about growing up female and male.

for Lance: To Sandy,
            whose precious ways
            and love, tender and true,
            are living proof that God
            still performs miracles.

Preface

Becoming an adult—you might think—would be enjoyable, yet many people reaching this stage in their lives find themselves facing crises in male-female relationships that seem more problematic and anxiety provoking than they should be. Whether in friendships, dating relationships, or marriage, many adults in relationships with women or men, may feel that their expectations of themselves are out of step with cultural, church, or family expectations. They may be in "the marriage crisis," fearing they are incomplete or inadequate if they are not married by the age of twenty-four. They may be in "relationship crisis," experiencing difficulties in developing healthy professional or personal friendships with members of the other sex, perhaps because they carry expectations of themselves or others that are no longer true. Or they may be in "whole-life crisis," feeling a vague sense of unease about their personal and work lives because they feel that one or the other is incomplete, that their work life is too encroaching, or that the two are too separate.

In this book we examine modern gender roles in our society, focusing on recent changes in roles and the problems and possibilities these changes create. We will consider the implications of these changes for friendships between the two sexes in a wide variety of circumstances: at home, at work, in dating, and in marriage. Our orientation is primarily toward people in their mid-twenties to mid-forties—the "baby-boom generation"—but the issues we address certainly affect people both younger and older. Indeed, while there have been a number of books written for Christians to guide them with dating, getting married, and living a healthy, godly life as a "single" (Why has singleness come to imply "being alone" rather than "being a whole person?"), there have been very few books that have tried to address the complexities and the simple joys of how we get along with one another as males and females experiencing together these changing times.

Our current society has witnessed marked changes in gender roles. To a degree astonishing to members of earlier generations, women go to college, establish careers, work after college before marriage, and work after marriage even if they have young children.

Men, perhaps surprisingly, participate in greater numbers in child-birth and child care. Men and women together are active in a range of traditional and not-so-traditional relationships, establishing cross-sex friendships at work and in their personal lives that are not necessarily sexual, and marital relationships that range from traditional to egalitarian. Many young adults are unaware of the degree to which their lives have been shaped by these changes in our society.

The ideas we present in this book reflect our experiences and professional training. We nevertheless believe—first and foremost—that Scripture should be the basis for our understanding of gender roles and relationships and the touchstone for our experience. We believe that the biblical model for these roles and relationships is one of mutual equality, respect, and responsibility. Further, we believe that the Bible focuses more on how we treat one another as persons than on prescribing specific behaviors for men and women.

We believe that there are not only social or ethical reasons to seek improved relations between the two genders, but also clear biblical injunctions to do so. By this we mean that we should consider improving our relationships with members of the other gender not just because doing so would be "nice" or "socially beneficial," but indeed because God commands us to care about and nurture others, even if that might be difficult (e.g., "you shall love your neighbor as yourself," Rom. 13:9; "do not be conformed to this world, but be transformed by the renewing of your mind," Rom. 12:2). At the same time that we affirm the value of Scripture and of our relationship with God, we also believe that non-Christians reading this book may find useful ideas for their own relationships with other members of the other sex.

We would like to thank those who have been helpful in putting this book together. Our heartfelt thanks to those who have participated in relationship with us. You have taught us much. Thanks to our clients, who have shared their concerns and their growth, and who have helped us refine our ideas. They are not responsible for any shortcomings the book may have. Special thanks to Beth, Ginny, Hyung Goo, Joe, Margaret, Nancy, Ray, Rob, and Ruth, who participated together in the small group on gender roles that inspired this book. We have used their particular experiences extensively throughout the book and think you will learn much from their experiences, as we have. Special thanks also to Gretchen Gaebelein Hull, Catherine Clark Kroeger, Nan, Joyce, Monica, Charity, Brenda, Chris, Steve, Ann, and Doug who carefully reviewed sections of the manuscript, improving it by their comments, and to Beth deAngelis who helped prepare the index and eagerly participated in multiple other small ways, making the preparation of this manuscript more enjoyable. Thanks to Rob Portlock who created cartoons to help our readers visualize our message. Thanks to our editor at Victor Books, Robert Hosack, who believed in our calling and diligently shepherded this book through the publication process. Finally, we would like to thank our collaborator and manuscript coordinator Dr. Howard Frost, whose idea this book was originally. Without his perseverance, this book would not have been written; without his editing skills, it would not have so clearly communicated its message.

Kaye V. Cook, Ph.D.
Ipswich, Massachusetts

Lance L. Lee, Ph.D.
Los Gatos, California

*Gender Roles in
Transition: A
Model of
Adaptation*

1 *Gender Roles: A Contemporary Crisis*

David drops Karen's proposal for their next project on her desk and walks away with a colleague. His comments — in red — cover the page. Karen looks at it and wails, "I thought we were friends. All you've done is criticize!" David hears her and turns. "But we *are* friends. You did a good job!" he says as he smiles and walks away. "Men!" says Karen to herself. "I just don't get it. If only he'd written 'Good' at the top — or said something nice. He could have saved me some grief!"

Bob sits in a restaurant near a group of men discussing their wives. He laughs to himself at their conversation. "My wife can change her mind faster than you can say 'jack rabbit!' " one of the men complains. Another agrees. "Women," he grouses, "you can't live with 'em — you can't shoot 'em!"

Misunderstandings between women and men are common and are often not easily resolved. Familiar sayings sometimes capture this confusion: "Men reason with their head; women reason with their heart," or "Women are made to be loved, not to be understood," or "He marries a sex object; she marries a standard of living." It is no wonder we often find ourselves exclaiming, "Men (Women)! I can never understand them! Why do they have to be that way?"

These misunderstandings can be painful and traumatic. Sharon eagerly anticipated her brother's wedding, and she and her boyfriend had planned to spend the weekend celebrating with the wedding couple. Instead they ended up fighting.

Sharon: "What is going on? We usually have fun together. . . . "

Al replied: "You may, but I don't anymore. . . . "

Sharon was surprised to learn that although she and Al had dated exclusively for four years, Al wanted to break up. She left the weekend feeling shocked and hurt, confused by what had happened. Only later, with a counselor's help, was her boyfriend able to express his fears of commitment, and Sharon able to hear that her own abilities to express emotions and feelings intimidated him.

Women and men may find honest, warm, trusting relationships difficult to form and maintain, whether they are coworkers, members of a couple, or just friends. Singles hurt in the past may carry "baggage" from one relationship to another, hindering the development of trust and good communication. Married persons find themselves taking each other for granted, or one partner begins to resent the other, believing his or her spouse has a better job or a more supportive work environment. Friendships between coworkers of different sexes turn out to be more difficult or complex than either person expects.

Changing Gender Roles Contribute to Misunderstandings

Many of these problems occur because of changing gender roles. Roles have become increasingly complex and confusing in our society, and many Christians experience problems in dealing effectively with these changes. Sometimes, well-meaning people in the church contribute to the problem by advocating traditional gender roles without hearing the pressures that contemporary young Christians face. As Christian psychologists and individuals who have struggled with these issues, we want to share with adolescents and adults, pastors and parents, our concerns about male-female relationships. Individual and corporate struggles with increasingly complex gender role issues provide greater potential for richness and reward in relationships than many Christians now experience. Issues may be more confusing than ever, but it *is* possible for Christians to resolve much of the anxiety and crises that surround relationships between males and females. In this book we will offer specific suggestions and recommendations to encourage this resolution. In particular, we argue that a more flexible view of gender roles will help us as Christians to adjust to these changes in a way that is pleasing to God.

We would like to note that most of our remarks are directed to Caucasian middle-class society in the United States, since that is the population with which we are most familiar. While many of our comments and suggestions may be useful for American society in general, there are special issues and problems in male-female relationships in minority communities—and cross-cultural issues—that we do not address.

When did all these problems in male-female friendship, dating, marriage, and work relationships begin? It has always been difficult to build and maintain honest and trusting relationships, but it may now be harder than ever. In recognition of conflicts between the sexes, a recent book on sex differences is titled *The Longest War*. This label sometimes seems especially appropriate for people in or past their mid-twenties, the group to which this book is primarily written. Some of these people have been dealing with relationships a long time! Also, as they enter relationships—whether the relationship is primarily a friendship or has romantic potential—the two people may be more competitive and mistrusting than is helpful because of past hurts and lingering scars.

It may be hard to have healthy, fun, carefree relationships with members of the other sex because of pressures that John Fischer calls "weirdness." In "A Single Person's Identity," he writes, "By 'weirdness' I mean the pressure which results from the prospect of marriage—raising disquieting inner questions like, 'Is this the one? Is this "That Relationship"?'—yet without our communicating our feelings and questions to the other person. This 'weirdness' starts to creep in, both people get uptight, and one member of the couple splits!"[1] Sometimes such miscommunication between women and men can continue for a long time without either partner recognizing what's happening, a problem that can affect both romantic and non-romantic relationships.

Difficulties in relationships many times do not solely stem from the participants themselves. A woman and a man may find it hard to carry on a friendship without friends or acquaintances pestering them about whether the relationship is romantic. In romantic relationships, parents and friends, well meaning but interfering, may make couples feel pressured or guilty if their relationship does not culminate in marriage.

Must Things Be So Difficult?

Getting to "I do" often seems harder today than ever. In the past, meeting others was easier and more automatic, and getting married was taken for granted. Now there are fewer men than women above the age of eighteen, especially in the church, and people are marrying later than ever before. According to the infamous Yale-Harvard study, the chances of marriage for a woman over thirty-five are less than 5 percent (the actual percentage, however, may be higher).[2] Once married, one is not "safe." Modern marriages seem especially vulnerable to divorce.

Other changes in our society make relationships more diverse and less predictable than before. A striking number of women now work outside the home, including more than half the mothers of infants. Men's roles are changing too. The distant provider has become the part-time caregiver. Fifty years ago, 10 percent of fathers spent *no* time with their children. Even in the 1970s, the average American father spent only twelve minutes per day with his child. Today, fathers are increasingly active in parenting. A recent study of dual career couples showed that fathers provide 38 percent of total child care time.[3]

In these and other ways, society has changed — radically. Relationships between women and men show greater diversity than ever before, producing uncertainty and often anguish. Some in relationships experience the anguish of a seemingly unresolvable conflict between their expectations of the relationship and their partner's expectations, while others are disappointed they are not in the relationships they desire. Many of these uncertainties and anxieties can be resolved by making thoughtful, biblical choices, choices that *can* make relationships more rich and rewarding.

Change Brings Questions

Societal changes bring feelings of insecurity and self-consciousness. We, as women and men, are forced to address questions about ourselves and our sexuality that other generations never asked as openly: Am I "okay"? Will I marry, or is it "okay" not to? What about premarital sex? Struggling to cope with the changes, we may blame ourselves, our background, or God. Some even find it necessary to choose not to explore relationships for awhile, an uncommon step in the past, but more frequent now because relationships seem "too much work" or "too unrewarding."

Relationships *are* work—more difficult, complex, and confusing than we were led to expect. For example, we have been taught it is "normal" and "Christian" to have a spouse and have started a family in our mid-twenties. Yet some of us find ourselves unmarried at even later ages, questioning God and our own personal worth. Or we may feel quite self-confident but despair of finding a suitable spouse and dread the marriage of one more of our single friends or the moving away of one more coworker. Married persons may recognize that their marriage does not fit the "script" they thought they wanted or that their struggle to live their "script" is stressful and frustrating.

Our identities as human beings and children of God are challenged by these struggles. Is anyone else in the church experiencing similar crises? If I don't want to be "traditional," will I be able to find a partner? If I prefer the traditional role, will I be looked down upon by more career-oriented friends? Does "making it" in a career mean having too little time for friends? Doesn't God want all singles to marry? Why must Christians have to face these issues anyway? Surely God could not have meant relations between women and men to be this hard.

Our struggles in relationship confront us with a perplexing and compelling question. *How different are men and women, and is it possible to communicate across these differences?* We begin to search for answers in our own experience and in the Scriptures.

Some people, even those who profess to be "experts," argue that males and females have important psychological and emotional differences. Men and women, we are told, live in different worlds, "hear" different conversations, and have different priorities. We picture two worlds, incompatible and mutually exclusive, with an unbridgeable chasm between them.

Gender Roles and the Church

Sometimes, parents and clergy may widen this chasm, telling us that "God made males and females different, and that's how it should be." Instinct tells some of us that this view is too extreme. "There must be a way toward greater harmony between the sexes," we wonder in frustration. And there is. In spite of the differences between males and females, we *can* share our humanness in Christ and achieve greater peace together.

God, in His holiness, *is* all-caring and all-powerful, *despite* the confusion we face in our society. *How can our awareness of God's sovereignty and providence help improve relationships between men and women?* God in His wisdom and love has endowed humans with unique characteristics that differentiate males and females. At the same time, many of these differences have been exaggerated, and our society (including many Christians) has attributed to biology many behavior patterns that are actually learned.

Contemporary research in gender-role issues indicates that a few innate sex differences do exist in psychology and behavior, but these differences, especially when viewed in the context of the whole range of normal human behavior, are minimal at best. Many of the alleged differences between females and males have been greatly magnified by our expectations. Males and females share needs and feelings, and our similarities are much more important than our differences. We need to exercise our own understanding and love as Christian people—and our sense of humor—to form the healthy attitudes that are crucial to the development of good relationships.

Attempts to establish good relationships between men and women may be hindered by too-rigid, societally learned roles that become barriers to communication. Gender roles that made sense a generation or more ago may not altogether fit with contemporary society. How are we as Christians to distinguish between those roles and values that are healthy for us to maintain and those roles and values which we need to modify? This question is a key focus of our book.

The church—sometimes consciously and sometimes inadvertently—has endorsed many gender role stereotypes of the past. In so doing, it has intensified the relationship problems people encounter. As committed Christians, we affirm the church's role in our personal lives and in community. As psychologists and believers, we see that individuals, struggling to live as Christians, need flexibility and tolerance within the body of the church to resolve these struggles biblically.

What is the relationship between the church and society with regard to gender roles? One expects that sex role confusion in our society would be reflected, to an extent, in the church, since the church is part of that society. Such is indeed the case, but the church need not contribute to anxiety and confusion in this area. The church instead needs to provide a context for growth and adaptation toward more wholesome and more positive relationships. A biblical approach to these issues calls for an attitude of tolerance and flexibility. Men and women should be free to choose traditional or nontraditional roles in response to God's calling, without criticism or blame from their Christian friends.

Real-Life Complications

Contemporary societal changes complicate individual lives. These changes effect us all. For example, changing women's roles have raised a complex of questions. Louise is a professional woman, who works long hours and has a good sense of self-esteem. She knows that sometimes she is too hesitant to say "no" at work and too slow to express her opinions, but in general she manages the demands made on her and does a good job. However, she is frustrated by attempts to meet men. She is a woman who has "made it" but doesn't "have it all." She identifies with the sentiment expressed in a recent popular book titled, *I've Done So Well, Why Do I Feel So Bad?* Louise doesn't really feel *so* bad, but a little more male attention would be nice. Relationships seemed much easier to develop in her late twenties and early thirties. Now, in her mid-thirties, with fewer men available, relationships appear more complicated and less rewarding. What can she do to enrich her social life?

Marriages too have changed radically, as both spouses now often work. Harvey married Sue three years ago, when both were field support representatives for IBM. Sue recently received a promotion and currently travels two to three weeks a month. They now have to plan for time together, and Harvey struggles to feel "okay" about his lower job status and lesser financial contribution to their household. How can they work together to ease these changes at work and at home?

Parenting seems complicated, with more major decisions than

before. George and Linda want to have children, but they can't meet the mortgage if Linda stops working. Although Linda thinks she can work out part-time options, George isn't sure he wants to commit the time to child care that will be necessary for her to take advantage of a part-time opportunity. How should they resolve their dilemma?

Too often, however, Christians particularize these concerns, seeing them as the result of individual situations and needs. If we would only be more traditional, some people say, we wouldn't have these problems, or we could at least solve them sooner. These Christians fail to recognize that many of us are in the same points of crisis, and that the traditional roles are not good options anymore for many of us, for economic and other reasons. Because they have not examined changes in gender roles and the contemporary pressures and challenges that have brought about such changes, these more traditionally oriented Christians limit the roles their friends, children, or church members should "properly" pursue, based on the person's sex. Moreover, they argue that it is only the more traditional options for males and females which are the appropriate "biblical" ones. People frequently have internalized these traditional roles in their youth and find it hard as adults to match their expectations of themselves with the reality of their lives.

On the other hand, Christians with more liberal ideas on gender roles can sometimes intimidate those with traditional views. Because these more liberal individuals focus on change, they may pursue their objectives without adequate sensitivity to the deeply held feelings and beliefs of their more traditional friends. Social change doesn't occur overnight, and when the desired changes are in such a fundamental and personal area as relationships among males and females, this insensitivity can make liberals appear as inflexible as some conservatives.

One therefore regretfully ends up with a church that is "conformed to this world" in a variety of ways — a church not "transformed by the renewing of its mind," in that it often propagates much of the same inflexibility and prejudice found in the larger society about gender roles. As a result, the church becomes full of individuals who do not feel free to respond to God's calling for ministry and service.

How This Book Can Help

The problem is real. Our counseling experience, and that of pastors and other counselors with whom we are in contact, confirms our opinion that many Christians are struggling with gender roles and with "appropriate" behaviors for men and women. Many individuals have been hurt by being led to believe that there are certain ways that Christian women and men should be, think, or act—ways they find difficult to emulate. Some of these behaviors and attitudes have been taught by their parents; many others have been learned from friends, both Christian and non-Christian, and from the media. We are not talking about those struggling with homosexuality, or men who wonder if they are females in male bodies, or women who question if they are males in female bodies. We recognize these struggles but do not address them here. We are talking about common, everyday people—our family, our friends, ourselves—who want to make their relationships run more smoothly and be more glorifying to God. For these people, we as authors want to facilitate healthy Christian growth and adaptation.

As Christian psychologists and counselors, we have given much thought over the past few years about the best way to present our ideas on the challenges and possibilities for Christians as males and females in contemporary society-in-transition. We have shared our experiences and struggles with others and have learned from these exchanges. As we have continued to hear these struggles again and again, we feel there is a need for wider discussion of these issues and of ideas to facilitate their resolution.

Recently, two graduate students in our community, a man and a woman, jointly organized a small group in their local church to discuss these issues. This group was undoubtedly like many other such groups in the anxiety and confusion its members felt about Christian perspectives on contemporary gender roles. It was unusual, though, in the academic intensity and thoroughness with which this group examined these issues. The group, five men and five women in total, were graduate students and young professionals who came from different parts of the country and had diverse backgrounds, interests, and activities. They were united by a solid commitment to evangelical Christianity and a desire to understand better their maleness and femaleness. Their plan was to discuss selected readings on various topics and share personal experiences, with the hope of developing healthier Christian relationships with the other sex. At the group's conclusion, one of its leaders summarized the members' concerns and observations and shared these summaries with us. We decided that these summaries would provide interesting case material to supplement our own experiences as professional psychologists, and we have integrated the conclusions and comments from the small group with our own thoughts. We quote extensively from this group and from our own experiences throughout the book. Almost everyone whose stories we quote is Christian. Their stories are true, but their names have been changed.

Our model for healthy relations among the sexes is based on several assumptions with which you may or may not agree. We have summarized our assumptions on page 26. In these assumptions we attempt to outline basic principles that underlie dynamic biblically based change.

Give your opinions in response to the following survey found on page 23. If you find questions difficult to answer, qualify your answers in the margins and read on. You may find your concerns addressed. (If not, write us!)

Score your survey. Once you have completed the survey, add up your scores. If, for example, you respond to question 1 with a 2 (agree), question 2 with a -2 (disagree), and question 3 with a 3 (strongly disagree), then your total score for questions 1 to 3 is 3. (Notice that some of the questions have positive scores to the left of 0; the other questions have positive scores to the right of 0. Simply record the score that matches your answer and add up this number.)

Your score indicates whether we begin from similar assumptions. If your score is 0 or lower, you'll find this book challenging and controversial. Please read on. If your score is between 8 and 16, you agree more than disagree, but will experience points of disagreement. If your score is 24 or higher, you substantially agree with us. You should find this book informative but not revolutionary. You may find, however, that evaluating your relationships — with friends, in dating or in marriage, and with coworkers — in light of our comments revolutionizes these bonds. If your score is 40 or higher, we'll call on you to help with this book's second edition!

What Do You Think about Gender Roles: An Opening Survey

What's *your* opinion about gender roles? Are they stable or flexible? Are a range of characteristics gender-specific or are many characteristics widely shared? This survey is designed to help you assess your own beliefs.

Place an "X" on the line indicating the extent to which you agree or disagree with the following statements:

1. Men and women are each given specified roles. There should be little deviation from that role when everything is working well.

```
|- - - - |- - - - -|- - - - -|- - - - -|- - - - -|- - - - -|
3         2         1         0        -1        -2        -3
```

| Strongly Disagree | Disagree | Mildly Disagree | Neutral | Mildly Agree | Agree | Strongly Agree |

2. No two men or women are alike. People should base their choice of roles on what works best for them and how they feel God leads them.

```
|- - - - |- - - - -|- - - - -|- - - - -|- - - - -|- - - - -|
-3        -2        -1         0         1         2         3
```

| Strongly Disagree | Disagree | Mildly Disagree | Neutral | Mildly Agree | Agree | Strongly Agree |

3. The Bible has little to say about special behaviors men and women should use in their general relationships with one another. While it shows *people* how to live together, it is not a book on "how to be a man" or "how to be a woman."

```
|- - - - |- - - - -|- - - - -|- - - - -|- - - - -|- - - - -|
-3        -2        -1         0         1         2         3
```

| Strongly Disagree | Disagree | Mildly Disagree | Neutral | Mildly Agree | Agree | Strongly Agree |

4. A woman should be able to make as much money as a man does, but she should never have more power than he does.

```
|- - - - |- - - - -|- - - - -|- - - - -|- - - - -|- - - - -|
3         2         1         0         -1        -2        -3
```

Strongly   Disagree   Mildly   Neutral   Mildly   Agree   Strongly
Disagree   Disagree   Agree   Agree

5. A man should be able to provide financially for his family; if he cannot, he really has no business being a husband.

```
|- - - - |- - - - -|- - - - -|- - - - -|- - - - -|- - - - -|
3         2         1         0         -1        -2        -3
```

Strongly   Disagree   Mildly   Neutral   Mildly   Agree   Strongly
Disagree   Disagree   Agree   Agree

6. The most important thing about your behavior as a man or woman is whether or not it fulfills the expectations of those around you.

```
|- - - - |- - - - -|- - - - -|- - - - -|- - - - -|- - - - -|
3         2         1         0         -1        -2        -3
```

Strongly   Disagree   Mildly   Neutral   Mildly   Agree   Strongly
Disagree   Disagree   Agree   Agree

7. A husband's responsibility is to nurture, cherish, love, and protect his partner. His wife's responsibility is the same.

```
|- - - - |- - - - -|- - - - -|- - - - -|- - - - -|- - - - -|
-3        -2        -1        0         1         2         3
```

Strongly   Disagree   Mildly   Neutral   Mildly   Agree   Strongly
Disagree   Disagree   Agree   Agree

8. No one (not even God) has a right to tell you how you should behave as a man or woman.

```
|- - - - |- - - - -|- - - - -|- - - - -|- - - - -|- - - - -|
3         2         1         0         -1        -2        -3
```

Strongly   Disagree   Mildly   Neutral   Mildly   Agree   Strongly
Disagree   Disagree   Agree   Agree

9. In general, it is up to the stronger sex to initiate positive changes in a relationship.

|－－－－ |－－－－－|－－－－－|－－－－－|－－－－－|－－－－－|
| 3 | 2 | 1 | 0 | -1 | -2 | -3 |

| Strongly Disagree | Disagree | Mildly Disagree | Neutral | Mildly Agree | Agree | Strongly Agree |

10. Men and women are basically alike. The primary differences between them are physiological.

|－－－－ |－－－－－|－－－－－|－－－－－|－－－－－|－－－－－|
| -3 | -2 | -1 | 0 | 1 | 2 | 3 |

| Strongly Disagree | Disagree | Mildly Disagree | Neutral | Mildly Agree | Agree | Strongly Agree |

11. Men have tough roles in life. Therefore, they need to be strong and show little emotion.

|－－－－ |－－－－－|－－－－－|－－－－－|－－－－－|－－－－－|
| 3 | 2 | 1 | 0 | -1 | -2 | -3 |

| Strongly Disagree | Disagree | Mildly Disagree | Neutral | Mildly Agree | Agree | Strongly Agree |

12. A woman who can't cook or clean needs to have some basic lessons in how to be a woman.

|－－－－ |－－－－－|－－－－－|－－－－－|－－－－－|－－－－－|
| 3 | 2 | 1 | 0 | -1 | -2 | -3 |

| Strongly Disagree | Disagree | Mildly Disagree | Neutral | Mildly Agree | Agree | Strongly Agree |

13. There are really no gender-specific rules for men and women for dating. What you do on a date should depend on who you are and what you want out of the encounter.

|－－－－ |－－－－－|－－－－－|－－－－－|－－－－－|－－－－－|
| -3 | -2 | -1 | 0 | 1 | 2 | 3 |

| Strongly Disagree | Disagree | Mildly Disagree | Neutral | Mildly Agree | Agree | Strongly Agree |

14. The best thing that a man and a woman can do is to decide how they're going to work together to fulfill God's calling for each of them.

```
|– – – – |– – – – –|– – – – –|– – – – –|– – – – –|– – – – –|
  -3        -2        -1        0         1         2         3
```

Strongly   Disagree   Mildly   Neutral   Mildly   Agree   Strongly
Disagree   Disagree   Agree   Agree

15. The church does not contribute to gender role conflict in its members, and should have no role in reducing their gender-role conflict issues.

```
|– – – – |– – – – –|– – – – –|– – – – –|– – – – –|– – – – –|
   3         2         1        0        -1        -2        -3
```

Strongly   Disagree   Mildly   Neutral   Mildly   Agree   Strongly
Disagree   Disagree   Agree   Agree

Our model is based on the following basic assumptions (review your answers to the survey to see if you agree):

■ For the Christian, gender roles must be grounded in biblical principles and continually subject to God's wisdom and guidance (questions 2, 3, and 9, specifically discussed in chapter 2 but assumed and mentioned throughout the book);

■ Most of us in gender-role conflict need greater flexibility in gender roles than we presently experience (question 1, defended throughout the book);

■ Gender roles are not ultimately flexible (question 3) but subject to biblical principles and societal pressures (see, e.g., chaps. 2–3);

■ Christians disagree about how much gender-role flexibility is biblical. We have acknowledged this difference in chapter 2, provided categories for addressing this difference (i.e., traditional, neo-traditional, biblical feminist, secular) in chapter 3, and urged that we all show respect and tolerance for these differences as we together struggle with gender roles.

We address issues central to societal definitions of masculinity and femininity (specifically in chapters 4–7), including money and power (questions 4–5) and the myths of masculinity and femininity (questions 11–13), and, in every chapter of the book, make suggestions for modifying societal definitions of gender roles in light of biblical principles (question 6). In chapters 8–11, we provide biblical guidelines for males and females as singles, in friendship and dating relationships, and in marriage — issues which questions 7, 9, 13, and 14 address — and conclude with a discussion of the church's responsibility for encouraging gender-role flexibility among its members (question 15).

As Christian authors, we want to encourage healthy Christian transformation, but we do not recommend that the church blindly follow the spirit of cultural change. We do try, from a dynamic biblical perspective, to provide direction and emotional support for individuals caught in these relationship struggles. We have to admit that male-female relationships are beset with many problems, *but* the present anxiety and gender-role confusion carries important potential for healthy growth and productive change for us as individuals.

Some components of earlier roles, for example, the wife's staying home with the children for their preschool years, are workable and often desirable. Such roles deserve more thought than earlier, however, as they may bring sacrifices not required thirty years ago. We want to discuss these more traditional attitudes, set them alongside possible new roles, and try to help Christians evaluate the choices in the context of the options for gender roles that are currently available.

Some people may agree with the ideas and suggestions raised in this book but find them too difficult to implement. We readily understand this. Attitudes about such a basic part of us as our sexuality cannot be changed easily, and we respect the struggles of those who find these attitudes hard or impossible to modify. Even healthy growth can be difficult. If you find it hard to change, and indeed all of us do, we challenge you to remember the hope of faith, the "upward call of God in Christ Jesus," (Phil. 3:14) and Paul's charge to "be transformed by the renewing of your mind" (Rom. 12:2). Being the best Christian one can be has never been an easy task.

Questions for Reflection:

1. In what ways have you been aware of changing gender roles? Which changes have been positive for you? Which have been a struggle?

2. How different do *you* think men and women are, and in what ways have you had difficulty communicating across these differences?

3. How does our awareness of God's sovereignty and providence change our participation in relationships with women and men?

4. How have changing gender roles affected your church? Has your church's adjustment been positive or negative? What further changes would you recommend to your church leaders?

2 Identity and Interdependence: In Quest of a Biblical Model

Difficult and controversial questions surround the Bible's view of men's and women's relationships with one another and within the church and society. Without trying to avoid or minimize any of these issues, we nevertheless propose a perspective on these relationships that we believe is entirely consistent with Scripture. We suggest a helpful and hope-giving framework for understanding and dealing with the broad range of difficulties affecting male-female relationships in our society. Specifically, our agenda is to:

■ Explore what is clear and not so clear in the biblical passages related to male and female roles in marriage and society.

■ Discern some tension points which exist between Christians in interpreting these passages.

■ Present a framework for confronting contemporary challenges posed by gender roles in our society.

■ Provide suggestions for people earnestly desiring change and creative solutions to the problems they face in their Christian communities and in our society at large. These suggestions are rooted in biblical concepts and therefore may seem to non-Christians to be less helpful than advice based more broadly and generally on social ethics. We would argue just the opposite — that it is God's power and grace working through Scripture and through those who use it that provide the best hope for solving most of these male-female interaction problems.

A Caveat: Where We've Come from Determines What We See

As we begin this discussion, we must remember that all of us have come from different backgrounds, and are likely to react to the material presented here on the basis of our experiences.

Perhaps the story of the three blind men who set out to explore what an elephant is like describes at least some of our disagreements. Each of the three blind men is led to a different part of the elephant. Says one (grasping the trunk), "See, the elephant is wide and strong and flexible." The other two, being led to the tail and the ear, respectively, had distinctly different experiences and different conclusions about "what an elephant is like." Our efforts to determine what the Scriptures say about male and female relationships are likely to be biased by where we begin, what we've been told, and who led us to discover "the elephant."

Those of us from traditional backgrounds may be surprised to find that the Scriptures say surprisingly less about differences between men and women and "who should do what" than we may have been taught to believe. Those of us from more egalitarian backgrounds may be surprised to discover, on the other hand, that the Bible is not a "unisex" document; it does, in fact, recognize differences between men and women, although we may disagree on the meaning of these differences for today's Christians.

This chapter is meant to provide a philosophical framework and biblical foundation for the remainder of the book. There is insufficient space to analyze the vast amount of biblical scholarship on this topic; therefore, our effort will be to provide a balanced understanding of the issues, with an emphasis on their implications for modern men and women. Our attempt is to be enlightening, not exhaustive. Readers interested in a more comprehensive consideration should refer to Bilezikian,[1] Hurley,[2] Piper and Grudem,[3] Foh,[4] Gundry,[5] and Mickelsen,[6] authors who reflect a spectrum of opinion about what the Bible says about male-female roles and female leadership in the church.

Bilezikian, Gundry, and Mickelsen argue that the Bible advocates egalitarian roles and treatment for men and women in the church and home. Piper and Grudem, Hurley, and Foh support more "traditional" principles governing male and female relationships (e.g., headship as "authority", female submis-sion).

The Devil in Two Places: Extremes to Avoid

Dr. Walter Kaiser writes in *Worldwide Challenge:*

> The daily controversy over what the Bible really says about God's purpose for women [and men] has brought forth two dangerous positions. The first is an evangelical backlash mentality against libertine statements on women and society, and the second is an easy capitulation to whatever current fad holds sway over society, with very little authoritative biblical basis for the latest change. These views are dangerous for opposite reasons: The first espouses a low view of women, and the second takes a low view of Scripture![7]

Our effort in this chapter will be to avoid both of these tendencies. The Bible's message, properly understood, is one of hope for all Christians — men and women. Yet there has been substantial disagreement over how the two sexes are to interact in appropriating the "fullness of the Gospel." Our anchor for faith and practice must always be Scripture itself; within it, with humility and an openness to discovery, we seek the wisdom of God. Others may disagree on Scripture, but it is still with Scripture, rather than with some other source (e.g., experience, tradition, psychology), that we Christians should start.

Starting Points: What Scripture Says . . . and Doesn't Say

Any effort to uncover the Bible's wisdom must consider the totality of Scripture and the mix of passages which are relevant to an understanding of maleness and femaleness.[8] Our reading of these passages leads us to the following foundational observations.

Equality of Men and Women

The Bible teaches that, although there may be differences between males and females, their relationships with one another should be marked by their complementarity (without either being superior or inferior) and equality (without their being the same).

■ God chose to create both men and women in His own image (Gen. 1:26-27).

■ All men and women, whether young or old, black or white, rich or poor, are equal in the sight of God and may approach Him with similar confidence (Gen. 1:27; Gal. 3:28; Eph. 3:12; Acts 10:34-35).

■ Men and women are equally called to be in relationship with God (1 Peter 3:7).

Both are important and precious to Him and called to kingdom service. Though Jesus spent a large proportion of His ministry with twelve male disciples, He nonetheless spent time instructing and teaching women, for example, Mary (Martha's sister), the Syrophoenician woman, and the woman at the well. Women were the first to witness and testify to His resurrection.

■ The New Testament encourages both men and women to exercise their spiritual gifts.

All gifts are important, indeed vital, to the health of the whole body (Eph. 4:12). There is no evidence that these gifts are given any differently to men or women (1 Cor. 12).

Differences and Distinctions— at the Creation and Elsewhere

■ Woman was created as a "helper fit for" and "corresponding to" the man (Gen. 2:18, authors' trans.).

The understanding of that phrase and calling is still subject to discussion. Both man and woman were commissioned to the task of filling the earth and subduing it (Gen. 1:28) and were encouraged to be interdependent upon one another (1 Cor. 11:11). Some understand "helper corresponding to" to suggest someone who plays the role of a cooperative assistant. Others suggest that the concept refers to a complementary being whose abilities and needs match ours. The Hebrew word for "help" or "helper" (*ezer*) is used twenty-one times in the Old Testament, almost always in reference to a mighty God who nurtures Israel rather than to a subordinate or inferior (e.g., see Ps. 121:1-2; Deut. 33:7, 26, 29).[9]

■ The interdependence and equality of the sexes were distorted by the Fall into male dominance and female subjection (Gen. 3:16).

The new covenant in Christ, according to many, is meant to reverse that distortion. But whether the pre-Fall covenant was actually hierarchical, and whether the New Covenant in Christ results in a more or less egalitarian partnership between man and woman, or in a leadership framework where some version of male authority is exercised, is widely debated.

Some argue that since man was created before woman, the Jewish concept of primogeniture (primacy of the first-born) applies. The contention here is that the husband has authority over the wife as a timeless, God-given principle.[10] Bilezikian and others argue that biblical support for the practice of primogeniture is weak and that the practice, when Jewish families followed it, involved property rights among siblings, not the relationship between husband and wife.

■ The Bible supports the existence of some authority relationships between people, without altering their equality as persons.

■ Jesus Himself always submitted to God (John 6:38; 8:28-29) but remained equal with Him (John 5:18). Men and women are called to submit, for the Lord's sake, to one another (Eph. 5:21) and to authorities (1 Peter 2:13; Rom. 13:1). What is clear from this is that men and women are equally valued. What is not entirely agreed upon is the degree to which authority in male and female relationships should be emphasized (e.g., with one sex being assigned responsibility or leadership over the other).[11]

What about the Home? Marriage and Family

■ Christian husbands and wives are called to submit to one another (Eph. 5:21). However, within the context of the home, the relationship between husband and wife may in some ways be asymmetrical.

Wives are instructed to "submit to your husbands" (Eph. 5:22, NIV), a command that must without fail be interpreted in light of Ephesians 5:21, which emphasizes mutual submission, because of the grammatical connection between the two verses.

In the same context, husbands are commanded to love their wives as Christ loved the church (Eph. 5:25), an equally important commandment.

■ The husband is the "head" of the wife in a way that is parallel to that in which God is the head of Christ (1 Cor. 11:3); this headship is also related by Paul to the Creation (1 Cor. 11:11-12). In 1 Corinthians 11:3 the Greek term used for "head" (*kephalē*) is closer to the meaning of "source" or "origin" than "ruler" or "superior rank," suggesting that Paul meant to emphasize the husband as receiving glory or honor from the wife (since man was originally the "source" from which woman came), rather than to assert an authority relationship between the spouses.[12]

The concept of "headship"—what it refers to and what it means—is a matter of much discussion.[13] It is clear from the Scriptures that "headship" is a designation, function, or responsibility accorded to the man. In the Greek text, the call to headship is clearly presented in the context of mutual submission and the complementary partnership of husband and wife (i.e., self-giving love and self-giving submission).

Even Christians who believe that "headship" implies an authority differential disagree on how much emphasis to place on it.[14]

■ The ideal wife, in relationship to her husband (according to Prov. 31), had considerable authority in managing her household, including servants.

Although this ideal woman of Old Testament times was primarily a homemaker, she was not exclusively so. With her multi-faceted activities as a good businesswoman, wife, and mother, she provides a biblical model for "working mothers" of the twentieth century.

In the Church: Different Roles for Men and Women?

■ On the basis of 1 Corinthians 14:34-35 and 1 Timothy 2:12, it is held by some that a woman's demeanor in church ought to differ from that of a man's.

Alternate translations of these passages prescribe a woman to silence, to "a quiet spirit,"[15] or to maintain a general decorum in church. It is abundantly clear from other passages that women are called to prophesy (Luke 2:36; Acts 21:9), that the gifts of prophecy and prayer were meant for all, irrespective of sex (1 Cor. 11:4-5), and that the Spirit was to be poured out upon both men and women, even so that "your sons and daughters shall prophesy" (Joel 2:28, RSV).

■ Paul indicates that he does "not permit a woman to teach or have authority over a man" (1 Tim. 2:12, NIV).

The implications of this passage have been construed by some to be one more example of culturally encapsulated teaching, no longer relevant to our day and age. Traditionalists have used this passage to support a male-only authority or leadership role in the church. Most, however, argue that Paul's statement is for a particular situation but has timeless relevance, that is that unqualified people (in Ephesus, women) should not preach and that church services should have decorum and be edifying.[16] To challenge the more traditional position, they point to examples in the Bible such as Huldah, the prophetess, who appears from all descriptions to have "taught" the word of the Lord to the priests and king's officials when King Josiah could not understand the "words of the Book of the Law" (2 Kings 22:11). Priscilla too is considered a great teacher. She and her husband Aquila (of the pair, Priscilla is generally thought to be the better teacher), instructed Apollos, who became a great evangelist (Acts 18).

■ In all the passages about elders, there is no clear mention of women.[17]

Some have argued that 1 Timothy 5:1-2 indicates a parallel between elders and older women. There do appear to have been women who were deacons (1 Tim. 3:11), though some believe this refers to deacons' wives. Phoebe was mentioned as a deacon (Rom. 16:1),[18] and Junia seems to have been an apostle (Rom. 16:7).[19]

Paul regarded a significant number of women as co-laborers in the Gospel (Rom. 16 and Phil. 4:2-3).

Because these passages uphold the place of women on the "frontlines" of the spiritual battlefield and because God today appears to be using so many women (e.g., in leadership in overseas missions and Christian education), many see this as evidence of His equal calling to women in the church.

■ There is disagreement as to whether or not there is a difference between the provision of gifts and the delegation of offices, roles, or responsibilities within the church to men and women.

While men and women were both empowered and given opportunity to prophesy, pray, evangelize, and instruct, some have argued that certain functions in the church (e.g., pastor, elder) were reserved for men, at least in the first-century church.[20] These same people then argue that this guideline was meant to sustain a God-given order within the church. Others argue that women did play such roles in the early church, but that the abundance of men in these roles may have been an artifact of the culture of that day and therefore not meant to be static and institutionalized for all time. Indeed, there is no evidence that these were formal or professional offices, in our sense. Originally, church offices were charismatic (filled in accordance with people's individual gifts, or *charismata*), and such people were normally laypersons, since there was no organized priesthood then.[21]

Men's and Women's Roles in Society at Large

■ The Bible provides evidence of women as well as men, who followed God by taking an active part in society.

Deborah was a ruler of her country as well as a prophetess. Esther was a diplomat who was able to save her people from extinction. Lydia was a trader, and Tabitha a well-known seamstress and social worker; and it is probable that Priscilla was a leading public figure. As earlier noted in Proverbs 31, the ideal woman was shrewd in public affairs and as effective in the marketplace as she was in the home.

■ There are no overt biblical injunctions or limitations set on the roles of either men or women in society.

Much of what has been discussed in the foregoing paragraphs is useful—if one is setting out to write an essay on men's and women's roles in biblical perspective. But what of everyday life? What of the conflicts we face, you and I, just because we happen to be Christian believers in a time when so many things are changing?

When all is said and done, what are men and women to do who earnestly desire to:

■ Glorify God in their personal and professional lives;

■ Seek fulfillment in their identities as men and women, and yet who find themselves . . .

■ Exhausted, exasperated, and defeated by the confusing signals and scenarios of the "gender war" in our society?

Framework for a Redemptive Revolution

We propose that there is indeed a way out of the "gender-role swamp." Men and women, on one hand, need to get back to biblical basics—those things which unite all women and men as followers of Christ—and, on the other hand, to challenge patterns and prescriptions (be they "conservative" or "progressive") which end up violating these very Christian principles. In fact, we suggest that three things will help all of us who earnestly seek to be redeemed men and women of God:

■ *Spiritual Primacy*. Finding our core identity in Christ, and seeking His call and completion in our lives, over and above those demands placed upon our identity as members of a particular gender, race, or socio-professional station in life.

Florence Nightingale once wrote: "Keep clear of all jargon about men's and women's work and go straight to God's work in simplicity of heart."[22] Or, as one friend said recently, speaking of male-female role controversies in the context of God's overall mission for us as Christians to make Him known to the world: "Don't be guilty of straightening the pictures when the house is burning down!"

■ *Relationships Rooted in Holiness.* Weighing our decisions on "how to be"—what to say and think and do—on the following guides, emphasizing principles above practices:

(1) What the principles of Scripture teach us, including mutual love and respect, and individual responsibility to God.
(2) What God is telling us to do, as we pursue Him in a humble, obedient, open walk of faith.

■ *Flexibility versus Fixation.* Seeking dynamic identities as men and women of God—finding refuge in "the rock" (Ps. 61), but flexing to meet the demands of the age in which we live—finding ourselves open to "revisioning" ourselves and our relationships so that we might continue to glorify God throughout the changing seasons of our lives.

Spiritual Primacy: The Call to All Christians

Pastors are quick to say that the Bible is not so much a set of directions—a "color-by-number" formula—as it is a guide to great art (living, loving, growing) by the Greatest Artist of the universe. When it comes to man and woman, the Creator intended that *both* be His handiwork, reflecting and emanating His image of justice, love, mercy, grace, peace, and goodness in every aspect of their lives. For whatever increment of differences and directives that distin-guish man and woman in the Scriptures, there is an over-whelming inheritance of privileges, prerogatives, commandments, and com-missions which apply to both, equally and abundantly, as children of God, as Linda Raney Wright has pointed out.[23]

At the Creation, both women and men were formed to be the bearers of His image (Gen. 1:27). In the new creation, both are to be heirs of God and joint heirs to grace in Christ Jesus (Heb. 1–2; Rom. 8:17). Both man and woman are born again into a spiritual identity, within which they are members of Christ's body (1 Cor. 12:27), saints of the kingdom (Eph. 1:1), "children of God" (John 1:12), and sharers of Christ's destiny (Eph. 1:5). Alone and together, both woman and man are to be students and followers of Scripture (2 Tim. 2:15; 3:16-17) and couriers of the Great Commission (Matt. 28:18-20).

Just as a classical ballet would never survive without a female and male partner, so no portion of our service to God in community or marriage was intended to occur without the synchrony and industry of man and woman "in the dance" together. From the viewpoint of an audience watching the ballet, there is clear distinction: his physique and hers, sexless and sexual, different yet strikingly similar. Both are essential to the dance. At the peak of a performance, the grace and strength, poise and beauty of each is evident. In God's design, in the dance of life, the two — man and woman — were meant to be equal and complementary, each the crowning glory of their Creator.

The promises of God, the blessings of God's presence, the anointing of God's power, the indwelling of God's character in the heart and mind of the believer: all are privileges He has granted to man and woman in equivalent measure. From creation to commission, from enfolding to equipping, both were meant to have God's greatness and goodness as their eternal provision.

Relationships Rooted in Holiness: Principles versus Practices

Regardless of one's preference for traditional role orientations or more egalitarian understandings of male and female identity, at least two things are clear.

We need to hear from God Himself and follow Him. A right relationship with God is essential for emancipating us from the tyranny of prescriptions that may be ours and not His. Hearing God's voice, a man can know when to act more strongly and when to hold back, when to be tough and when to be gentle, when to be more "traditionally masculine" and when to be less so. A woman can know when she is to be assertive or quiet, when she is to be submissive or stand firm, when she is to lead and when to follow.

In marriage, the principle of relationship means two individuals maturely walking in Jesus Christ. Linda Raney Wright perceptively comments:

> The real foundation of a Christian marriage is the relationship with God of both individuals. Both partners must be sold out to Jesus Christ and individually led by Him. This will enable both parties to submit to each other as well as encourage, serve, please, build, and love each other. . . . [italics deleted]
>
> Marriage is a relationship, not a role, a set of rules, a system. It is two Christians operating fully as Christians. And it is a beautiful order in which decisions can be brought not by arbitrary rules, but by the Spirit of God, alive and functioning in each believer's life.[24]

We need to honor one another and seek to give highest preference and service to each other. This is the principle of cherishing—of making precious, of viewing others as infinitely valuable, just as they are in God's eyes. We then make their needs and goals and personal development as important as our own. Paul, speaking to the whole Christian community, describes it this way:

> Therefore, as God's chosen people, holy and dearly loved, clothe yourselves with compassion, kindness, humility, gentleness, and patience. Bear with each other and forgive whatever grievances you may have against one another. Forgive as the Lord forgave you. And over all these virtues put on love, which binds them together in perfect unity (Col. 3:12-14, NIV).

Cherishing insures that we do not regress to the mere application of rules for the sake of rules, or tradition for the sake of tradition. It requires us to keep our hearts sensitive while using our heads. We are then freed to lead from conviction, affirm from belief, submit in love, and sacrifice in honor and with authentic desire for the other's best.

In marriage relationships, cherishing takes on an added dimension. With marriage, we become one—"bone of my bone and flesh of my flesh" (Gen. 2:23). Not to honor and love one's spouse is not to honor and love one's own body, one's own self.

A daily and dynamic walk with God and a steady and sustained commitment to cherish the men and women He brings into our lives are important. Together, these qualities can help us to navigate the gray waters of role uncertainty.

Roger Chen was the pastor of a large, successful urban congregation in California. Members of his church were upper-class, conservative, evangelical Christians. The men worked, while the wives tended the homes, raised the children, met in women's prayer groups, and the like.

Roger's wife, Melissa, did *not* fit the mold. She neither wanted to stay at home, nor did she wish to have children. (In fact, she resisted being a "pastor's wife" and attending all church functions by her husband's side). It was not that she did not love Roger or support him in his work. She was intimately interested in him—as a person—and consequently in his life and ministry. She simply had never dreamed of being a pastor's wife. When Roger felt a calling, seven years into their marriage, to pursue the ministry, Melissa prayed about it and decided that it was indeed God's will for the *two* of them that Roger should enter the pastorate. Nonetheless, she recognized that a role as a pastor's wife was going to be a difficult adjustment for her to make, since she knew how much God used her daily in her job as a social worker.

Roger appreciated greatly Melissa's willingness to support his calling to the ministry. Several years following his ordination, however, he began to feel pressure from members of the church. Individuals wanted to know why his wife was seldom present at church functions. He himself wondered why Melissa could not act like other pastors' wives he knew. Roger commented:

> For a long time, I struggled with God on this one. I knew we had mutually agreed that I should enter the ministry. But I also knew that Melissa had some of her own ideas and dreams for God's calling for her. I wanted a wife who would be like the wives of the other members of our ministry staff—right there, home when I got home, someone who could minister to me, and someone to be a mother to our children. Melissa wanted none of those things.

God and I made peace about this on two counts. The first was that He simply told me that Melissa's dreams and ministry were as important as (maybe even more important than) my own. His will for me was to cherish her and support her in her goals — while seeking to create a home in which both of us could feel nurtured and protected. The second thing He told me was that Melissa was my first ministry (as I am hers) — not the church. It took me a long time to hear that one, but in the final analysis, I knew He was right.

Roger's decision to follow the Lord's leading led to the fostering of a secure and happy marriage between him and Melissa. Ten years into Roger's ministry, the couple decided to adopt a baby girl. Melissa remembers: "I know we'll never be quite like the 'perfect' pastoral couple — but then God has His own plans for us. I've learned in the last few years that I can support Roger without acting like a 'pastor's wife.' At the same time, I've learned that I like being a mother. I still work, but not full-time. The most important thing I think we both gained was a realization that God's guidance is best for both of us and for our relationship, not just for one or the other of us."

Flexibility versus Fixation: When to Flex and When to Stand

In the 1989 San Francisco earthquake, two bridges were badly shaken. One was immeasurably damaged; the other emerged unscathed. The damaged bridge, a steel-and-concrete monolith, was created stiff and still, an absolutely immovable structure and conduit for transportation. The other, the Golden Gate, was a suspension bridge. Hanging by cables which flexed under the strain of motion, the bridge withstood the temblor. There was no damage, only a slight swinging sensation for motorists on the bridge.

Men and women who rigidly adhere to a fixed pattern of practices are likely to find, in the tremors of life, that their experiences are like that of the first bridge. Unable to move, their relationships break under the strain of change and stress. Other individuals, learning to adapt, find fresh ways of relating to meet the circumstances. Like the Golden Gate bridge, their malleability gives them "sway" in the moment, and durability over the long haul.

David Augsburger describes the journey to a flexible relationship in marriage as comparable to two individuals riding a bike. In the first stage (in some marriage relationships), a man and woman may be like two riders on the same bike: one partner (the dependent one) sits on the handlebars, while the other (the dominant one) supplies the power and steering. Later, the two choose to ride separate bikes; they ride side-by-side, regulating their speed and choosing a common direction. Then they ride separately together, with each partner supplying his/her own power; one may get ahead or lag behind, but each keeps the other in sight. In the final stage, a man and woman may be ready for a bicycle built for two: they both can supply equal power, or one can rest without being left behind, but they ride individually, together.[25]

In "fixed" relationships, there is predictability and safety. Women and men know what to expect: who makes decisions, wields power, determines outcomes. Identities become welded to the permanent definitions we develop of who we are and what we are together and apart. Those definitions may be helpful in some instances; in other moments, they are a hindrance to growth and creative evolution in a relationship. In the worst scenarios, fixed and maladaptive roles become a paralyzing straitjacket, binding partners into conspiracies and collusions of dependency and dominance. Included in these are patterns such as:

■ "I'll be the parent, you be the child. I'll police, support, nurture; you be spontaneous, carefree, childlike. . . . "

■ "I'll be responsible; you can be irresponsible. The concern for managing our schedules, time, money, talent will be mine. You go ahead and follow your impulses freely."

■ "I'll be the healthy one; you be the sick one. I'll nurse you and take care of your needs; you may act out the patient role. I'll be the helper; you be helpless."

■ "I'll be the social one; you may be withdrawn. I'll take care of our communal, church, school obligations, and you do your work, your art, your sports, or whatever. I'll be friendly; you be distant."[26]

Of course, some kinds of task specification can be helpful, even necessary. Flexibility does not imply anarchy. It does imply that the stipulation of any roles is open to change, and that no one — man or woman — should be defined simply by "what they do." Each is given the prerogative to explore his or her capabilities and callings within a jointly developed, dynamic covenant that compels them to honor and serve one another.

Finally, flexibility means that roles serve the individuals and not vice versa. Men and women who find this flexibility celebrate identities which are found in Christ, not in a particular role, performance, or position. They discover that tasks are not static roles but dynamic functions. Functions — chosen by the participants because they further the purpose for which the individuals exist — can be shared, exchanged, delegated, or reconsidered by both individuals, as they seek the best for one another. Augsburger contrasts these nicely:

> The role [fixed] perspective sees tasks and persons as inseparable; the function [flexible] attitude recognizes that people choose certain tasks and refuse others. All [tasks] can be assigned, exchanged, shared, renegotiated according to the gift, preference, or circumstance. Now the two [man and woman] experience an openness and a freedom that allows their lives to move near and far without threat of either abandonment or engulfment.[27]

Getting from Here to There: Empowerment for the Journey

After reading the above material, one may say: "That's enlightening, but I was raised to believe (and even to become) one particular way as a man (or woman). I don't know how to do it differently." How's a Christian supposed to change for the better?

Throughout the rest of this book, we share insights on how believers can find their place as men and women in a contemporary world, while being true to their highest callings in serving a sovereign and worthy God. Here, we highlight three tips for producing in one's life a space for change — ways to achieve hope, wholeness, and new direction both in self-understanding as a man or woman and in understanding of communities, Christian and secular.

Tip One: Check Out God's Word as a Fresh Document, Seeking Truth Anew

It's surprising how well the Bible addresses us—whatever state we are in, whether we purport to be liberal, conservative, or otherwise. With the enlightening of the Holy Spirit, whole new vistas can become apparent to the willing believer.

A fresh study of Scripture may yield the understanding of particular strategies, rules, or roles that are important to take in a specific instance. But a compelling meditation upon the Gospel will be incomplete if it does not suggest new positions of the heart in the end. Preferable to the elucidation of precise prescriptives is the attainment of perspectives that are God's very own. Jesus made it clear that love, not legality, would be the measure of His followers. Therefore, any interpretation of Scripture which results in mere rule following will have missed a great deal. Ultimately and most importantly, the primary goal for men and women, alone and together, is maturity and unity in Christ. A traditional or contemporary rendering of Scripture that escapes this has escaped the essence of the Gospel.

Tip Two: Ask God for His Unique Revelation to You about Your Identity and Calling

Whether we are stationed in the home or the workplace (or both!)—and how we act there—should depend less on what others say and more on what He says, directly to us, in the deepest places of our heart. If the Christian perspective is correct, then paradoxical truths can be reconciled in one revelation, unique from God:

■ One can break certain customs or social "rules" of our society, yet follow God if and when He calls one to be different.

■ It is possible to be a leader, yet a servant, in marriage and relationships.

■ One can have authority, yet be submissive in a relationship where both parties are under God's direction.

■ One can follow traditional roles, even if one biblically interprets male "headship" as "source" and espouses egalitarian roles in the family. For example, the career-oriented woman can choose to stay home with her children, or the child-oriented man can choose to work long hours, so that his wife can stay home.

Conversely, one can choose *not* to follow traditional roles, even if one espouses the "traditional" hierarchy in the family—believing male "headship" to mean male "authority" and female submission—if one perceives God is calling them to such non-traditional roles in their particular circumstances. Examples of such a decision could be the woman who would like to stay home with her children but, for economic reasons, instead feels compelled to work. Another example could be the man who loves his job but who, with a more flexible work schedule, chooses to divide evenly the responsibilities of child care with his wife so that she can work a few hours outside the home, maintain a place in the job market, and get better health care benefits. In these cases, the husband and wife see the husband as head of the household, not because of his economic provision for the family, and not because of a stereotypical division of responsibilities in the family, but because of his God-given role in the family.

The key in working through these truths is to seek Him first and not always the safety of our preconceived notions on these topics.

Tip Three: Pursue the Company of Those Radically Following Christ in Their Search for Authentic Identity

There will always be those seeking to typecast us on the basis of our characteristics: our social class, ethnic backgrounds, or gender. To break free from their expectations and from cultural constraints which are binding—but not always biblical—takes support from our friends and family. Such support is found with those who continually and expectantly seek new identities in Christ.

Many of us need to consider seriously joining or establishing a group made up of persons with whom we can be honest. One young pastor, having experienced without warning a life-threatening heart attack, gratefully acknowledges that his small group was an invaluable source of support for him in his recovery. Recognizing that many expected him as a Christian and pastor to face death peacefully, but knowing at the same time that he very much shared the fear of death that all humans share, he chose to express his fears with his small group. As he expected, they "heard" his fear without being judgmental and provided him the support and assurance he needed, which hastened his recovery and deepened his faith.

A sharing group needs to be made up of those whom we trust and who will help free us from limiting or inappropriate expectations we hold of ourselves and that others have of us. One minister, upon taking the pastorate at a new church, approached members of the pastoral search committee who were not elders or church leaders, asking that they meet together weekly, share their concerns, and pray together. He specifically desired a forum in which he could be authentic, asking questions, expressing concerns, and hearing the needs of the congregation and the ideas of the people present, sharing himself in a way that new pastors often find difficult. A year later, the members of that small group continue to meet, sharing with the church a deep appreciation for this sincere, honest man who serves as their leader and spiritual partner.

Small groups may consist of one other person or several people; they may consist of church leaders or "the rest of us"; their members may spend their time in Bible study or personal sharing. Who comprises the group and how they spend their time is less important than that the group is tolerant and open, that its members feel free (within appropriate limits) to share who they are and to talk about their concerns. In our modern world, too often characterized by shallow relationships and materialistic concerns, we need a place to air concerns and fears, to be assertive and quiet, to be a leader and a follower, allowing growth to take place within the context of authentic Christian community.

Questions for Reflection:

1. To which extreme are you more prone: rigid role expectations or too much flexibility?

2. What do you believe the Bible teaches about gender role differences? How has this chapter helped you clarify your beliefs?

3. In what ways do you think men and women (especially husbands and wives) can be equal before God yet complementary?

4. What examples of "identity-fixed" orientations can you recall among your friends and family? What examples of *identity-flexible* orientations?

For Further Reading:

Bilezikian, Gilbert. *Beyond Sex Roles: What the Bible Says About a Woman's Place in Church and Family.* 2nd ed. Grand Rapids: Baker Book House, 1990. One of the best examinations of male-female relationships from the biblical feminist perspective.

Lees, Shirley, ed. *The Role of Women: Eight Prominent Christians Debate Today's Issues.* Leicester, England: InterVarsity Press, 1984. Lees, recognizing that "over the centuries, Christians have given different interpretations of certain passages of Scripture referring to women," asked well-known Christians from various perspectives to present their interpretations and debate with one another. The result is a helpful volume for those who want to clarify their position on the role of women in the church and home.

Piper, John, and Wayne A. Grudem, eds. *Recovering Biblical Manhood and Womanhood.* Wheaton, Ill.: Crossway Books, 1991. The contributors to this volume offer arguments from a broad range of disciplines (theology, history, psychology) why men should have the principal leadership role at home and in the church. This is a sensitive and thorough explication of the neo-traditionalist position.

3

A Developmental
Model of Gender-
Mature Spirituality

Mature spirituality requires gender-role flexibility. The Bible outlines general principles for male/female relationships, without prescribing specific behaviors for males and females, recognizing that Christians live in many cultures and times. We therefore propose an *identity-flexible* model of gender roles. The "identity-fixed" position holds that the Christian's options are limited and can be described by a set of rules, usually based in part on Scripture or church dogma. The second stance, an *"identity-flexible"* position, finds a breadth of appropriate roles and functions for the biblical woman or man.

These options derive primarily from social experiences, but also from interpretation of specific Scripture passages and a consideration of overarching biblical premises, as we discuss in the following chapters. The *identity-flexible* position is less interested in asking "What is the appropriate behavior for a man or woman?" as it is in asking "How can both genders most creatively fulfill their potentials in the effort to glorify God?" This position is less interested in proclaiming the "rights" of either gender than in propounding the freedoms and responsibilities inherent in the fact that both women and men are "co-inheritors" of the kingdom. The identity-fixed position seeks a clear-cut role for the individual based on his or her gender; the *identity-flexible* position seeks ways to become women and men that are based upon a recognition of interdependence between the genders and mutual worth in the eyes of God.

How then are we to relate to one another as men and women? Our model centers on four virtues that are based on scriptural principles and derive from our experience as Christians in community and as professional psychologists: *respect, responsibility, tolerance,* and *flexibility.*

Respect suggests an admiration and affirmation of each gender's unique strengths and a refusal to "mind read" or act solely on the basis of stereotypes of any kind. It implies a reverence toward the freedom of individuals, of either gender, to make choices within the context of the wisdom granted by God. It implies a concern for the exercise of legitimate authority based on actual capabilities, rather than merely on one's gender, and a concern for maximizing one's own potential and that of others, rather than for circumscribing and abusing the rights of others.

Responsibility implies the obligation of men and women to assist in one another's lives without domination, and to protect one another without anyone's becoming patronizing, paternalistic, or subservient. It commends both genders to "love and work" together in a reflection of God's highest love, working together out of faith-fueled compassion, not merely from conformity to a specific gender-role definition.

Tolerance suggests an acceptance of differences and a willingness to appreciate others who act in roles or demonstrate behaviors which are suspicious or unfamiliar to us. We propose a "range of tolerance" in which gender-role flexibility is encouraged, but which recognizes that some qualities should not necessarily be tolerated, including those which fail to maintain biblical principles.

Flexibility is the acting arm of tolerance, the grace, desire, and strength to surrender or modify old behaviors in response to newly discovered needs or better ways one finds to conduct relationships. It is the commitment to meet the individual — man or woman — whenever possible, in a place which gives freedom and security to both. *Flexibility* also implies a willingness to take risks — to step out on faith. Challenging as this is, if you are listening to God's voice and following His advice, He will give you the comfort and persever-ance you need. *Tolerance* and *flexibility* sound like weak humanistic values, but alternatively, in our model they are meant as complex, active expressions of biblical faith.

Identity-flexible relationships are therefore person-oriented: centering on *respect, responsibility, tolerance,* and *flexibility,* whether in relationships with others in community, close friendships, or marriage. Paul Tournier, whose teachings on community continue to challenge us to wholesome relationships, writes of the day his wife shocked him by saying: "You are my doctor, my psychologist, even my pastor; but you are not my husband."[1] After a great deal of heart-searching and struggle, he came to realize that his relationship to her was too authority-oriented and not personal enough. He writes, "It was not until we came together in God's presence and I confessed my own feelings, that she felt that *I* needed her help as much as she needed mine, and that I had as much to learn from her as she from me. That is real equality."[2] Whether our biblical model is hierarchy-oriented or egalitarian, these words challenge us to emphasize the relationship over its form, the person over the model.

Identity-flexible relationships are dynamic and adaptable. Walter Trobisch, in *All a Man Can Be*, describes the flexibility of marriage this way: "Marriage is not something static like a body at rest. It is not an achievement which is finished. It is dynamic, a process between two people, a relationship which is constantly being changed, which either grows or dies. Fuel has to be put on the fire, and that takes work. Healthy marriages take work too, and dialogue is part of that work."[3]

Identity-flexible relationships are interdependent, marked by mutual respect and responsibility. Speaking again of flexibility within love and marriage, Walter Trobisch quotes from a letter he received from Ingrid when the two were separated during their engagement:

> I want to tell you why I love you. When I picture you in my mind, I can see you stretching out your hand to me. I trust your hand for it is the hand of a safe and secure man. It is true, you walk a little ahead of me, but when you realize I'm getting out of breath and can't quite keep up, you stand still. You turn around and give me your hand to help me over the hard places. Then I come very near to you and you talk to me and comfort me. You don't make fun of my thoughts, neither are you threatened by them if they challenge you to try a new path.

When I am weak and need protection, I know that you are stronger than I, and so I take hold of your hand because I know that you will never use your strength to make me feel inferior.

But you need me too and you are not ashamed to show it. Even though you are strong and manly, you can also be helpless as a child. Your strong hand can then become an open, empty hand. And I know no greater happiness than to fill it.[4]

The following questions, designed with this model in mind, can help you assess how identity-flexible or identity-fixed you are and suggest areas you may need to address.

Table 3-1
How's Your *Identity-Flexibility* Quotient?

1. *Valuing Diversity.* Do you maintain close relationships with people in other "life states" than you (for example, with members of the other sex, with singles if you are married, marrieds if you are single, people from other races, social classes, ethnic groups)?

Yes*		Yes**	Yes***	No
Score: 5	4	3	2	1

   *Yes, I have 4 or more friends in other "life states."
  **Yes, I have 2 friends in other "life states."
 ***Yes, I have 1 friend in another "life state."

2. *Listening.* When you differ with people—about gender roles or other issues—do you encourage them to talk, and do you hear them through, without requiring that they listen first?

Always		Usually		Never
5	4	3	2	1

3. *Communication.* When you feel your opinion is not heard, whether this opinion is about gender roles or other issues, do you work hard and patiently to get another to hear you, and do you try to communicate your position as clearly and in as unbiased a manner as possible?

Always   Usually   Never
| | | | |
5   4   3   2   1

4. *Encouraging Diversity.* When you have explored an issue with someone and find you disagree, do you continue to respect that person, without labeling them, telling others unnecessarily about your disagreement, or avoiding that person?

Always   Usually   Never
| | | | |
5   4   3   2   1

5. *Self-Honesty.* Are you generally honest with yourself?

Always   Usually   Never
| | | | |
5   4   3   2   1

6. *Self-Forgiveness.* When forgiveness is appropriate, can you forgive yourself for your mistakes?

Always   Usually   Never
| | | | |
5   4   3   2   1

7. *Availability.* Do you make yourself available to help others solve problems, without demanding that they choose your proposed solutions?

Always*   Usually**   Never
| | | | |
5   4   3   2   1

*I can remember five times recently I did so.
**I can remember twice recently I did so.

8. *Avoiding Labeling.* Are you quick to use the labels "machos," "wimps," "feminists," "liberals," or "traditionals"?

Never		Sometimes		Always
|	|	|	|	|
5	4	3	2	1

9. *Cherishing.* Do you pray for others, including those you do not know well?

Always		Usually		Never
|	|	|	|	|
5	4	3	2	1

10. *Openness.* Have you ever changed your mind about issues that are important to you and yet not pivotal to faith, in response to another's ideas?

Several Times		Once or Twice		Never
|	|	|	|	|
5	4	3	2	1

The higher you score on this scale, the higher is your *identity-flexibility* quotient. If you score below 20, take a friend out to lunch and pay for it! Ask how you can be more respectful, responsible, tolerant, and flexible. If you score between 20 and 30, take a deep breath and relax. You're on the right track. Learn to listen more and hear better, to avoid labels and cherish others for their individualities. If you score between 30 and 40, you're doing well! Examine those areas where you can improve, but recognize you're good at nurturing relationships. If you score between 40 and 50, you're phenomenal! Friends probably seek you out, and your prayer time is so full that you have to schedule requests!

As we have already mentioned, flexibility does and should have limits. Our gender roles need to remain true to biblical standards and our individual Christian callings. These questions are meant to recognize these limitations. For example, if you answered question 10 with "several times," (a score of 5), you are saying that you are flexible about issues that are not pivotal to faith.

The ten qualities represented by the ten questions on the *identity-flexibility* quotient scale elaborate the four virtues that comprise the *identity-flexible* model of gender identity. Thus, *respect* includes listening, avoiding labeling, and cherishing one another. *Responsibility* includes communication and availability to relationships with others. *Tolerance* includes encouraging and valuing diversity and avoiding labeling others with whom you disagree. *Flexibility* includes self-honesty, self-forgiveness, and openness to the ideas and opinions of others.

The ten questions of the *identity-flexibility* quotient scale assess your relationships with other people and are not limited specifically to questions about their gender-role beliefs or behaviors. Every relationship we have with one another, each communication, reflects our beliefs about gender roles and our respect and appreciation for one another.

The Challenge to Develop *Identity-Flexible* Relationships

Because there are similarities in our beliefs about gender roles and about our relationships to God, we can characterize our relationships to Him by using categories that help us further understand the identity-flexible model. In various examples we've used throughout the book, we've implied that four major positions of biblical understanding could be placed roughly along a continuum: traditionalists, neo-traditionalists, biblical feminists, and secularists. Although such an understanding is overly simplistic, a brief discussion of the implications of our model for the two central positions may be helpful. We focus in our book on these two central positions because they best represent what we feel to be a sensible range of differences in the interpretation of biblical views of male-female issues.

We define *traditionalists* as persons who extend the "male as authority/female as submissive" model to encompass all of life. For example, as Bill Gothard has argued in his *Institute in Basic Youth Conflicts*, women are to be submissive to their fathers until they marry and then to their husbands. If they then divorce or become widowed, they are to seek a place in a divine "chain of command" under a male.[5] In contrast, we find it difficult to support the universalizing of the biblical model for husband and wife to all male-female relationships.

Neo-traditionalists, or complementarians, support the "male as authority/female as submissive" model of male-female relationship primarily in marriage and in church leadership, while recognizing that friends and singles have a host of other models of relationship (generally more egalitarian ones than the traditionalists assert). Sociologically, they generally can accept women acting as leaders and taking initiative in some aspects of society, though they assert men in general are to lead, protect, and provide for women, especially husbands in relation to wives.[6]

Biblical feminists argue for egalitarian roles in the family and society. They may support the model of the husband as the "source" or "completer" of the wife.[7] Biblical feminists recognize that males and females are responsible to God for their own behavior and that neither has a more valuable relationship with his or her Creator.

Secularists reject the primacy of the Scriptures in guiding behavior, and therefore base their understanding of gender roles and marital relationship in secular sources.[8] Their ideal model for relationships changes with the times and at present seems, more often than not, to incorporate an egalitarian model.[9]

Persons representing each of the middle two perspectives, as well as the two extreme positions, can benefit from an *identity-flexible* rather than identity-fixed model of relating, since the *identity-flexible* model integrates the concepts of *respect, responsibility, tolerance,* and *flexibility.* Whether as neo-traditionalists who emphasize the hierarchy and headship (authority) in the kingdom, or as biblical feminists who emphasize our mutual submission to one another, we often erect barriers to brotherhood and sisterhood when we attempt to relate to one another in stereotypical, role-governed, impersonal ways.

A Developmental Schema of Gender-Role Maturity

Gender-role flexibility does not develop easily. Based on our experience, however, there do seem to be stages in our growth towards *identity-flexibility.* There seems to be a pathway to becoming more "fully human and fully alive" as God's children, capturing more of the freedom as well as the abundance with which He intended us to live as men and women.

We propose that gender-role maturity is a dimension of psychological and spiritual growth. While we hesitate to put formal marker points on such a dimension, we nevertheless contend that (a) there is a continuum, and that (b) individuals can grow in their capability to grasp God's full provision for them as men and women.

Our observations lead us to believe that the following stages of development hold true for many individuals as they mature in their conceptions of gender and identity. The stages are based in strong measure on *how* they believe, not simply *what* they believe. To use the following set of stages for personal growth, see where you fit along the continuum, then ask yourself what prevents you from moving ahead to the next stage. If you can identify specific obstacles, you can evaluate these prayerfully and see if you sense God moving you to change. Find other people who represent your stage and later stages. How does your thinking differ from theirs? What insights have they to offer you? We will continue to offer vignettes and specific suggestions that may help guide you in your self-evaluation and growth.

Stage 1: Sharply Differentiated Gender Roles Exist

The individual at Stage 1 believes that there is one and only one way to be a man or woman. The characteristics defining the appropriate behavior and roles of each sex are set out in concrete, black and white. Any deviation from this ascertained prescription is not only wrong, but probably unbiblical and unspiritual.

For the individual at Stage 1, there is no questioning of what one has been taught or has been brought to believe—not even to see if it is, in fact, consistent with Scripture or God's revelation through sincere prayer and seeking. Stage 2 is a transitional stage. Although one may remain in this stage for long periods of time, conceptually it is seen as a belief that most often eventuates in Stage 3 belief.

Stage 2: Sharply Differentiated Gender Roles Exist, but Sometimes May Be Modified by God

There is one and only one way to be a man or woman, but God may direct some individuals in the application of this prescription. Therefore, it is important, first, to know the specific gender rules and, second, to seek His direct guidance and leading, if for no other reason than to understand how to apply the singular prescription for male and female roles to one's own life.

Stage 3: Diversity in Gender Roles Exists, but One's Personal Gender Role Is Fixed

While the person at Stage 3 may be convinced that there is the possibility for diversity (or *identity-flexibility*), he or she is generally uninterested in changing his or her own behaviors. He or she generally does recognize, however, that there is probably allowable diversity in God's plan for the behavior of men and women. Certainly it is a suitable matter for individuals and the church at large to ponder.

Stage 4 (transitional): Beginning Consideration of Personal Flexibility and Choice in Gender-Role Expression

The individual at Stage 4 may have a more wide-ranging conception of gender roles, and may even be living within their "revised standard version" of gender identity (e.g., she is a working mother or he is a father who stays at home with the kids). However, they are more attuned to their own status (e.g., "I'm a liberated male" or "I'm a traditional housewife") than they are to God's calling to them or the needs of others around them. They may be willing to part with traditional gender norms, but they are unable to adjust their behaviors in light of more crucial directives (e.g., God's individualized direction to them or the needs of their family, partners, or friends).

Stage 5: Gender-Mature Spirituality

The individual at Stage 5 recognizes gender-role freedom and responsibility. He or she accepts that all individuals have a legitimate right to choose, before God and within the sanctity of their own consciences, a way of being a man or woman which is most consistent with God's direction in their lives. Stage 5 individuals recognize that gender roles are largely societally imposed and assert that biblical gender roles should be more constrained by scriptural than societal standards. Therefore, they advocate that behavior should be premised primarily upon God's Word and the guidance of the Holy Spirit, not upon the preconceived formulations of gender roles prescribed by the culture or period in which they live.

The individual at Stage 5 actively and willingly modifies his or her behavior to be consistent with perceived direction from God as to how He would have them behave — not only as a man or woman, but as a child of God and a citizen of the kingdom. To the Stage 5 individual, the question is less "What role should I play as a man or woman?" but rather "What should I do, under God's guidance, to bring about all that would glorify Him, magnify His name, and bring about His kingdom here on earth?"

Although these stages refer to individual growth, experiencing gender-mature spirituality often depends on those with whom we are in relationship, whether our relationship is a friendship or marriage.

Karen and Bill recognize the desirability of a Stage 5 relationship but know that their reality falls short of the ideal. In premarital counseling, they expressed their commitment to making their relationship to one another reflect God's presence in their lives. Recognizing that honoring God was easy when their relationship flourished, Karen and Bill chose to consciously submit their disagreements and conflicts to God.

Karen is active in her church and community, leading a weekly Bible study and directing activities for the local Y. Bill is a church leader and speaker, involved in a Christian mission organization, preaching almost weekly in various churches and spearheading ministry programs.

They disagreed rarely but realized that their disagreements followed a common pattern. Bill found that he sometimes resented her demands that they spend more time together, feeling that his commitments were more important than hers and his time more precious. Although he usually asked her to accompany him to his speaking engagements, they rarely had private time together. Karen realized that she often felt as if he wasn't listening to her or valuing their relationship. She honored his heavy time commitments and rarely asked him for time together, instead pursuing her own interests alone. Their struggles together epitomized classic gender-role conflicts, as well as common struggles for greater maturity as Christians.

When they realized their relationship was suffering as a result of their lack of awareness of the other's needs, they committed themselves further to mutual respect and honesty. Karen practiced talking more about her own activities and asking more directly that Bill spend quality time with her. Bill started to refuse commitments when he felt his time with Karen became too constrained. He is still learning how to listen to her when they are together, as he often tends instead to mull over his next commitment or responsibility. Both partners, however, find themselves talking more readily about important issues in their relationship, as well as in their individual lives. Both also feel that their relationship, which had always been good, is now even better.

Putting It in Perspective

These five stages of gender-role maturity have implications for neo-traditionalists and for biblical feminists, as well as for people who associate themselves with the other two biblical interpretative positions of traditionalism and secularism. The level of maturity implied in Gender-Mature Spirituality has particularly important implications for neo-traditionalists and biblical feminists. Although people from these two camps may disagree on the specific behaviors that define male and female roles, persons representing each point of view may be equally rigid about their beliefs.

Gretchen Gaebelein Hull, in *Equal to Serve*, puts our struggles in perspective:

> Yet today, like James and John, so many people pluck at Christ's sleeve: dogmatists, traditionalists, egalitarians, feminists, liberationists, all sorts of activists. They all say the equivalent of "Seat *me* nearest You, Lord; show those other people that *my* system is best." As they pluck at Christ's sleeve, thinking that places at His right and His left will bring them honor and power and worldly recognition, He looks at them — and all of us — and still asks: "Can you drink My cup? Don't you see that whoever stays nearest Me must follow Me in the closest sense — go where I go, serve as I serve? Don't you see that, loving the world as I do, I must serve it to the uttermost, because only then can I save it to the uttermost?"
>
> So the real measure of our suitability as Christ's ambassadors (and therefore His servants) is not whether we have a collar on backwards or have a certain title or are a man or a woman. The real measure of our suitability as ambassadors for Christ will be how we answer that hardest question of all: "Can *you* drink My cup?"[10]

As we grow toward maturity, we become better able to place God in the center of our gender roles, just as we increasingly place Him in the center of our lives, giving Him the central position of leadership and power that He merits. We move away from rigidity and self-centeredness, recognizing that diversity is often God-given and God-sanctioned, becoming better able to express with gentleness and love our calling as male or female, participating together as children of God.

Questions for Reflection:

1. In which ways do you agree with the *identity-flexibility* model? In which ways do you disagree?

2. Which of the four virtues (respect, responsibility, tolerance, flexibility) are easiest for you? Do you agree that these are virtues?

3. What's your *identity-flexibility* quotient? On which areas do you need to work?

4. What biblical position best characterizes your own? How can you better understand and appreciate those from other biblical positions?

5. What level of the developmental model of gender-mature spirituality best characterizes your present beliefs? How can you increase your responsivity as God leads you toward greater flexibility?

For Further Reading:

Balswick, Jack, and Judith Balswick. *The Family: A Christian Perspective on the Contemporary Home*. Grand Rapids: Baker Book House, 1990. This book, written by a husband and wife, sociologist and social worker team, provides a thorough and scholarly discussion of family relations and problems from a Christian perspective. It proposes sound principles for developing mature marital relationships and reasonable child-rearing practices that encourage the development of responsible, *identity-flexible* boys and girls.

Tournier, Paul. *The Gift of Feeling*. Atlanta: John Knox Press, 1981. This well-known Christian psychologist challenges men and women to feeling — to experience the human need for subjectivity, emotions, tenderness, and caring. These qualities, traditionally attributed to women, can be developed in men, he argues, and women also benefit from examining them. His examples and sharing of his experiences and wise observations are intended to help men and women toward experiencing and better practicing their gifts.

Trobisch, Walter. *Love Is a Feeling to Be Learned.* Downers Grove, Ill.: InterVarsity Press, 1971. A brief volume and a classic for Christians — all of whom are called to love. This essay challenges us to love more fully and more biblically. Eschewing the popular cultural notion that love is something that happens to us, without our efforts, Trobisch gently reminds us that love is a powerful expression of our deepest selves, that demands intense efforts and a willingness to learn and continually change. This is a beautiful, inspirational, wise volume.

van Leeuwen, Mary Stewart. *Gender and Grace: Love, Work and Parenting in a Changing World.* Downers Grove, Ill.: InterVarsity Press, 1990. The author, a Christian psychologist, examines physiological, psychological, and sociological reasons for traditional and modern gender roles. She examines biblical passages that lead to a reinterpretation of traditional views of women's roles and male-female relationships in society and the church.

Gender Roles:
Their Problems
and
Possibilities

4 Becoming Male and Female: Myths and Realities

If you ask a four-year-old if she's a boy or a girl, she'll look at you indignantly and say, "a girl." If she knows you well, she'll laugh. She knows you're teasing her, for who cannot tell what sex she is?

As children, we just "know" what being female or male means. It's having long hair, or wearing skirts, or wearing jewelry; or it's mowing the lawn, or not wearing skirts. One "just is" male or female, without ever thinking about what that means.

At some point, we hit adolescence, finding not only that we ourselves are sometimes confused about what it means to act like a female or male, but that many other people our age are confused as well. There are, of course, developmental and individual reasons why adolescence is hard and gender roles are confusing. But society also gives us information that is inconsistent or that conflicts with our experiences. Or we may find that we have difficulty putting our assumptions into practice.

Gender roles are societal, shared by everyone in the same culture. Such widely held knowledge is called cultural knowledge. If you are in your late twenties or your thirties, you probably watched the same television ads, learned the same jingles ("Where's the beef?"), and saw the same models (Twiggy, Farah Fawcett, Cher, Madonna) as everyone else your age. You told similar horror stories at camp ("A boy was parked on a dark country road, making out with his date, when suddenly he heard something scratching the top of the car. It's " . . . the Brutal-Killer-Who-Only-Attacks-Couples-Who-Are-Making-Out!"), and laughed at the same jokes (Remember the "dead baby," "knock-knock," and "pink elephant" jokes?). Knowing this information is important to "cultural literacy," to quote the title of a recent book.

Widely shared knowledge need not be accurate and can be misleading, particularly for Christians. Consider, for example, the beautiful women shown in fashion magazines. They teach us that attractiveness is crucial for femininity. We deplore this message for its emphasis on looks rather than on spiritual maturity, but many women who accept it become trapped in a never-ending struggle to be beautiful. Yet we all hear this message and, to some degree, accept it.

Another example of widely held knowledge is the belief that children learn to be moral if they are punished for wrongdoing. Parents tell one another, "You can't let them get away with anything. They have to know who is boss." This advice is not necessarily true, particularly for adolescents. Children learn to be moral if they are given clear, consistent guidelines, explanations for discipline, and appropriate (not harsh) punishments.[1] If they are punished too severely, given harsh or vague guidelines, or not given enough warmth, they may become increasingly immoral and difficult to change. Children from these kinds of households tend to behave in the presence of adults but, in their absence, misbehave more extremely than their peers.

Much widely shared knowledge about gender roles is also misleading. These "myths" may interfere with establishing good relationships and a positive sense of self. Four major myths are particularly problematic for Christians seeking wholeness in relationships:

(1) Males and females are significantly different;
(2) Men are "macho," powerful, and invulnerable, while women are not;
(3) Gender roles are static; and
(4) We have a choice about whether gender roles change.

In our book, we'll use the term "gender roles" rather than "sex roles." Unger pointed out that many male-female differences have little to do with the biological differences between the sexes and proposed using the word "sex" to refer to a person's biological maleness or femaleness and the word "gender" to refer to the nonphysiological aspects of sex—the cultural expectations for femininity and masculinity.[2] This distinction is one we also think is useful.

1: The Myth of Gender Differences

Males and females are significantly different. Most people would probably agree with the preceding claim. But in fact, many studies of gender differences suggest that fewer differences exist than many of us expect, apart from the physical ones, and that our similarities far outweigh our differences.

Before we begin to discuss this myth, let us clarify: in challenging the myth of gender differences, we are not questioning biblically based distinctives between men and women. Whether you are a neo-traditionalist, and recognize relatively more distinctives, or a biblical feminist, and recognize fewer distinctives, let us celebrate our sexuality, recognize the diversity of men and women available to us as models, and aspire to be wholly male or wholly female.

Nor do we question the biologically based, obvious physiological distinctives between men and women, and the social and personal effects these differences bring. Women, for example, bear children, and men do not—a biological difference that has implications for their daily lives from a young age. Their capacity for childbearing accounts in part for parental tendencies to protect young girls more than boys; females experience the physical effects of the menstrual cycle; and they experience the effects of pregnancy and childbirth.

We challenge instead the culturally prescribed entrapments, the stereotypes that magnify gender differences or introduce differences where there are none, the beliefs about one another that bind and separate us from one another. These beliefs may include the assumptions that: women are less competent in business than men and men are not nurturant, or that men never cry and women must always be full-time homemakers.

These societally learned stereotypes often concern such qualities as nurturance and dependence. Yet Maccoby and Jacklin's classic study of gender differences found few sex differences in these qualities. Although males and females express these qualities in different ways, males can be as nurturant and dependent as females.[3]

In other areas, also examined in this study, gender differences occurred but were more minor than expected. Girls, for example, use more complex and precise language, and boys showed better spatial ability.[4]

Most of the gender differences that Maccoby and Jacklin reported don't show up until adolescence, but we expect boys and girls to be different, and we treat them differently, long before adolescence. In many studies, however, when gender differences are expected, they simply don't occur. We have great expectations of gender differences, far out of proportion to reality.

Other studies of male-female differences have noted that girls, from infancy, appear more attracted to human faces and voices than boys, who consistently show more interest in their toys or mobiles on their cribs.[5] Additionally, women's brains have been shown to have more extensive neural connections linking processing centers to emotions and language, suggesting a greater facility than men for verbalizing about their emotions.[6] Men's brains seem to have more specialized processing patterns than women's brains, which may explain in part why men tend to deal with their experiences in more focused and abstract terms, while women usually tend to be more aware of the rich contexts of their experiences.[7]

Beryl Lieff Benderly says she began her book *The Myth of Two Minds*

> as a straightforward summary of the new evidence for three increasingly apparent scientific truths: First, despite the social changes sweeping America, men and women think, feel, and act differently. Second, these differences have definite physiological bases. Third, physiology explains the very different male and female roles observed in many cultures, and these differences, therefore, doom recent, well-meaning American attempts to narrow the gap in power and opportunity that now separates the sexes. I threw myself into reading the latest scientific literature, which, everyone said, ever more clearly affirmed these ideas. But a strange thing

started to happen; the more I read, the uneasier I felt. I soon began to suspect, and finally came to know, that the three truths were false.[8]

We all share in the Myth of Gender Differences. We believe in it, write sermons about it, and teach it to our children. It shapes our lives in dramatic ways, and yet in reality, when our assumptions are more carefully explored, they often are only a myth. Where did our assumptions come from? Why are they so powerful?

Carol Gilligan, in her classic book *In a Different Voice*, argues that (in a sense) women and men inhabit different worlds. Whereas men live in a linear, rational world in which success is a priority, women live in a world of relationships, a "spider's web" of commitments and obligations, a network of caring.[9] Thus, our powerful stereotypes may reflect Gilligan's observation that, although few differences occur in their abilities, men and women (probably as a result of both biology and socialization) sometimes have different values and priorities. Our stereotypes may reflect our awareness of difference and our inability to understand and appreciate the perspective of the other person.

Men, for example, when in a particular situation, may focus on the practical aspects of a question while women in the same situation focus on the relational aspects. Judy reports a recent conversation with her husband, "We were on our way home from a party when I asked if he thought Sharon was doing well. 'Sharon? Was she there?' he said. 'I was having such an intense conversation with Bill (her husband) about how they built their well that I never thought to look.' "

Males and females are not identical. Their similarities, however, far outweigh their differences. In perpetuating the Myth of Gender Differences, in overemphasizing the differences between men and women, we do ourselves, one another, *and* God disservice. We can create boundaries between women and men that interfere with mutual trust and interdependence.

The following cartoon — in which Red Riding Hood acts in unexpected ways — is humorous because it challenges our expectations about men and women. As women's and men's roles change, as individual people we thought we knew very well behave in unexpected ways, we find ourselves surprised — perhaps amused, per-

Yeah, you're the Big Bad Wolf and I'm Red Riding Hood. I'm also a black belt in karate and a member of the N.R.A. If you lay one paw on my grandmother, we'll be having wolf soup tonight.

haps anxious—as we struggle to develop alternative story lines for ourselves. What happens next? Maybe, by not making assumptions about others' difference from us, we too can begin to establish better, fairer relationships with members of the other sex, and with our own sex as well.

Women and men in our culture describe one another as the "opposite sex." Our very words magnify the differences that exist between us, portraying the other sex often as incomprehensible and perhaps frightening.

Perhaps we emphasize differences because we would like to believe in them. We want to be convinced that strong differences exist. If men are mysterious and incomprehensible to women, and women to men, then maybe we are free. We don't have to try to understand them, pay attention to their needs, or be hurt by them. We can make jokes about them and dismiss them. ("He didn't call me last night when he said he would. What else can you expect from a man?" "She's always talking on the telephone. Yack, yack, yack! Just like a woman!")

One of the first things we notice when we meet a new person is his or her gender. We wonder: is this person "us" or "them?" Or, in another mindset, is this a potential "date?" In neither case do we have to pay attention to the individual. We just pull out our expectations of "us" or "them," or our stereotyped responses and proceed to act accordingly.

A Biblical Approach

For us to begin with our shared humanness is both biblically (as defended in chapter 2) and psychologically sound. "For all have sinned and fall short of the glory of God" (Rom. 3:23). Indeed, at times in our relationships with one another and with God, our distinctives seem unimportant. "There is neither Jew nor Greek, there is neither slave nor free, there is neither male nor female; for you are all one in Christ Jesus" (Gal. 3:28). We are all—male and female—made in the image of God. That image, according to Stephen Evans and other well-respected writers, consists in part of our ability to "know God," to make choices for our own lives, and to act on those even when it is not pleasant or comfortable.[10]

Sin magnified sex differences. In Genesis, after the fall, the woman is called to pain in childbirth; the man to earn his keep "by the sweat of your brow" (Gen. 3:19, NIV). If, in part, the wages of sin are exaggerated gender differences, then the gifts of God include deliverance from overemphasizing these differences. We can return to a pre-Fall state through redemption by the blood of Christ.

We are not arguing for androgyny, which has come to mean replacing gender differences with sameness. Imagine that qualities such as dependence, nurturance, and aggressiveness are on a continuum, with one end the presence of the quality, and the other end the absence of the quality. Put males on one end, the end of independence, lack of nurturance, and aggressiveness. Put females on the other: dependent, nurturant, and nonaggressive. An androgynous person would be in the middle on every quality, sexless and bland, neither independent nor dependent, neither nurturant nor lacking in nurturance, neither aggressive nor nonaggressive. What results from androgyny is the notion that males should be like females, or females like males, or, perhaps, that neither gender should have distinctive qualities.

Dealing with Stereotypes

As you read on in this book, there will undoubtedly be times in which you will wonder if we aren't perpetuating the Myth of Gender Differences by writing this book. In some cases, we address widely held stereotypes, hoping that, by exposing them and discussing the evidence in support of them, we will help people recognize that differences are more minimal than they seem. In other cases, we address gender differences imposed by traditional socialization (e.g., the biasing of women toward passivity and dependence and of men toward the "macho" syndrome) and discuss the negative and positive effects of this socialization. Our hope is that as informed Christian parents, teachers, and pastors, we can bias our children against maladaptive stereotypes, on the one hand, and on the other hand, encourage them to display masculinity and femininity in increasingly exciting and diverse ways.

We must then be against mind-numbing and misleading stereotypes, but be open to appropriately diverse and exciting images for men and women of today. There is room in our cultural repertoire of masculine and feminine images for a girl to dream of being Sigourney Weaver, Sally Ride, or Barbara Bush; for a guy to think of himself as Bill Cosby or Clint Eastwood. Not every societal image we hold of what's masculine or feminine is bad. Some of our images — widely shared but extreme — require balance, and most of us need to go beyond our initial images to develop a range of roles and visions of what it means to be male and female.

In our relationships with one another, we need to replace an emphasis on explicit prescriptives and expectations (e.g., "men shouldn't cry and women shouldn't lead") with an emphasis on *tolerance* and *flexibility* (e.g., "I never realized males could be nurturant, but *you* are"); an emphasis on our differences with mutual *respect* and *responsibility* (e.g., "I appreciate your opinion and the articulateness and gentleness with which you express it, even if

I disagree with you"). This is biblical, psychologically sound, and good common sense. As male and female, let us concentrate on, and better express, our individualities and commonalities in Christ.

Relationships thrive on mutuality and complementarity. Particularly when talking of our relationships in the body of Christ and in marriage, it is helpful and biblical to emphasize our inter-relatedness, our sharing of roles and responsibilities (Eph. 4:11-16). Let us together build up the body of Christ, not by erecting barriers of "differences" but by working together to the glory of God.

2: The Myth of Gender Stereotypes

Men are macho, powerful, or invulnerable; women are not. This image of maleness and femaleness is not particularly flattering to either gender! Who wants to be either macho or wimpy (are those the only alternatives?); totally powerful or powerless; invulnerable or vulnerable? Maybe we've stated this myth too strongly. We suspect, however, that many people read the myth without questioning it.

Perhaps these myths have some basis in reality. Certainly, men have more power and a higher status (as defined by our secular culture) than women.[11] Men, from early childhood, also appear to be more interested than women in hierarchies, dominance, and status relationships in general.[12] Men are generally stronger than women in some parts of their bodies. Women usually live longer than men. While gender differences are not as major as everyone assumes, some gender differences may become magnified and form the basis of stereotypes.

Men are macho, powerful, and invulnerable. This myth feeds upon the Rambos and Incredible Hulks, cultural figures that we collude in calling "real" males, even if we mean it derisively. We all understand the allusion. Men who are macho try too hard to meet the cultural standards of maleness, qualities which make them hard and unresponsive to the needs of others, which deny their inter-relatedness.

Powerful, like macho, connotes hardness. Powerful men make their own choices, whatever others may want or need. Yet Jesus Himself had the means to be powerful, but chose instead to be meek, and to minister to the lowly.

Invulnerability sounds positive but is no more desirable than power. A fortress under siege, a person who cannot be reached — these are the images of invulnerability. What is the advantage of invulnerability? Why would someone worry so much about being attacked? If the image of invulnerability is a fortress that cannot be scaled, replace that with another. Imagine instead a house with open doors.

This myth of male invulnerability is particularly negative because it encourages men to be their own masters rather than serving God. It fosters distance and impersonality, rationality at the expense of sensitivity, and the effort to protect oneself at the expense of membership in the body of believers. Because it is so highly valued in society, we accept this myth in the church. We look for "strong leaders," "powerful men of God," "machos for the Master." We give such men higher status in the church, forgetting the Good Shepherd and the "widow's mite," forgetting that the powerful God we see in the Old Testament is the same one who promises to comfort Israel "as a mother" (Isa. 66:13, NIV). God can use "machos" and "wimps," strong and weak leaders, the powerful and the powerless, transforming all such men for His glory.

Women are not. The second side of the myth could be completed with many terms, none meant as a compliment. Too often, women are defined by their absence of male qualities, and the male terms are invariably seen more positively, as psychological studies have shown. Even aggressiveness, although presumably an undesirable trait, is often acceptable in men. After all, some think, one *has* to be aggressive to be a leader and to be powerful. Right? By paying so much attention to success (how many people have made decisions for Christ under one minister, how many buses a church may have to bring attendees to church), we exalt negative qualities in men, even in the church, ignoring more positive qualities in them and ignoring the contributions of women.

Our negative stereotypes of women may be based on the assumption that men are more powerful and more successful, by the world's standards, than women and therefore that men *should* be valued more highly.[13] As the sayings suggest — "Behind every good man there's a good woman" and "Behind every good woman there's another good woman" — power and success are not qualities that occur in isolation but rather depend upon other people. At least some of these people may be choosing to deny themselves for the benefit of others, a preference which can be unhealthy, but which in Christian terms is not necessarily so. "For all who exalt themselves will be humbled, and those who humble themselves will be exalted" (Luke 14:11, NRSV).

Stereotyping: Benefits and Pitfalls

The myth that *men are macho, powerful, and invulnerable; women are not*, and the resulting higher status of males in society, may also refer to (and result from) women's voluntarily choosing submission. Perhaps women use this approach in relating to men because they sometimes think, many times correctly, that men like for them to do this. In a Christian sense, submission characterizes the marriage relationship and need not characterize the relationships among men and women in general, apart from injunctions to humility, like those in Luke 14:11 mentioned above or James 4:10 ("Humble yourselves in the presence of the Lord"). Further, since the Bible calls those who are married to mutual submission, to care for one another and to lay aside one's own wishes when another's needs and wishes are in conflict, men too at times appropriately place themselves in subordination to women. Why is the myth one-sided? Even if one accepts the husband as the authority in the household, the images of macho — powerful and invulnerable — are inappropriate and extreme qualities that are unlikely to characterize a successful participant in a mutually rewarding, intimate relationship.

Stereotyping (i.e., magnifying the differences between the sexes) is harmful and negative, both to women and men. Stereotyping causes us to judge or reject others without getting to know them. This process makes us respond to another based on our expectations, not on the realities of the other person's needs and personality.

Why do we stereotype, then? Stereotyping is a natural process our mind engages in as it tries to sort out reality. Faced with continuous variety in life, the mind attempts to categorize our experiences so that we can deal more easily with similar experiences later on. Our minds categorize places, smells, people, and situations. Our minds even have a natural tendency to disregard evidence that conflicts with previously established categories.[14]

The problem arises when we focus on these categories rather than on the particular situation or persons we encounter. In contemporary society it is a faux pas to make generalizations about a particular race or ethnic group. We need to be even more careful, though, in our attitudes about males and females, taking care that our language and actions are not prejudicial.

Interestingly, our traditional stereotypes of women, rather than being negative qualities, often describe positive qualities that should be cultivated in both women and men: nurturance, empathy, and vulnerability. On the other hand, the macho male stereotype, despite its higher value in society and the church, is in many ways negative and unbiblical.

Stereotypes are harmful and negative when they make us judge or reject another, or when they limit our own or another's response to God's calling. God calls us — female and male — to be powerful and powerless, invulnerable and vulnerable, strong and sensitive. The alternative to stereotypes is encouraging the individual to explore another's (and his or her own) talents and skills, regardless of gender.

We do not intend with this perspective to suggest the elimination of gender roles in our society, but to encourage *flexibility* in our perspectives and behavior as males and females. Every society has gender roles, and every member of the society learns about those roles. But when gender roles become too restrictive, when they exalt worldly success over spiritual qualities and heavenly rewards, then we need to reevaluate our roles and our callings, praying to be more open to and *tolerant* of those around us.

3: The Myth of Constancy

Gender roles are static. The time of most rigid gender-role categories, although not of most rigid behaviors, is in the early school years, when children first learn the terms "boy/male" and "girl/female," and the exemplars of these categories. Children seem to learn a "laundry list" of sex-differentiated characteristics. Karen vividly remembers a situation that occurred soon after she finished her doctorate. When her boss's seven-year-old son was introduced to her, the boy commented to his father's embarrassment: "She can't be a doctor; she's a girl."

It probably does not matter what gender-role norm is violated: having long hair (for males) or being in a male-dominated career (for females); young children struggle with fitting reality into their categories. They quickly learn the categories of their family and society, whatever those categories are. While making such distinctions appears to be an inevitable facet of a child's efforts toward appropriately filling his or her own gender role, it would be much better if those distinctions were more balanced and if children were taught more toleration in using them.

Gender-role behaviors are most rigidly adhered to in adolescence, when peers punish any violation of gender-typed behavior with ostracism and rejection. Remember how hard it was to be fifteen? You might have worried that your clothes or haircut would be laughed at by your friends. Some girls resisted doing better on exams than boys, and boys had to be *so* tough, whatever happened. How nice it would have been for many of us if teenagers could only have been more tolerant of others and themselves!

With age, particularly in adulthood, gender roles become increasingly complex and, some psychologists suggest, traditional gender roles become more flexible, with women becoming more agentic—effective in modifying their environment—and men becoming more communal or relationship-oriented. Levinson suggests that one result of the "mid-life crisis" for many people may be an increasing freedom for males to experiment with nurturance.[15] Life circumstances in adulthood can, for many, encourage reevaluation of one's assumptions of masculinity and femininity.

Some people marry with strong gender-role expectations. As the wedding plans progress, the wife rushes out to take cooking lessons, and the husband worries about his ability to make enough money to feed the family. Although strong gender-role behaviors are sometimes possible to maintain, in many cases circumstances may force a changing division of labor—a husband is laid off or a wife gets sick. Wives and mothers who work outside the home may find their expectations of themselves are impossible to maintain in the face of escalating jobs or family responsibilities.

Parenting, for many, leads to reevaluation of gender-role expectations, particularly for women. "Before pregnancy," relates one woman, "I experienced my femaleness most strongly in complementary relationships with men. After the birth of my daughter, I became more aware of my connectedness with women. I felt compelled to connect with other mothers, by talking and reading, even reading the stories of mothers in other cultures and times."

Young children early on begin to show skills and strengths. Parents who recognize that children's self-esteem hinges on their competencies encourage the development of these abilities. Why focus in art class on "girls keeping their clothes clean" and "boys making a mess?" "Great drawing" is so much more positive, teaches them *flexibility*, and communicates to them that you are *tolerant*. After all, children ordinarily learn to be appropriate adults in their culture in ample time. Their parents and others model such behavior, and society and the media give them more than enough information about it. At home, they can (and should) learn that maleness and femaleness are not associated with strict role behaviors but rather that being a mature adult means exercising their abilities for the glory of God.

The Myth of Constancy encourages us to believe that gender roles have been and should be constant throughout history and one's lifetime. Such is clearly not the case, as a study of U.S. history, particularly in the last fifty years, and other cultures quickly shows. Indeed, it is the *lack* of constancy in gender roles that makes us—rather than our grandparents, the Pilgrims, or the pioneers—so self-conscious about these roles.

In these modern times—rapidly changing and unpredictable—changes can be less frightening and overwhelming when we realize our own capacity to adapt. *Flexibility* is not only a goal to be reached in developing *identity-flexible* relationships. It is also a reality of our humanness. Strict gender-role divisions are not taught in Scripture, perhaps for precisely the reason that they *should* not be. Gender-role expectations can limit our ability to participate in relationships and adapt to crises in marriage, to worship and serve God.

4: The Myth of Choice

We have a choice about whether gender roles change. Gender roles have changed, whether we want them to or not. Most men and women, boys and girls, now expect to go to college, get a job, and live in two-paycheck families. As a parent of a high-school senior and below-average student said, "I know she may have trouble in college, but I think college is the gateway to careers. I don't feel she has a choice whether to go or not." Most women work, including mothers of young children. Girls now question which career to choose. Whereas in earlier generations only boys were asked their career goals, now, at younger and younger ages, girls are asked to explain and defend their choice of a career. Men find that increased education and the demands of building a career delay marriage and often childbirth. Husbands more often than not expect to have a working wife and to become involved to some degree in housecleaning and cooking chores. Boys and girls, born into these homes, have expectations that they too will work and make joint decisions about housework and child care.

Although we may not have a choice about demographic, sociological, or financial changes in the world about us, we can choose what roles we will play within that world. Sociological factors may alter the context of our decision-making, and may even modify the choices we make, but they do not remove our choice. One coauthor works in a clinic with ten therapists, nine of whom are married. Of those nine couples, four have chosen traditional styles of being husband and wife (i.e., the husband works and wife is at home full-time with the kids), a difficult choice in an area with an extremely high cost of living. But they have made their decision — validly and powerfully, despite the difficulties — because they hold a basic belief about what children need, and more so, because they hold a basic belief about the kind of lifestyle they want to live (e.g., the husband "providing and protecting" and the wife being the homemaker as her "profession").

Generally, when someone suggests that they espouse "traditional" gender roles, they mean that they believe the wife should stay home with the children while the husband provides financial support for the family. The traditional gender role meant, however, a more complex and global lifestyle which was for some women and men more rewarding in the culture in which it predominated. Our culture has changed radically in the last twenty years, becoming increasingly technologically oriented and bringing with it strong economic pressures, all of which are or have been changing our families and work roles in the process.[16]

Changes in our view of what the average woman does with her life indicates the radicalness of the change. Thirty years ago, the issue was whether women chose to go to work or not. Most women married early, had children, and did not work outside the home. The professional woman—particularly the married professional woman—was relatively rare.

Now women question, not whether to work, but whether to stay home with the children. Societally, we have changed our lifestyles. For many, work is a given. With women working and men and women delaying marriage, the questions for many people become: When, in my work life, do I have children? How much time do I spend with them as they grow up? What was once the majority choice—women staying home full-time with the children—has become the choice of the minority. Despite these changes in demographics, the choice—to stay at home full-time or continue to work—remains a real decision.

The "traditional" woman, staying home with her children in the 1950s, received community support and approval for her choice—through neighbors, friends, the media, and the church. The modern "traditional" woman who is home in the 1990s lives a different lifestyle—unless she has a supportive church community—and is potentially more isolated and lonely, perhaps sharing her experience of child rearing with greater difficulty. This modern "traditional" woman often works part-time; her husband may be criticized rather than honored by their acquaintances for the time he spends with the family rather than at work; and it is likely that the family has a poorer lifestyle than those of their peers.

One of us (Kaye) was a "traditional" mother for a time, completing her portion of this book while at home with her daughter for the child's first six months. On Kaye's street are five families with children, and none of the mothers in these families stay home full time. In looking for companionship during the day, she found it only among those women who work part-time. She, as did these women, squeezed in time for visiting among all the other demands for running errands, working, and caring for her home and family. Kaye too sometimes felt the loneliness of caring for children without extended family members present and without the easy availability of neighborhood mothers.

Yet many parents *do* choose to stay home with their children, despite the difficulties. Kaye asked several mothers of infants to have coffee together one Saturday morning. Most of these mothers—particularly those working full-time—yearned to spend more time with their young children. One or two mothers, having been quite career-oriented before their child's birth, found themselves strikingly less career-oriented after their child's birth. Knowing full well what they were "giving up," these mothers were considering making arrangements to spend more time at home, because they knew equally well what they would gain by staying home.

Children need to be cared for and protected, whether by the modern "traditional" lifestyle or some other alternative. Even the two-career couple can, by evaluating their children's needs in light of career demands and placing their children's needs first, live a biblical life.

Summary

These four myths—of gender differences (males and females are significantly different), stereotypes (men are macho, powerful, and invulnerable; women are not), constancy (gender roles are static), and choice (we have a choice about whether gender roles change)— delude us into concern about our sexuality and the appropriateness of our actions. They limit us, encouraging our conformity to external measures or vague societal standards. They seduce us away from concern for our gifts into concern for propriety and conformity.

Our concern should rather be for spiritual growth and maturity. We should focus on the growth of the internal person rather than the external, on developing competencies rather than fitting gender-role standards. We should spend as much time hearing and responding to God's calling as worrying about our relationships with the other sex. We should dedicate ourselves to developing Christian maturity rather than ultra-femininity and macho-masculinity. These myths can then be revealed for what they are: conformity to standards that are culturally rather than biblically imposed. "Do not be conformed to this world, but be transformed by the renewing of your mind, that you may prove what the will of God is, that which is good and acceptable and perfect" (Rom.

12:2). By taking the Apostle Paul's advice to heart, we can make major progress in "re-visioning" the stereotypes we may have of gender roles.

The Chers and Rambos of this world beckon us to emphasize and exploit our femaleness and maleness. They entice us to believe that males and females are fundamentally different (the myth of gender differences) and to exalt "male" qualities over "female" (the myth of stereotypes). They encourage our belief in the rigidity and impersonality of gender roles (the myth of constancy), and our hope of returning to an earlier era, when life was simpler and choices more clear (the myth of choice).

We need instead to recognize the truth of male-female interdependence and strive to develop within ourselves solid biblical qualities. With God's help, we can continue to grow and change throughout life, witnessing the dynamic nature of our sexuality, and making choices that edify ourselves and our friends. Together we can protect our children and foster their growth in an increasingly complex and secular society.

Questions for Reflection:

1. Which of these gender-role myths do you think are the most powerful? Of which have you not been aware?

2. If gender differences are more minor than some have previously assumed, how does this change your relationships/work/ life/church?

3. If males and females do not have certain distinctive personality characteristics, how does this affect child rearing? What concerns do you have about socializing males and females for freer gender roles? How might these concerns be addressed?

4. How might (or have) stereotypical expectations of males and females negatively affected marriages (yours, if you are married)? How can these expectations be minimized?

5. Do you agree that gender roles have changed? How has this change affected you, both positively and negatively? Where are the

problem areas for you? Consider what individual might help you or provide a model for addressing these concerns.

For Further Reading:

Balswick, Jack, and Judith Balswick. *The Family: A Christian Perspective on the Contemporary Home*. Grand Rapids: Baker Book House, 1990. This book provides a thorough and scholarly discussion of family relations and problems from a Christian perspective. It proposes sound relationship principles and child-rearing practices that encourage the development of mature, responsible, *identity-flexible* boys and girls.

Benderly, Beryl Lieff. *The Myth of Two Minds: What Gender Means and Doesn't Mean*. New York: Doubleday, 1987. This book, written by a journalist, translates for the lay reader the latest research on gender differences in thinking, feeling, and relating, and argues that this research shows that these differences are heavily cultural, rather than heavily biological.

Rubin, Lillian B. *Intimate Strangers: Man and Women Together*. New York: Harper and Row, 1983. Rubin provides a superb analysis of male-female relationships and the difficulties of these relationships. She concludes by discussing "people in process," and why people find it so hard to change.

Tournier, Paul. *The Gift of Feeling*. Atlanta: John Knox Press, 1981. This well-known Christian psychologist challenges men and women to feeling—to experience the human need for subjectivity, emotions, tenderness, and caring. These qualities, traditionally attributed to women, can be developed in men, he argues, and women also benefit from examining them. His examples and sharing of his experiences and wise observations are intended to help men and women toward experiencing and better practicing their gifts.

_____. *The Meaning of Persons*. New York/San Francisco: Harper and Row, 1957. Tournier here writes, as a clinician, to help persons—men and women—to develop their authentic personhood.

Paralleling psychological with spiritual growth, continually calling us back to worship God, he has wise words for those who hurt in any way.

van Leeuwen, Mary Stewart. *Gender and Grace: Love, Work and Parenting in a Changing World*. Downers Grove, Ill.: InterVarsity Press, 1990. The author, a Christian psychologist, examines physiological, psychological, and sociological reasons for traditional and modern gender roles. She examines biblical passages that lead to a reinterpretation of traditional views of women's roles and male-female relationships in society and the church.

5 The Total (and Totaled) Woman

I'm active in my church, a good mother, and a hard worker at my job. I love my husband, and we enjoy being together. After 20 years, how many people can say that? Yet I keep feeling that I'm missing out on something. My job should be higher paying, or I should not have to worry so much about my health, or it shouldn't be so hard to get everything done. Especially at Christmas, always my favorite time of the year, I feel like hibernating. Stop, world, I want to get off! I don't know what I expected, or what I'm missing. But it's always there . . . the sense that there's something more.

(Corinne, forty-six years old)

Her dilemma is not uncommon. As is true for many women, her cheerful exterior masks deeper questions. Many women who seem to be coping well with busy schedules or demanding relationships — many of whom *are* coping well — nevertheless struggle with issues that seem unique to our generation and experience. Are women in crisis more than they were thirty years ago? In what ways are their gender role expectations to blame?

We — men and women — are more aware of anxiety and crisis than ever before. Ours is a self-conscious society, in which people seek help in unprecedented numbers. Our expressions of stress sometimes appear gender specific. Men appear more prone to develop alcoholism, while women are more prone to depression than men. Twice as many women as men request help in clinics and are hospitalized for clinical depression.

One Christian man, when asked whether he would "mind being female," said he definitely wouldn't have wanted to be a woman before the early 1970s. He said he would be somewhat less averse now, but that he still would prefer "to wait" another decade or so more.

Why would he mind being a woman now? In a time when it seems possible to achieve women's highest potential, why is it that seemingly simple goals, such as developing positive self-esteem, or having a good job and a good marriage—things women and men have been taught to take for granted—seem so elusive? We contend that the problems—increased anxiety and frustration—accompany the benefits of greater flexibility in women's roles and that change is difficult and frightening.

Women in the last twenty years have been told that they can "have it all": excellent marriages, children who are "above average" (to quote the Lake Wobegone line), and careers that are rewarding and well-paying. This promise has made many women unrealistic about their futures. Female students in college classes, when asked what they want to be doing in ten years, say they believe that women have achieved full equality in the workplace and that they can be lawyers and full-time mothers simultaneously. These female students are shocked to find that, in exploring their possibilities, they do not always feel "happy" or "satisfied" and their achievement seems blocked in some ways. "I never thought it would be so hard to find a job," says one woman, a recent graduate of a Christian college who is searching for a job in a recessionary climate; "Or to find a boyfriend," chimes in her friend, also doing part-time work. "I feel like I flunked Femininity 101."

We do not believe the picture is bleak, or that women are in major crisis. We do believe that women have common but often unshared anxieties that reflect their socialization into a femininity that is still much affected by the "traditional" values of passivity, dependence, and homemaking. Such traditional qualities are difficult to attain in our contemporary society, and these qualities are probably not even desirable, were it possible to achieve them. We believe that the church has too long ignored women's issues that result from changing gender roles and thus hindered women's service and growth in the church and community. By addressing these concerns, we believe, as this cartoon illustrates, we can help free women to follow God's guidance, allowing them to experience more satisfying personal lives and participate more honestly in relationships.

© Rob Portlock

Modern Gender Roles Are More Flexible and Diverse

In the 1950s, the model (and modal) woman among white middle- and upper-class Americans was a housewife, raising children and caring for the home; now in the '90s, women's roles have become much more diverse. Many are career women, facing the issues of women in the workplace. More women are single than in earlier decades, either having never married or having divorced. More single mothers with children are in our churches, with their own unique issues to address. Even among married women with children, more than half of women work, creating the issues of integrating work and family life.

Traditional gender roles (which, as we generally use the term "traditional," have actually been dominant only since World War II), where women were predominantly housewives, (stereotypically) entrusted with emotional issues while men made the necessary "rational" decisions, and dependent while men were dominant, were somewhat abusive to both women and men. Husbands and wives related to one another in more rule-governed ways, with strong "do's" and "don'ts" about their relationships, and relatively clear demarcations between the acceptable qualities of men and women and the acceptable spheres of influence. Women found their sphere restricted to the home and family, and men found themselves effectively excluded from this domain. Although traditional gender roles may seem to be easier to achieve, in some ways, than the more flexible roles we advocate, they bring a price — for both men and women. The price for women is in terms of lack of fulfillment. As our technological society created more "labor-saving" devices and American families had fewer children, women were freed from drudgery but not labor. Women spend as much time as ever in housework, partly because acceptable standards for household cleanliness have become more stringent. The combination of constricted, rule-governed roles, and endless housework has contributed to the high incidence of depression among housewives.[1]

Modern female roles also have their price. Women who prefer the "traditional role" may feel criticized and devalued by society for their choice. Working women may feel pressured by the many demands of their lifestyle, including the need to nurture relationships with friends or spouses or to care for children. They may struggle to integrate the demands of the workplace with the rest of their lives. Even in the best of working conditions, jobs are stressful, and, in most situations, women continue to face pressures different from and possibly more negative than those faced by men. Many of these pressures are the result of socialization for a society that was more predictable and stable. It was a culture with a more constrained set of roles for women than is true of our contemporary society.

Many of these contemporary pressures are also the result of a society that puts unrealistic expectations on women and men. In our society, one's work can be all-consuming; one's private life is often not talked about at work. To succeed at both is difficult. We—male and female—need to question our definitions of work and the separateness of home and work life. We need to redefine present society so that work and home are not so separate. This process is already beginning, as businesses begin to provide flextime, paternity and maternity leave, computer hookups for office work at home, and daycare centers for their workers. Society needs to explore these issues, encourage public debate to help people clearly see how the work world and family world could interact, and help employers and employees find better ways to support the family.

Perhaps eating disorders are the most striking evidence of the pressures of modern gender roles. Although anorexia was virtually unheard of twenty years ago, and remains uncommon (affecting only 1 percent of women ages fifteen to thirty-five), it is a striking disorder, and most laypersons now know its definition. Bulimia too was not a common psychiatric diagnosis twenty years ago but is now thought to characterize 10 to 20 percent of college women. The increase in these disorders is rapid enough to have been labeled an epidemic. Because of their rapid increase, and because they occur ten times more frequently among women than men, experts believe that a major cause of these disorders is unrealistic sociocultural expectations of women.

Some women hear the dual societal messages of both traditional and modern socialization: you are to be *ultrathin* ("one can never be too thin," as the old saying wrongly asserts), which perpetuates the older societal expectations of attractiveness, and you are to be *successful*, which adds new pressures. Unable to understand or integrate these messages appropriately, women often blame themselves for their inability to meet these unrealistic standards.

As we have already argued, contemporary roles are not necessarily better or worse than earlier roles. Each is adaptive—at least for a time—for its societal context, and each has its nonconformists. But society today demands more flexibility and diversity in our spiritual, personal, and work lives than thirty years ago. This is inherently more difficult than fitting into constrained roles. Finally, we are often self-conscious about the change toward contemporary roles, making today's gender roles a frequent topic of women's Bible studies and coffee times. Our challenge is to ground the dynamic nature of modern life in the unchanging stability of God.

We suggest that the contemporary difficulties women have with gender roles often originate in misunderstandings of qualities toward which women have traditionally been socialized: passivity, dependence, nurturance, and body emphasis. Although these characteristics are closely related to one another, we feel each is important enough to be separately addressed.

We recognize that, in discussing these qualities, we are also stereotyping and that changing roles have actually brought increasing diversification in the personality characteristics of women and men. We recognize that women's issues of the '60s focused heavily on competence, independence, and autonomy, whereas now they focus heavily on relationships as well.[2] For the sake of discussion, however, we will use some stereotypes here, hoping that our comments will help people toward greater self-understanding.

Are Women Best Taught Passivity and Dependence?

The term "feminine" probably immediately elicits images of pinks and pastels, ruffles and color-coordinated clothes, demureness and quietness. Women have traditionally been taught that certain qualities define femaleness, including dependence and passivity. As members of society, we inappropriately stereotype when we emphasize these qualities. Women are socialized for other qualities, and men may also be socialized in these ways. But women *are* socialized much more strongly for those qualities than men. Dependency and passivity are not inherently negative, but when they are taken to an extreme they bias women toward depression and interfere with Christian service.

From early on, in middle-class Western Anglo-Saxon culture, girls are taught to "be," while boys are taught to "do."[3] Toni enjoyed building with blocks as a child, and her father sometimes sat on the floor to play with the children. With the hindsight of adulthood, she remarked that when the structures that her brothers made fell, her father would take time to show them how to arrange the blocks so they would not fall again. But when her blocks fell, he would take her in his arms and tell her that everything was okay — that it didn't matter that her structures had fallen. In taking this approach, her father retarded the development of her instrumental capabilities — using her mind and abilities to rectify her problems and affect her environment — and limited her learning to take responsibility for the results of her endeavors. These lessons are ones frequently missing from the repertoires of women raised in traditional homes.

In the preschool years, boys are allowed to go further from home to play or to visit friends than girls.[4] They "check in" with home less often, and they are encouraged to climb and to engage in rough and tumble play more often than girls. Whatever the influences of biological factors, from early on, socialization maximizes sex differences in activity level and dependence.

Reflecting on her parent's teaching her dependence on others, Jan remarked, "I'm thirty-four years old! When I now drive the family car, Dad constantly offers 'helpful' advice about driving, but he never does when my brother drives. I've had my own car for ten years now!" Her friend Carol commented, "My dad is now sixty-five. Yet, when I cross the street with him, he grabs my coat, as if to protect me, like he did when I was a kid. It seems funny to me. My dad is frail and needs my help more than I need his, but he'll always see me as his little girl — dependent on her big daddy. I love him for it, but I wonder how much I avoid doing my own work, depending on others instead, as a result."

Low Self-Esteem

With the emphasis on dependence and passivity that women more often receive, it is not surprising that they report lower self-esteem than men. Dependence and passivity encourage women to expect that others will solve their problems for them.

Having been socialized to these qualities from birth, women have had less experience with independence, taking initiative, problem-solving, being responsible, and being active — qualities which are effective in counteracting depression.

Naomi is a thirty-five-year-old woman who has a whirlwind social life and a well-paying job as an administrative assistant. Her friends envy her good looks and her active lifestyle, yet she periodically experiences depressions that interfere with work and keep her away from her friends. As she once said, "Everyone thinks I am doing so well, but I don't feel like I am. If I had a steady boyfriend, my problems would be solved." Later, she admitted, "I grew up expecting adulthood to be wonderful. And sometimes it is. But I thought I'd be married by now, and still doing as well at my job as I am. You know, two kids *and* a good job. I feel like a failure."

Despite her seeming self-confidence, and despite being well-liked, Naomi's problem, and that of many women who are depressed, is that, having learned well the lesson of socialization (her need for dependence on others, particularly her need for marriage), she is not free to enjoy being who she is while not in relationship.

Although relationships are certainly worthwhile, Naomi has been taught that the clear measure of mature womanhood is marriage and, secondarily, a good job. Rather than appreciating relationships for themselves, she lets her self-liking hinge on her dating status. Many women who are unable to articulate their internal "rulers" carry some such expectation, with similar if not the same criteria, rather than the more appropriate internal "rules" of their Christian maturity and relationship to God. Given their socialization, it is not surprising that some women appear addicted to relationships.[5]

Women may cognitively understand that they are made in the image of God, without feeling—if they are not in relationship—that they are worthy of God's love or the love of others.

Learned Helplessness

Some women experience learned helplessness, a cause of depression and low self-esteem.[6] Learned helplessness refers to a condition in which one comes to believe that he or she has only limited control over life. Socialized to passivity as well as dependence, many women find they feel "stuck" in their low self-esteem and lack of relationship. Rather than taking control of their lives, they accept their state, blaming themselves for their inadequacies. As a psychologist friend recently commented, "When a woman gets depressed, she is immobilized; when a man gets depressed (unless he's seriously depressed), he gets busy playing basketball, problem solving, working. Too bad we can't get some of men's reactions to rub off on more women."

Learned helplessness is further exacerbated by societal expectations of women and men. Society has traditionally limited the roles of women more than men, and it continues to do so: allowing men to dominate conversations while women patiently wait their turns;[7] making men's contributions in public meetings more valuable than women's;[8] and limiting women's pay for jobs in comparison to men's.[9]

Even if women are motivated and self-confident, they find themselves—particularly earlier but to some degree even now—discriminated against and cut out of doing things.

If society limits women's options, if "daddy will do it," and girls are relieved of choice, girls learn little sense of self-control and little acceptance of responsibility for their own lives. This socialization "worked" in a society in which women had fewer choices, were more likely to be primary caregivers, and did not work outside the home, but it is less effective when women must make choices for themselves. Women's feelings of being depressed, "out of control," and "trapped" are often the result of being socialized for passivity and dependence.

Christian women too experience feelings of passivity and dependence in their experience of faith, an orientation which can in part be imposed by their church, inhibiting their growth as Christians. Men are to be spiritual leaders; women are to depend on men's leadership. By denying women's past and potential achievement, we interfere with their growth as persons and as Christians. Christian author and lecturer Patricia Gundry highlights the problem when she reports the disappointment of women who have been given the distinct impression by male church leaders that women are not capable of much more in the life of the church than organizing church suppers.[10]

"Re-Visioning" Passivity and Dependence

In general, qualities used to describe women are seen as negative, whereas those used for men are seen as positive.[11] For example, dependence (attributed to women) is seen as negative and independence (attributed to men) as positive. Similarly, passivity (attributed to women) is seen as negative and activity (attributed to men) as positive. Indeed, in part because boys are punished for being "sissy" while it is acceptable for girls to be "tomboys," some scholars have suggested that women are taught to be female, while men are taught, not to be male, but to be "not female."[12] Yet, mature development requires a combination of dependence and independence, passivity and activity. Socialization pressures for females encourage qualities of the self that put women at risk for depression and low self-esteem. (The parallel risks for men will be discussed in chapter 6.)

We contend that the qualities of dependence and passivity are not biblical when taught in isolation from other balancing qualities, and that they bring costs to women. We propose that a clearer biblical understanding is that women (and men) are called to interdependence rather than dependence, and to activity rather than passivity. As the model of womanhood in Proverbs 31 clearly illustrates, women are called to active service and personal responsibility for Christian maturity and to interdependence in relationship with other members of the Christian community.

Can One Be Too Nurturant?

Women are also socialized for nurturance, a second quality that is positive but has potentially negative effects. Nurturance is clearly biblical, and one would hope that men would be as nurturant as women. Too much nurturance, however, giving far beyond one's capacity to give, causes loss of identity, personhood, and self-esteem, and is ultimately unhealthy and unbiblical.

Society's devaluing of nurturance contributes to women's low self-esteem. One woman described her grandmother as a dedicated family member and selfless servant, whose life revolved around service to her busy husband and family. Yet, this woman, in some sense a feminine ideal, considered herself worthless because she was unable to give as much to her family as she thought she should. This frustration drove her to attempt suicide and, as a result, to receive treatment for her unrealistic concerns. An extreme story, but one which suggests that nurturing others is central to many women's sense of their own femininity, even nurturance that is self-destructive and extreme.

Although most assume that women are more nurturant than men, psychological studies suggest that women and men can be equally nurturant.[13] They may, however, be nurturant in different ways. For example, women are more likely to spend time with their children caregiving, while men are more likely to spend time playing with their children.

Stereotypically, women are socialized to take care of other people, whereas men are socialized for individual success. Women's "other-orientation" is less valued in our society than success, and qualities that follow from this may be negatively stereotyped.[14] Anne Wilson Schaef, in her book *Women's Reality*, describes women as less time oriented, less likely to insist on the rationality of arguments, and less goal oriented.[15]

These stereotypes are common enough that we each can recall a time in which they have been jokingly or seriously invoked: "late, just like a woman" says the patiently waiting male; "women are so irrational," he says, struggling to understand; and "make up your mind and then just do it, don't keep talking about it," he says in frustration as she reviews the options for the umpteenth time.

Yet, these qualities may reflect a priority for relationships over time, reason, and products. She may be late because she was talking to a friend in need. She may prefer to seem irrational rather than admit she disagrees with him. And she may have trouble making decisions because she sees the situation as a complex composite of individual wants and needs, with any solution to the dilemma causing pain to one of the participants involved.[16] In each case, the biblical value of nurturance has received a negative societal label.

Women's other-orientation, in most cases a virtue, becomes negative when it causes stress. Kathy, a successful field-support representative for a major computer company, has refused several offers for promotion to a management position. Although she clearly has management skills, she fears that others will criticize her, calling her "proud" or "bossy" if she moves up. "If I accept the promotion, who will love me?" she asks. "I know my choice is extreme, but it's the way I feel." When approached to give group presentations, she declines, saying she gets too nervous. When pressured, as she has been on a few occasions, she agrees only if someone else works with her, and she generally begins her presentations with a needless disclaimer, mentioning her lack of knowledge in the area and her limited experience.

As is true for many women, Kathy's extreme other-orientation creates distinct problems on the job, causing her anxiety and stress and frustrating herself and other people. In the workplace, it has been suggested that women's orientation toward others causes them (1) to fear power, (2) to blame themselves for failures and to share inappropriate credit for successes, and (3) to be masochistic.

Fear of Power

Women fear that power is harmful, negative, and isolating, separating them from other people.[17] Linda, a successful child psychologist, nevertheless describes her job as "child-care worker" to new people, particularly men, to downplay her career success.

Her friend Brenda is willing to organize conferences and plan workshops, so long as she does not have to speak in front of groups or take the credit for her efforts.

Women's fear of power may be easiest to see in adolescence, where it has been called the "femininity-achievement conflict."[18] Girls in adolescence feel the strongest pressure to be feminine, with all the qualities that define femininity. Traditionally, and still to a surprising degree, it is not considered feminine to achieve. Susan, an exceptionally bright adolescent, when asked what she wants to do as an adult, says she wants to be a lawyer and senior partner in a law firm but, when pressed, remarks that she will stop working when she has children and return to work when they get older. Her goals are unrealistic, and her sense is that nurturance and achievement are incompatible. Most teenage girls desire a career (never a "job," although the reality is that most women work in low-paying jobs), but only until they are married. They have little idea of how to achieve their goals, and their goals are often less realistic than the goals of their male peers. Women feel in conflict over their desires both to nurture others and to achieve. Additionally, they fear that achievement prevents their developing relationships — particularly dating relationships.

In a more recent, more holistic formulation of this adolescent conflict, Carol Gilligan has observed that, around the age of eleven, girls go through a "moment of resistance" that is, a "sharp and particular clarity of vision, an almost perfect confidence in what they know and see, a belief in their integrity and in their highly complex responsibilities toward the world."[19] Previously outspoken and honest, the girls, as they age, seem to undergo a kind of crisis in which, "by fifteen or sixteen," says Gilligan, their "resistance [to the strictures and demands of the culture which tell women to keep quiet] has gone underground. They start saying, 'I don't know. I don't know. I don't know.' They start not knowing what they had known."[20] This fear of power, integrity, and independence seems to lead women to deny themselves, undercutting their relationships with themselves and others. It is not surprising that the greater incidence of low self-esteem and depression among women begins in adolescence.

Women, fearing the abusiveness that comes from exercising power, are more comfortable with the version of "empowerment" in which a woman's own power is used to empower or support other people. Empowerment in this sense is close to a biblical definition of power. At the same time, while supporting others is important, women vitally need to feel comfortable with empowering themselves and learn how to do so.

The goals of nurturance and relationship are valuable goals. Similarly, achievement is important for positive self-esteem, and power, often associated with achievement, can be used for other's benefit as well as their harm. It is unfortunate that most women feel that nurturance and achievement, nurturance and power, or nurturance and "having a voice of one's own" are incompatible and in conflict.

Sharing Credit, Taking Blame

Some psychologists suggest that women are more likely to share the credit for successes and to take the blame for failures, even when they deserve the credit and not the blame.[21] One woman, awarded a citation for shepherding a large and difficult project through the bureaucratic red tape necessary to get funding for children with severe disabilities, minimized her contribution, saying "I only started the process." A Sunday School teacher, complimented on the skit she wrote for the Christmas program, answered, "They're good actors." These everyday examples illustrate how hard it is for women to say "thank you."

Yet, when mistakes are made, or sometimes when they are not, women take the blame, apparently because they perceive it as a way of protecting or caring for others. Steve, home for Christmas, got up from a family discussion to get a piece of fruitcake. "Oh," his mother volunteered, "I should have known you wanted that, and I could have gotten it for you." A student berated herself for not being insightful enough to know without her boyfriend's telling her that, since he lived far away, he would have liked her to call him. In these two instances, it is clear that blame is not the same as guilt. While these women may have felt guilty, in reality they were not to blame.

The tendency of women to take the blame has become a stereotype of women in the workplace. A professor at a Christian college once commented that he finds women harder to work with than men because women are "too sensitive" when problems occur. "I'm sorry," women say, when there may be no need to feel sorry. Even when this response may be appropriate, to emphasize it may interfere with correcting the problem.

Although women may be more likely to share the credit and take the blame, some suggest that men are more likely to do the opposite, that is, to take credit but share or deny blame, projecting it on someone else. While this observation may not be entirely true of men, in actuality this response in some cases may represent a more adaptive response and may contribute to better job performance and self-esteem. In contrast, sharing or refusing the credit, or attributing success to "luck," encourages low self-esteem and less respect from others.[22]

Susan Schenkel calls women's demeaning their contributions "discounting." Discounting constitutes an unhealthy, unnecessary, and debilitating practice that emphasizes weakness and incompetence, even when these characteristics do not describe the women who practice them.[23]

Another manifestation of the problem of "sharing the credit and taking the blame" can be observed in the frequent tendency of women to depend upon others (particularly male friends or relatives) for confirmation that they have done a good job with something. Unable or unwilling, usually from a lack of self-confidence, to evaluate frankly their own achievements, women too often depend on others for affirmation, thus lessening their sense of self-worth as women. As Kim, a Christian woman in her mid-thirties, wisely put it, "One problem much too often characteristic of women is that they are not self-referential, that is, they are incapable of making basic, healthy self-judgments."

Some women, prone to refuse the credit and take the blame, experience the "imposter phenomenon," the sense that their skills are overvalued.[24] These women feel incompetent, while others view them as quite competent. One woman, promoted into a prestigious job in a law firm, carried the secret fear for years that she was not really qualified for the position and that she would soon be "found out." Feeling that she could not say "no" when asked to take on new assignments, she often worked sixty-hour weeks and found herself isolated from church and family support. Now, at forty-five, although experiencing the benefits of her hard work, she is saddened by her difficulties in breaking her isolation and frustrated by the knowledge of those "lost years."

Women's tendency to take the blame contributes to low self-esteem. By refusing to take the credit, by not saying "thank you" when this is appropriate, women feel less worthy. By taking the blame, particularly when there is no real blame to take, women devalue themselves and foster the sense that they are never quite "good enough." Even if others value them, women belittle themselves, eventually undermining others' confidence in them. Undervaluing oneself leads to lack of self-confidence which leads to low self-esteem, becoming a self-destructive cycle.

Our goal as Christians is not to view ourselves more highly than we ought to, but, as women and men, to show sound judgment about our skills and abilities. "For by the grace given to me I bid every one among you not to think of himself or herself more highly than he or she ought to think, but to think with sober judgment, each according to the measure of faith which God has assigned him or her" (Rom. 12:3, our paraphrase). Appropriate self-evaluation — knowing our strengths and weaknesses, when combined with humility — fosters positive self-esteem.

Masochism

Women are socialized to be considerate of others, sometimes to the detriment of themselves, a quality which has been called "masochism" (this in quotes because most masochistic acts appear less painful than the term generally connotes). Women learn that the highest sign of caring for others is to do so at a price to themselves.[25] To see how masochistic one is, answer the following questions on the Masochism Scale. The more questions one answers with "true," the more masochistic she is. (If a person responds with six or more "true," then she is somewhat masochistic; if she responds with substantially more than six, then she is seriously masochistic.) Although we may sometimes be called to serve others to our own loss—a valuable and biblical calling—women are being masochistic when they consistently nurture others to the exclusion of their own needs.

Selected Items from the Masochism Scale[26]

T F 1. If you drop something, do you find yourself saying, "I'm sorry," even though there is no one to hear you?

T F 2. Do you find yourself saying "thank you" frequently, even unnecessarily?

T F 3. Do you go into lengthy explanations for being as little as five minutes late?

T F 4. In an important discussion or argument, do you back down easily?

T F 5. Do you tend to postpone asking for things that are important to you until it is too late?

T F 6. In a restaurant, are you afraid to ask for a glass of water because it might annoy or trouble the waiter?

T F 7. Do you usually choose the cheapest dish on a menu rather than the one you would like, even though you can afford the latter?

T F 8. Do you spend an inordinate amount of time buying presents for others and worry that they will not be "right" or good enough?

T F 9. Do people tend to ignore you when you talk?

T F 10. Are you afraid to say no when you are asked to perform an unpleasant job that is inappropriate for you to do?

T F 11. Do you have difficulty talking to the landlord or insisting that the doctor tell you what is wrong with you so you can understand what he or she says, or reporting an accident to the police?

T F 12. If your spouse wants sex, do you give in rather than make a fuss about it?

T F 13. Do you fantasize being tied up, raped, or in some way overwhelmed to increase sexual responsivity?

T F 14. During sex, have you ever felt more aroused when lightly bitten, or accidentally hurt, or have you ever arranged to be hurt?

T F 15. Are you afraid to end an unhappy, destructive relationship because you fear being alone or never having another relationship?

T F 16. Have you had more than your share of accidents or broken bones?

T F 17. Do you tend to have accidents when you're upset or angry?

T F 18. If you were on a dark, deserted street, would you feel obliged to stop and answer a man who asked for directions, a match, a quarter?

T F 19. In your dreams, do you find yourself falling into black holes, paralyzed and unable to walk, unable to scream for help, pursued by cops or robbers, nude?

T F 20. Do you think you're excessively apologetic?

The most common evidence of "masochism" is women's apologies. Women apologize for every missed shot in tennis, "ring around the collar," bad weather, and another's illness. Apologies show women's tendency to take blame inappropriately. The statement, "I'm sorry" may be a gentle way of sharing the pain, but it sometimes functions for women as a way to "punish" themselves inappropriately.

A second evidence of "masochism" is women's denying their own needs in order to meet another's needs, as the all-giving grandmother did. Despite her extreme depression, she continued to take care of others, at first refusing, and later on being unable, to take care of her own. When challenged, women respond, "I'm okay," or "I'm stronger so I can take it," or "It's the Christian thing to do."

It *is not* Christian to ignore our needs and to deny others the opportunity to minister to us. If we habitually ignore our own needs, we experience "burnout," when we can no longer care for self or minister to others.

Many women have become so practiced at ignoring their needs that they are out of touch with themselves. They have become automatons, caretaker machines who while able to meet obvious needs are unable to experience their own emotions and needs or to really care about other persons.[27]

One social worker talks of sometimes leaving the telephone off the hook to have some time to herself. "I take care of everyone else," she says; "Who takes care of me?" She went on to explain how she decided to take this step:

> When I arrived at Bible study last week, when someone asked "How are you?" I said, "Fine." Later in the meeting, I told everyone about losing my job. They were astounded and appalled. "You've been sitting here, hearing all our struggles for an hour, and they are nothing in comparison to yours. If we hadn't pushed you, you would never have told us this. In fact, you rarely share yourself, good or bad. We feel like we don't know who you are." I realized they were right. I'm so busy taking care of everyone else, I never replenish myself, or open myself to the benefits of Christian community. I'm not just leaving the telephone off the hook at times; I'm trying to talk about myself more (laughter). It sounds selfish, but I'm beginning to see it's self-preservation.

Women in crisis, taught to meet others' needs, may support others endlessly yet be unable to tell their own needs, at great cost to themselves. They nurture everyone but themselves. Unfortunately, they then deplete themselves, having little to continue to give. We all need time for self-nurturance.

Women may experience a low sense of self-care because they have learned powerlessness and limited self-efficacy. In a society which devalues women, socializing them for passivity and dependence, women may feel they violate societal norms and expectations by self-nurturance. Empowerment of women begins by modifying society's attitudes toward women and by teaching self-nurturance.

Nurturance, traditionally defined as denying oneself to meet the needs of others, also includes appropriately meeting one's own needs. It is a noble deed, as the Bible suggests, to give up one's life for a friend (John 15:13), but that doesn't mean we're to seek a slow death from exhaustion.

What's a Body to Do?

A third area of socialization in which women's experiences are so extreme as to be problematic is their sense of body/self relationship. Historically in the church, women have often been characterized as "body" and the "weaker sex" (despite their greater biological superiority as shown, in part, by women's longer life span), subject to the baser human instincts, causing men to experience their baser instincts, or as an example of the mind/body dualism. For example, it was commonly thought in the early centuries of the Christian church that:

> [a woman] is to be suspected and avoided as a subtle and dangerous temptress, always inclined to beguile man and to inflame him with evil passions. Hence the injunction of the Father against cosmetics and every kind of adornment and dress, on the ground that they are calculated to excite lust in the beholder; men must be protected against the wiles of the sirens who would ensnare them, and draw them into the ways of immorality. Nor is it enough for woman to eschew these artificial aids to enticement; "even natural beauty," writes Tertullian [early third century A.D.], "ought to be obliterated by concealment and neglect, since it is dangerous to those who look upon it." In church she must be veiled, lest by uncovering her face she should invite another to sin, while she should avoid banquets, marriage feasts, the bath, and all other places where her presence and charms might stimulate the desires of men.[28]

This emphasis on "woman as body" may have a biological basis. Women may have a stronger sense of body and of their own mortality, because of their menstrual cycle, the body-centeredness of pregnancy, or their comparative muscular weakness.

This sense of "woman as body" is magnified, however, by social-ization.[29] Women are taught to pay attention to their bodies, caring for their looks, in order to be a "good" female and to get a man.

"Why is it," one student asks, "that every time marriage is mentioned, even though I'm far from overweight, I am told to lose weight?"

This emphasis on appearance is socialized from early on. Young girls are dressed in ruffles and long skirts, even for outdoor picnics; young boys would never be dressed so impractically. In a recent research project on babies, when parents were asked to bring their infants in jeans, the girls were dressed in frillier, more colorful (pink!) outfits.

This emphasis on female appearance is shared by peers and the media. One look at designer jeans advertisements is enough to convince one that there is a consistent societal ideal for womanhood, which is characterized by youth and thinness (and one brand of jeans). Models are demonstrably thinner than they were in the 1950s, a thinness that is not achievable by most women. Indeed, women, on the average, weigh more now, while models are weighing less, a difference described as a major cause of eating disorders.[30]

The problem of appearance makes itself felt in other ways too. Laurie, a bright, attractive woman in her mid-twenties, was looking for a position as a financial analyst as she completed her MBA at a prestigious Ivy League school. She always attended her interviews dressed in a nice business suit. At one firm, where the interviews had gone well with the managers responsible for hiring, she did not receive an offer. When she later checked with a trustworthy contact at the firm, she discovered she had not received the offer because several female assistants to one of the most important managers had advised that Laurie's appearance and taste in clothes would prevent her from fitting in well at the firm.

We need to recognize the overemphasis on "body" issues and strive for the right balance. We are all human, with fallibilities and weaknesses. We need to be comfortable meeting our body needs. We need to acknowledge our sexuality — our maleness and femaleness — and integrate our sense of ourselves as one or the other into our sense of ourselves as Christians. And we need to recognize that mind and body issues, as well as believing and acting rightly, are central aspects of the Gospel.

The cultural overemphasis on women's appearance is extreme and unbiblical.[31] First Peter 3:3-4 is but one of the passages that call us to focus on concerns of the heart, not on concerns of this world. It is important to pay attention to the whole person, and not to become trapped by appearance.

The Complete Woman ... Achieving God's Best

Are you caught between emulating Barbara Bush and Meryl Streep? Do you wonder how God is preparing you for a future relationship—or how He ever got you into your present one? Do you wonder how you will ever get everything done that you've committed to do, or wonder why you are so lonely? If so, you need to survey your femininity quotient.

If you can answer "yes" to any of the next ten questions, you are probably an occasional victim of gender-role conflict. Read on to discover which brand of gender-role conflict you are experiencing. If you answer "no" to all the questions, you are a rarity, the ultimate exemplar of the Complete Woman.

Answer Yes or No to the following:
 1. I sometimes wonder if I am "feminine"
    enough.   _____
 2. I question whether I am attractive enough.   _____
 3. I have trouble expressing appropriate anger,
    even with my closest friends.   _____
 4. When I am not in relationship (or before I
    was married), I feel (felt) incomplete.   _____
 5. I have trouble expressing my own needs,
    particularly when I am around other needy
    people.   _____
 6. I found myself agreeing with several items
    on the Masochism scale.   _____
 7. I have trouble expressing my opinions, even
    with my closest friends.   _____
 8. I spend more time making sure I look "good"
    than I spend in church.   _____
 9. I worry sometimes that I am being too asser-
    tive and self-confident.   _____
10. I get uncomfortable when my close male
    friends make less money than I, are not very
    attractive, or are sometimes indecisive.   _____

Your Answers Indicate Your Brand
of Gender-Role Conflict

SELF-ESTEEM: "If I were [blank], I'd be a Real Woman."
If you answered "yes" to questions 1 or 6, you probably think you
are inadequate as you are. While everyone else is a peach, you feel
you're a potato. You may even think you're a nice potato, but you
know quite well you are only a potato. Sure you have nice qualities:
you're solid, interesting, lovable. But you would love to have just a
touch of the color, the sweetness, the pizzazz of the peach.

PHYSICAL APPEARANCE: "I've got to look more like Michelle
Pfeiffer than Bette Midler."
If you answered yes to questions 2 and 8, you may believe that
weight looks best on book ends, and the latest fashion assures you
of social acceptance. You probably diet constantly, check yourself in
the mirror regularly, and "die" if you develop a pimple or wear non-
designer clothes. You subscribe to *Vogue* and *Elle*, just to check out
the fashions. You'd settle for a smaller wardrobe than you'd like,
however, if you could just lose weight — or hang around with Tom
Cruise.

SELF-COMPLETION: "I'd be a Real Woman if I had a Real
Man."
If you answered yes to questions 4 or 10, you probably feel
incomplete in yourself. You don't want to admit it but you know
that, if you were in relationship with a Real Man, people wouldn't
notice your inadequacies. You're fairly certain that, if you were
dating Ken, people would think you were Barbie; if you were dating
Don Johnson, people would assume you were Melanie Griffith; if
you were married to George, people would assume you were
Barbara Bush. You could even see yourself married to Ronald
Reagan, so people would confuse you with Nancy. What's a Real
Woman to do without a Real Man?

SELF-NURTURANCE: "I'd be a Real Woman if I could take care
of everyone else's needs and ignore my own."
If you answered yes to questions 5 or 7, you probably feel your
needs and opinions wound other people. If you were the Complete

Nurturer, you would put yourself on hold until you'd taken care of everyone else. Then you'd be sure to express yourself, but only carefully, so that your needs never hurt anyone else. Of course, once you try this, your needs would probably end up never being met, and you may even wonder what your needs are. You also notice your opinions never get heard, even when they are the wisest, most perceptive opinions possible. But that's okay. You know you could be great at nurturing, just like a Real Woman.

SELF-EXPRESSION: "Silent Women are Complete Women" or "Better to Be Seen and Not Heard."
If you answered yes to questions 3 and 9, you probably believe that women should never be angry, or have power. Better to spend your energy taking care of others, while obliterating your own personality and distinctives. Of course, you also become bland and uninteresting to your friends, but isn't that part of the price of being a Real Woman?

Summary

Women have been socialized to be dependent and passive, to nurture others, and to focus on body issues. These are all positive qualities, but they have gone awry. Women have learned their lessons only too well, and often others too strongly impose expectations. By emphasizing dependence and passivity, we teach women to experience low self-esteem, without giving them the qualities which help to counteract low self-esteem. By teaching women to nurture others and not themselves, we contribute to inadequate self-nurturance and female "burnout." In the workplace, women have been taught to fear achievement and power, rather than to use it wisely and carefully. Women have been conditioned to take the blame and reject the credit, even when accepting credit is appropriate, making women's participation in work settings unnecessarily traumatic. We have taught women to pay attention to their bodies—then devalued these women for their body orientation and "baser" nature—rather than having emphasized an appropriate, holistic mind-body perspective.

We suggest that women (and men) should be taught to be interdependent, to be active, and to nurture themselves and other people. Femininity and positive self-esteem can be experienced in a variety of ways; femininity and achievement need not be in conflict; and women can be encouraged to achieve, particularly to achieve Christian maturity.

Women need *respect* for who they are as "whole" people and for who they can become. They need to respect themselves and be respected by others. Women need to act *responsibly* in their own lives, not shying away from decisions or endeavors that will help them to fulfill what they sense God has called them to be. Men need to act responsibly with women, valuing them as God's creation and of equal value. Women need *tolerance* from society as they negotiate the transition from traditional to contemporary roles and *tolerance* if they decide traditional roles suit them best. Similarly, women need to assess carefully the pros and cons of "traditional" and more "modern" social behavior patterns, not being afraid to change, or to maintain certain qualities, as they try to become the kind of person God wants them to be.

The church has been too quick to label women struggling to find themselves in a changing world and choosing "modern" roles as "feminist" or "liberal" and therefore bad. Rather than contributing to the church's history of problems in dealing with women, we (Christians) need to accept and respect women as full members of the body of Christ, encouraging them to exercise their gifts and participate together in God's earthly kingdom.

The Christian church has emphasized developing women's "inner strength," without changing the system, as a biblical approach to addressing the concerns raised in this chapter. Women should change themselves; the church has little responsibility, it seems to say. It is true: women need to understand these issues and care for their internal needs and their spiritual growth. But the system too is at fault. The church, reflecting unhealthy prejudices of the secular world, has inadvertently contributed to our confusion around the meanings of dependence, passivity, and nurturance by not emphasizing personal responsibility and individual growth, and by discouraging self-nurturance.

Finally, socialization pressures in the church and society are changing, not always in positive ways. Women are being encouraged by some to be aggressive, demanding of rights, and self-serving. If we want to encourage assertiveness rather than aggressiveness and anger, self-nurturance rather than masochism, and self-control rather than learned helplessness, we must be aware of the issues that are being raised. The church provides a context in which to address and begin to change these concerns. It may even provide a better context than any secular one, given the scriptural injunction to "encourage one another" (1 Thes. 5:11; Heb 3:13). Since women comprise more than half of our congregations, we ignore their distinctive needs to our own peril.

Questions for Reflection:

1. How might the church empower women? What responsibilities do they currently carry in your church, and what additional responsibilities might they be encouraged to assume?

2. Many Christians worry that empowering women necessarily disempowers men, that encouraging women to take on the roles available to them in the church means that women will take over and men will drop out. Is this a realistic fear? If not, what can be done about the fear? If so, what can be done to prevent men dropping out?

3. If you are female, how do you self-nurture? What additional ways of self-nurturance would you like to explore?

4. If you are male, do you encourage your female friends to self-nurture, or to serve others without self-nurturance? What might you do to support self-nurturance in women?

5. When does nurturing others become "masochistic"? How can masochism be prevented?

6. How might child rearing, and contemporary American society with its societal expectations, be changed to encourage the development in women of activity and appropriate passivity? interdependence and appropriate dependence? nurturance and self-nurturance? integration of the body and spirit? How is it already being changed? How might these changes become more biblical?

For Further Reading:

Balswick, Jack, and Judy Balswick. *The Family: A Christian Perspective on the Contemporary Home.* Grand Rapids: Baker Book House, 1989. This book provides a thorough and scholarly discussion of family relations and problems from a Christian perspective. They summarize contemporary societal pressures on families, acknowledge the difficulty of opposing these struggles, and propose a biblical response.

Gundry, Patricia. *The Complete Woman: Living beyond Total Womanhood at Home, on the Job, and All by Yourself.* Garden City, N.Y.: Garden City & Co, 1981. Gundry challenges women to wholeness. Using the woman in Proverbs 31 as a guide, she relates her own personal experience to basic issues for women today, giving the reader page after page of wise insights and good advice. Examples of the issues she addresses include women's attitudes toward work, health, personal appearance, and financial investment.

Hardesty, Sarah, and Nehama Jacobs. *Success and Betrayal: The Crisis of Women in Corporate America.* New York: Simon & Schuster, 1986. Hardesty and Jacobs provide an extensive overview of fundamental issues for working women, addressing such questions as: What do women expect from corporate work? When do they begin to doubt themselves? Why do they become disillusioned? Where do they go? What is their career development like? Highly readable, full of examples, any working woman is likely to see herself at some point in the discussion.

Hoffman, Lois Wladis. "Effects of Maternal Employment in the Two-Parent Family." *American Psychologist* 44 (February 1989): 283-92. This article, written by a well-known researcher, updates and summarizes contemporary knowledge of working mothers, primarily mothers of preschool children. A scholarly article, it addresses the psychological well-being of the parents, their marital relationship, the father's role, and parent-child interactions. It concludes that maternal employment is often beneficial for children, depending on the attitudes of the parents, the number of hours the mother is employed, the social support provided the mother and family, and the child's gender. "It is the disequilibrium of social change that creates problems; the typical American family is a dual-wage family, but neither social attitudes nor social policy are in synchrony with this fact."

Lees, Shirley, ed. *The Role of Women: Eight Prominent Christians Debate Today's Issues*. Downers Grove, Ill: InterVarsity Press, 1984. Lees, recognizing that "over the centuries, Christians have given different interpretations of certain passages of Scripture referring to women," asked well-known Christians from various perspectives to present their interpretations and debate with one another. The result is a helpful volume for those who want to clarify their position on the role of women in the church and home.

Miller, Jean Baker. *Toward a New Psychology of Women*. 2nd ed. Boston: Beacon Press, 1986. This secular classic outlines many of the concepts discussed in this chapter in more detail: women's fear of power and conflict, sense of failure, nurturing others without caring for themselves, need for empowerment. A clear, highly readable exposition that most women and men should find helpful in clarifying their understanding of women's changing perspectives on themselves in today's society.

Scanzoni, Letha Dawson, and Nancy A. Hardesty. *All We're Meant to Be: Biblical Feminism for Today*. Revised. Nashville: Abingdon Press, 1986. The Christian equivalent of Jean Baker Miller's *Toward a New Psychology of Women*, this book addresses issues central to being a female in the church in the 1990s. Despite its problematic section on sexuality, it recognizes the stresses of modernity and proposes, in many cases, biblical means of addressing those. Whether one is neo-traditional or egalitarian, one is likely to find good ideas here.

Storkey, Elaine. *What's Right with Feminism?* Grand Rapids: Eerdmans, 1985. This biblical feminist explains feminism for the uninitiated, clarifying how it can be biblical, and calls the church to recognize that the basic tenets of biblical feminism challenge the church to greater inclusion of women and to Christ-centeredness (not self-centeredness, as many believe).

van Leeuwen, Mary Stewart. *Gender and Grace: Love, Work and Parenting in a Changing World*. Downers Grove, Ill: InterVarsity Press, 1990. The author, a well-known Christian psychologist, examines physiological, psychological, and sociological reasons that explain how people grow up as masculine and feminine human beings. She examines biblical passages that address present issues in masculinity and femininity and suggests a biblical model for modern maleness and femaleness.

Ward, Patricia A., and Martha G. Stout. *Christian Women at Work*. Grand Rapids: Zondervan, 1981. An older book, this nevertheless provides an excellent introduction to the issues facing working Christian women. Based on interviews with 100 women, they discuss a Christian perspective on work, the issues facing married and single working women, and the necessity for women and men working together.

Modern Masculinity: In Transition from Macho To Sensitive

Andy looks up at the billboard as he drives along the interstate—and there the guy is. In his white Stetson, cowhide vest blowing in the breeze, he gallops along a ridge in the clear, crisp Western springtime. His powerful horse strains at the chase, his lasso whirls as he goes after a calf for the roundup. The deep blue sky creates a brilliant backdrop for the intense browns and greens of the countryside.

The sign above the highway reads:

"Come to where the flavor is. Come to Marlboro Country."

"Y'know," Andy thinks, "I don't smoke, but there's something really appealing about that guy—the Marlboro Man. There he is, off with his buddies, enjoying the wide outdoors. He's out doing his job, working with his hands, and nobody's really around telling him what to do. He's quite a guy—a rugged, strong individual—no doubt as much in control of his life as he is of his horse. Wouldn't it be great to be in his shoes—even if only for a few minutes?"

The people who design the ads for Marlboro are *smart*. With a ruggedly good-looking cowboy in the great outdoors—a real man's man—they've triggered an image with which many men strongly identify. The notion of being your own person, of having friends but no burdensome commitments, of running your life autonomously, with vigor and gusto, appeals strongly to many males. What is the problem with such a seemingly wholesome image of manhood?

John, a successful and respected neurosurgeon, asks to have lunch with a Christian counselor and friend. After some preliminary conversation, the surgeon takes a deep breath — "like a man about to plunge into the swimming pool," thinks the counselor — then begins:

> I guess I'm here because I'm messing up my relationships. All these years I've fought to get to the top of my profession, thinking that when I got there people would respect me and like me. But it just hasn't worked. Oh, I suppose I command some respect in the hospital, but I'm not close to anybody, really. I have no one to lean on. I'm not sure you can help me either.[1]

Ronald Blake was a thirty-nine-year-old radio talk show host, known throughout the South as the "Tennessee Iron Man" because of the all-night call-in shows he did with listeners as his only guests. Blake was in the hospital for a corneal transplant; his young, attractive wife was at his side throughout his stay.

"You know, honey," he said, chain-smoking in his room, "I'm going to go crazy just lying here. I'll try to talk them into letting me broadcast live from my bed."

The radio station manager liked the idea because Blake was one of the station's most popular announcers. The publicity value of the "Iron Man" broadcasting from his bedside would be enormous. The medical staff thought it would be a good public relations move for the hospital. Besides, they thought, it would boost morale for other patients, some of whom tended to be fearful of resuming normal activities after an operation. Blake's doctor agreed to it as long as Blake would remain under the staff's constant supervision.

"Are you really up to it?" the station announcer asked Blake after his surgery.

"Of course," Blake replied. "I feel fine. No problem here!" Blake was really sold on this idea. He would be a model for all the sick people who wallow in self-pity, and that was an exciting thought. He was sure his audience would love him for his courage, and by doing the shows from his bed, he could attract even more listeners. It would reinforce his "Iron Man" image and assure his young wife that she didn't have an invalid on her hands.

Warned that a cold or infection could impede or even be disastrous for his recovery, he continued to take Vitamin C pills, considering himself a sort of expert on vitamin therapy. Whenever he felt feverish or headachy, he just increased his dosage of the vitamin and usually didn't bother telling his doctor.

A week or so after his operation, he was discharged from the hospital, having turned his recovery into a party and proven to everyone that he was indeed the "Iron Man," who had no use for complaints, self-pity, or special attention.

Three months after his discharge he collapsed after his nightly show and was put in the hospital with double pneumonia. Two years later he died suddenly of a heart attack.[2]

The Marlboro Man, neurosurgeon, and radio announcer all illustrate the traditional image of masculinity in our country. This image has four characteristics: (1) "no sissy stuff" (that is, avoid everything feminine); (2) the "big wheel" (achieve status at all costs); (3) the "sturdy oak" (cultivate independence and toughness); and (4) "give 'em hell" (be as aggressive as necessary).[3] "The American male [often] sees himself as a very high-powered piece of machinery," says psychoanalyst Roy Menninger, "rather than as a human need system."[4]

While males are usually encouraged to have friends, their friendships are generally action-oriented rather than intimacy-oriented. "Sure, I share a lot with my friends," laughs a popular college senior. "We shoot baskets, play soccer, and talk about women." While women may worry about the effect their careers have on their friendships, and may consider modifying their work lives to enhance their social lives, many males value career over friendship, and think that career goals should not be sacrificed for the sake of personal relationships.

Being Macho—Hazardous to Your Health

The term "macho" has come to be used to refer to the traditional male image taken to an extreme. Being macho may have short-term payoffs, but it has serious negative consequences in the long run.

Despite the macho image of invulnerability, men may be more vulnerable to physical and emotional stress than women. Reports from medical doctors and psychologists show that American men are less able than women to acknowledge their emotions and express them effectively, less willing to ask for help when they need it, and less willing to show or accept friendly affection with both females and other males.[5] Physically, males are more vulnerable than females to a wide range of disorders and infections. The death rate for American men is higher than for American women at birth and in every decade of life, and women in our society and almost every modern society outlive men.

Males in our society are not as indestructible as many people would like to believe. Further, men's attempts to escape their psychological stress — by violence, alcoholism, or smoking — noticeably shorten their lives.

In present society, when gender roles are in transition, men see a variety of roles being offered, ranging from "macho" to "sensitive" to "wimp." Macho seems hazardous, and if you believe the jokes about it, passe, as in this "Day Care" comic. "Wimp" is "sissy" and therefore bad, and "sensitive" possibly suspect. What's a Christian man to do?

Redefining Manhood

Both the neurosurgeon and the radio announcer are so invested in proving themselves that they ignore their own needs. When their careers are going well, they feel good about themselves. When their careers are going poorly, or they lose their jobs, their identity significantly suffers. Women too are vulnerable to loss of self-esteem, but seldom are their careers so central to identity. Like the rugged, individualist Marlboro Man, males like to be in control of their environment. Like the radio announcer, males may become wrapped up in the perks of power, prestige, and financial reward that come from devoting most of their energies to work. Sometimes women may even contribute to this orientation by expecting — as a matter of course — that male friends, husbands, or other male relatives will provide them significant financial support or make all their key decisions for them. With such an orientation, it's no surprise that continued success — being the "big wheel" — easily becomes life's principal objective for males; failure, the principal fear. As Vince Lombardi, former coach of the champion Green Bay Packers said, "Winning isn't everything. It's the *only* thing." The foremost secret fear of men, according to one report, is the fear of being a failure.[6]

Being a success at work clearly drives many American men. One man, talking about his inability to separate himself from his work to spend more time with his wife and family, remarks:

> I've worked [so] hard to get where I am, and I can't put it in jeopardy. . . . If you want to stay up there, you can't live on past accomplishments. [pausing, then continuing more slowly] It's not just that old competitive stuff, that's not all. It's something about the work itself. [throwing up his hands in a gesture of helplessness] It's so much a part of me it feels like I'd have to violate my nature [to spend less time with it].[7]

Caring about and doing well in one's work is important, but letting work become the focus of one's life and success the principal objective is not healthy psychologically or spiritually. This approach to life is almost certain to leave one destitute, as we saw from the neurosurgeon's example. Life at the top can be lonely, but without a support community, that loneliness can become unbearable.

For the Christian, an all-consuming career is necessarily unbiblical. When career becomes the primary foundation for identity and masculinity, work becomes an idol. Even when career is less time-consuming but still critical to identity, a man often doesn't have the time to be sufficiently active in the lives of his family, friends, and Christian community. Improving relationships with their male friends, wives, children, and God are four areas where Christian men need to give renewed emphasis.

Developing Friendships, Especially with Males

Herb Goldberg, an expert on masculinity in contemporary American society, notes a common response he receives in asking men if they have close friends: "No, why? Should I?"[8]

Based on his interviews with middle-aged men, psychologist Daniel Levinson comments that "friendship was largely noticeable by its absence. Close friendship with a man or woman is rarely experienced by American men."[9] Interestingly, difficulty in establishing intimate relationships is one of the principal characteristics of Christian men who abuse their wives.[10] Author David Smith relates the typical response of one man who, when asked if he had any close friends, responded, "Of course I don't have any friends. I'm a man. My wife is the one with friends."[11]

Men, socialized for individualism ("the sturdy oak") and competitiveness ("give 'em hell"), seem to have trouble making and being friends because of this socialization. Many males seem to be socialized to measure themselves relentlessly against the next guy, whether in terms of academic performance, athletic ability, wife's attractiveness, income, or even the size of one's genitalia. Relationships—with their intrinsic characteristics of vulnerability and of caring for peers—wither in the atmosphere of one-upmanship inherent in constant comparison.

In the competitive male world, many men believe either that others would think less of them if they divulged information about weaknesses or that such information might be used against them. Psychologist Joel Block notes that many men are prone to think that "[i]f I tell another man I'm having trouble with sex in my marriage, he might say, 'Well, perhaps I ought to come over and help you out.' "[12] The old adage rings true: "Tell a man your troubles and he'll offer a solution; tell a woman your troubles and she'll commiserate with you."

Fear of vulnerability usually results in males establishing friendships that are "safe" in terms of a lack of candor and sharing. Men's relationships include "convenience friendships," based on a service or business one provides for another, "doing-things friendships," based on shared activities, "milestone friendships," based on significant occasions shared together, and "mentor friendships."[13] As Harold Robbins notes, for the "average man, the very idea that he could forge emotional bonds with another man contradicts everything that makes him male."[14]

To move to something more intimate than these "buddyships,"[15] Robbins relates one observer's comment that in the area of friendships, men are like turtles:

> [e]ver so slowly and cautiously, they stick out their heads, a millimeter at a time, to see if it's safe to proceed. Miscalculation is deemed fatal. The slightest hint of exploitation, real or imagined, causes instantaneous withdrawal.[16]

In a time of changing gender roles, richer friendships among males could help them deal more effectively with these changes.[17] Christian men (and men in general) should participate in "sharing friendships," not just "buddyships." Change is easier when the worries it brings can be shared with friends.

Indeed, Christians are called to participate in community (James 5:16, 1 Cor. 12:12; Gal. 6:2; Heb. 10:24-25). Surely this community was not meant to consist only of "convenience" or "doing-things" friendships, but of sharing, intimate friendships with coequal partners. The deep friendship between David and Jonathan (1 Samuel 20) provides a biblical example of such a friendship. David's eulogy in 2 Samuel 1 at Jonathan's death clearly shows how important this relationship was to him. We too are called to such relationships.

Sharing Oneself, Particularly with Wives

These observations about male friendships are also relevant to men's relationships with women. Husband-wife relationships are one important area of male-female relationships that often stand in particular need of improvement.

"My husband never talks to me," frequently complain wives, Christian and non-Christian. When men do share their concerns, wives continue, these discussions are often one-sided: he talks about his life, telling the facts but not the feelings, and she is left to intuit his emotions. Then he, in turn, doesn't ask about her life, which adds to the wife's frustration in trying to create good marital communication.

In a related problem, males often seem to deal with fundamentally emotional issues in objective or analytical terms. Here, Janis initiates a conversation about feelings. Arlo's response is quite different.

ARLO & JANIS reprinted by permission of NEA, Inc.

One wife complains:

> I can't stand when he's so darned unemotional and expects me to be the same. He lives in his head all the time, and he acts like anything that's emotional isn't worth dealing with.[18]

When a man does make the mistake of "living in his head" too often, he is likely to miss important emotional connections his wife wants to make. One wife comments:

> When he gets into that oh-so-reasonable place, there are times when I feel like I'm going crazy. Well, I don't know if I'm really nuts, but I'm plenty hysterical. When I can get a hold of myself, I can tell myself it's not me, it's him, that he's driving me crazy because he refuses to listen to what I'm saying and behaves as if I'm talking Turkish or something.[19]

A man relates his perplexity in dealing with his spouse about such problems:

> Sometimes my wife wants to fight over the craziest of things. The other day it was over where to hang a picture on the wall. I couldn't care less where it hung, but she kept needling me every time I made a suggestion, even after she asked for my opinion! [pause] Do you think she wants me to get kind of . . . more involved with her somehow?[20]

Women, for their part, need to realize that they sometimes put men in "double binds." Karen finds, for example, that she encourages her husband to share his feelings and needs, and delights in his doing so, until he shares financial worries. She then immediately panics and tells him that "you have to take care of that; I don't know anything about it." Her dual message to him — "Be vulnerable when I feel safe but invulnerable when I need to depend on you" — leaves him feeling confused and betrayed.

Males need to realize that sharing about their lives, emotions, strengths, and weaknesses may not come easily, but developing the ability to be open can greatly enhance their marital relationships as well as those with "significant others."[21] Women need to recognize and acknowledge their own ambivalences and the mixed messages they sometimes send. Sharing improves marriage relationships (see Eph. 5:25-31) and helps improve and refine the sensitivity of the Christian community.

Growing as Fathers

Father-child relationships are another area where American men can improve. One psychologist conducted a two-year study in which he asked children ages four to six which they liked better, Daddy or TV, and only 56 percent chose Daddy. When the question was which they liked better, Mommy or TV, 80 percent chose Mommy.[22]

A man's remoteness from his children — or wife or friends — often reflects the "manly" character of remoteness he learned from his father.[23] The father who maintains a physical or emotional remoteness from his son communicates the message that part of manliness is a strong sense of individuality. The effect of this distance the father creates can be especially problematic for sons, leaving some men without the capacity for intimacy, as they grow into adulthood. One of the interesting but unfortunate results of this remoteness is that sons, as they grow older, usually don't realize their inability to develop healthy intimacy.

While there is evidence that fathers in the 1970s and '80s have begun to spend more time with their children[24] — and indeed the media has reflected this trend in advertisements and sitcoms — there are also studies showing that men report being happiest when they have the least to do at home.[25] The fact is, many fathers still don't spend as much time with their children as they should.[26]

A frequent result of fathers' lack of integral involvement in the lives of family members is that wives often bear the principal burden of attending to family members' emotional needs and maintaining good communication within the family. This all-too-common burden of being the family's "emotional switchboard"[27] is not one wives would have to shoulder if fathers were more integrally and supportively involved in their families.

Could any of this evidence about the modern father please God? Hardly. David Benson comments that the Christian father

> is part of a God-designed team, and his teamwork is essential to the personal growth of his children . . . Dad is urgently needed! Together with Mom, he can help instill healthy perspectives on sexuality, love, discipline, roles, communication, and caring. His kids won't accept a lecture on the run. They couldn't care less about a disciplinary swat on the rear from a dad who hasn't been around much. *They will accept only his consistent personal example.*[28]

While children don't necessarily need Dad — or Mom — around all day, when Dad is at home, he needs to be sure to devote a good chunk of undivided attention to his children. The benefits — in terms of his children's healthy psychological development and his own personal fulfillment — are hard to overestimate.

God could only be pleased with such committed involvement. Proverbs (see chapters 1–7), which is full of fatherly advice for children, demonstrates the importance of healthy father-child interaction. Remember also that Jairus, an important synagogue official, was so concerned about his daughter's health that he prostrated himself before Jesus, an itinerant teacher (Luke 8). The love, concern, and humility Jairus displayed in the effort to have his daughter cured clearly sets a good example for Christian fathers.

Maturing Faith

The macho image of maleness we've mentioned also contributes to spiritual stunting. Macho men think they can avoid God, and they are often encouraged by society to do so. Macho men refuse to recognize God's guidance in their lives, rightly realizing that faith demands vulnerability and approachability.

> [S]piritually, faith is considered by many men at the most to be a personal matter of which they would rarely talk, but more often to be a woman's area of concern, for it implies a lack of independence and self-assurance that does not coincide with their macho self-image. Unfortunately for themselves, their families, and their communities, [men] have been satisfied with surface definitions of their masculinity. . . . [29]

Men who have a better grasp of their masculinity as centered in God should be able "to enjoy their lives, not in selfishness, but in the wonder of contributing their strength for the well-being of others."[30]

Many men have trouble fathering because their own fathers were unavailable to them. When taught by their fathers to hide their insecurities and to be distant, they learn qualities that become obstacles to faith. Acknowledging their fallibilities as human beings is necessary for pursuing spiritual wholeness and for participating in the church.[31]

Gordon Dalbey, a Christian counselor, tells the story of the man in his late thirties who had come for help after a divorce. The man was looking for direction in his life, and during the conversation, Dalbey happened to ask about the man's relationship with his father. The man, touched by a childhood memory, put his head in his hands and cried for awhile before relating the memory to Dalbey.

The man had grown up on a farm in the Midwest and was the only high school graduate in the family. As graduation day approached, he wanted his father, with whom he had a fairly good relationship, to be proud of him and to come to the ceremony. When the day arrived, his father drove him to graduation in the family pickup truck. Instead of staying, though, he dropped his son off and picked him up afterward. Even though his father later explained that he hadn't stayed because of feeling out of place as an uneducated farmer, the son was deeply hurt.

Dalbey helped the man to forgive his father through God's grace. The counselor also showed him that God stood ready to use His power and love both to heal hurts in the man's past life as well as provide direction for him in the present.[32]

God provides a model that earthly fathers can emulate of a caring, involved Father, who stands ready to provide help and support in even greater abundance than requested. Males who are aware of their need for more warmth and a more spiritual focus for their lives can find in Scripture how God can provide the necessary affection, compassion, and strength (e.g., Isa. 30:19-21, 51:12; Ps. 111:4; Matt. 9:36, 11:28; 23:37).

The emphasis of Christianity on humility before God and service to others does not mean that the church is a place for "sissies." Rather, if men were more able to acknowledge the fallibility and incompleteness that is a natural part of being human and could avoid becoming defensive about these shortcomings, they would find a relationship with God easier to develop. Indeed, such a realization is central to the wholeness Christianity says that people can have if they submit their lives to God and trust Him for their guidance (see Phil. 4:19).

Back to the Beginning

As we've discussed the various roles males play, we've highlighted widely shared and problematic aspects of modern masculinity. Most men should be able to see themselves in at least some of these characterizations. How did males get to be this way? Rubin[33] and van Leeuwen[34] suggest that males' early socialization (with the possible influence of some biological predispositions toward certain behaviors) is crucial for creating the macho image, and will be crucial for changing it.

A girl starts to develop a significant orientation toward personal relationships in the first few years of her life. This development occurs because she maintains the bond with her mother — the original caretaker—when she becomes old enough (about age three) to realize what sex she is and that her sex is permanent. Girls may have an innate predisposition toward this bonding.[35]

A boy, on the other hand, begins to realize about the same time that he is more like his father than his mother, so he starts to shift his identification of himself as a male to his father. In the best possible world, the father is present to provide warmth and nurturance to affirm the father-son bond and to help the young boy become secure in this newly found, important relationship. This warmth and nurturance helps the boy affirm both his developing sense of masculinity and the importance of wholesome personal relationships.

What usually happens, however, is that the father, off at work for most of the day, is not at home to the extent that the mother is.[36] Instead of having a warm, nurturant father readily available as a model for his masculinity, the boy, by default, begins to define himself as *not a female*. Indeed, studies have shown that many boys do not have a warm, close relationship with their father.[37]

A boy's strong sense of independence may also follow from this early relative absence from his father. The boy finds it necessary to separate himself from his previously most central relationship— with his mother. This need for independence becomes central to the development of his sense of maleness, especially since his father is not there and available for close male bonding. Furthermore, the need for independence is enough a part of this process that de-emphasis of the relationship with the mother usually becomes a de-emphasis of interpersonal relationships in general. If the father, when present, communicates the message that males are by nature aloof or distant with people instead of warm and loving, the sense of independence and separateness is further enhanced. The father, acting like a "big wheel" and "sturdy oak," encourages the son to do the same. Additionally, the boy usually comes to perceive that unless he maintains the firm psychological boundary between himself and Mom, his sexuality might be "smothered" by her female influence.

This early independence and separation may explain the "no sissy stuff" rule: the avoidance of domestic responsibilities and even child rearing ("women's work"), the absence of males in fields such as nursing ("too nurturant, not to mention the low pay"), and the greater discomfort or hostility displayed toward gay males than females display toward gay women.[38] Boys learn this "no sissy stuff" rule early on, as part of their socialization experiences. For example, they hear "Don't cry, that's what babies and girls do," "That's a crazy idea, you're thinking like a woman now," or "Women don't belong in upper-level management, they can't handle the pressure." With continued exposure to such attitudes, a boy's natural tendency is to think of males as endowed with a wide range of special abilities and to devalue women and "feminine" characteristics, such as nurturance and emotional sensitivity.

Boys learn instead that masculinity is expressed through physical courage, toughness, strength, and control. Studies of male school groups and street-corner gangs have shown that males who are gentle or compassionate toward others are not invited to be group members. Images of males portrayed in magazines, television, and movies enhance the image of the tough, silent, in-control man.[39]

Perhaps because he learned early on to separate emotionally from his mother, and because he developed a more distant relationship with his father—a distance encouraged by society—males, much more frequently than females, can be interested in paying for sex. Because of the importance to them of close relationships, for most women, the notion of purchasing sexual favors—not to mention sexual favors from an unknown man—is virtually inconceivable.

These particular dynamics—a relatively absent father and a culture which encourages macho masculinity—with the possible additional influence of biological predispositions, reveal themselves later in life in several ways:

(a) *control* ("the big wheel" and "the sturdy oak"): He tries to enhance his independence by exerting control over his environment (especially later, when that key environment he seeks to master is his place of employment);

(b) *competitiveness* ("give 'em hell"): He competes with others to define and enhance his individualism;

(c) *distance* ("no sissy stuff"): He avoids close relationships in general and hesitates to give himself heart, mind, and soul to his wife, lest she "smother" him in her femininity. He considers emotional closeness too "sissy."

Combating these pressures is not easy, but the macho-male stereotype is already changing in our society. Understanding where these qualities come from can help us both to change them and to foster the development of the healthy, Christian, "new male."

The Real Man—Where Did He Go?

For all you real men who ever wondered if it was okay to eat quiche, cry when watching *Terms of Endearment* (especially in front of a woman), or stay at home and watch the kids while your wife is at work, here it is, your first Valid Inventory of Genuine Masculinity.

If you can answer "yes" to any of the next ten questions, you are probably the occasional victim of gender-role conflict. Read on to discover which brand of gender-role conflict you are experiencing. If you answer "no" to all of the questions, congratulations, you are incredibly healthy (and probably next to perfect).

Answer Yes or No to the following:

1. I sometimes wonder if my job is "masculine" enough. _____
2. I question sometimes whether I'm built like a "real man." _____
3. I have trouble showing my real feelings, even to close friends. _____
4. I wonder sometimes if "real men" engage in the pastimes I engage in. _____
5. I hate to have a woman get the upper hand with me in a relationship. _____
6. I think that if I made more money, I'd feel more secure about my masculinity. _____
7. I wonder if I dress like a "real man" ought to. _____
8. I try not to cry in public, or display too much weakness. _____
9. I'm quite certain that most men do not have my particular hobbies and interests. _____
10. I get uncomfortable when a woman I am close to has more power or prestige than I have. _____

Your Answers Indicate Your Brand of Gender-Role Conflict

VOCATIONAL: "I am my job" or "My job makes me a real man."

If you answered "yes" to questions 1 or 6, you probably think that you need a certain occupation to make you more a man. Your world may be divided into jobs which are "more masculine" and "more feminine." Chances are you think that real men make above $50,000, or at least more than their wives. Congratulations on admitting your bias. You're not alone. And welcome to the real world where some real men actually make less than $50,000. Some even make less than their wives or girlfriends. But don't worry, that American Express Gold Card is still manly to flash on a first date.

PHYSICAL APPEARANCE: "I've got to look more like Clint Eastwood than Woody Allen."

If you answered "yes" to questions 2 or 7, you may believe that pink is a color that only girls can wear. You think that certain hairstyles are "what's right" or "what's in" for men. Chances are you work out at the local gym mostly to get the right shape and size for your upper body. Occasionally, you wonder if the guys in *GQ* — even the ones that look a little anorexic — are more masculine looking than you. You'd settle, however, for just an above-average build just so long as you could drive some muscle vehicle.

EMOTIONAL: "Real men don't cry" or "Silent and strong the whole day long."

If you answered "yes" to questions 3 or 8, you may believe a stiff upper lip is the entrance requirement to heaven (for a man). You probably are afraid to admit it when you're confused or don't know what's going on inside. You certainly wouldn't tell your boss — maybe not even your wife or best friend. Feelings? They're impractical and get in the way. Chances are you had a father who kept telling you "boys are brave" or a friend in school who said "don't be a sissy." You certainly decided not to be that. Come to think of it, you got real good at not showing emotions and being an analytical problem solver. Cool, calm, collected — all the time. Just like Sean Connery. That's it, Real-Man Heaven, here we come.

ACTION AND ACTIVITY: "Where do the Real Men in this town hang out on a Saturday night? That's where you'll find me."

If you answered "yes" to questions 4 or 9, you might think it's an indication of manhood to belong to the NRA, the Elks Club, or some other Real-Man organization. You know you need to hunt and fish, or at least pretend to know something about these. And "Monday Night Football" is a must. Also, there are certain things you would never do: sew, crochet, attend a baby shower. And you're fairly certain that your little boy (if you have one) is going to learn to play Nintendo (not hopscotch), soccer (not badminton), and do karate (not jazz dancing). You'd like to try some of the things you see the ladies do (like cook), but you're fairly certain that if God had intended you to do those things, He would have made you a woman.

RELATIONAL: "I know how to handle my women and I'm always in control."

If you answered "yes" to questions 5 or 10, chances are you like it when a woman needs you more than you need her. You feel a little intimidated when you go out with a lady who can pay her own way — and yours, also. You might not admit it in public, but it'd be hard for you to marry a woman smarter, richer, or taller than you. And you certainly wouldn't want someone who "wears the pants with you" when it comes to family decision-making. Enough is enough. Let's get back to basics. Man in control; woman in submission. Isn't that the way it was supposed to be?

The Next Step

In *Rainman*, Tom Cruise learns about respect as he interacts with Dustin Hoffman, who plays an autistic person. In the movie, Hoffman has some valuable lessons about people to teach Cruise, when he is sensitive enough to listen. Similarly, the well-known

Christian author Henri Nouwen discusses in his book *The Road to Daybreak* the work he did with a handicapped group in France. Nouwen comments that handicapped people create a lot of respect in others because of the kindness and mercy they inspire in those who become involved in assisting them. The handicapped person, Nouwen observes, generates respect because such a person threatens no one and brings out the best in people.[40] Both these examples demonstrate the value of a broader definition of what sorts of individuals and behaviors are worthy of respect. Such a development falls into what we have argued is an *identity-flexible* attitude, rather than an identity-fixed attitude tied to the performance of a narrowly defined set of gender-appropriate behaviors. In such an identity-flexible context, the importance of competitiveness for worldly status decreases markedly.

With a more wholesome definition of manhood (and with greater involvement in parenting by fathers), we could also begin to avoid negative stereotypes of men and women. Moving to positive conceptions of masculinity (caring, logical, nurturant, analytical) instead of the "I-am-not-a-female" mode of thought, would be a particularly healthy development. Perhaps, "the big wheel" could be replaced with "I'm doing the best I can;" "the sturdy oak," with "Let's work this out together;" "no sissy stuff," with "I care about you;" and "give 'em hell," with "telling the truth in love."

Responsible masculinity would also include an awareness of the importance of nurturing and mentoring in relationships, rather than a focus on sizing up other people and/or competing with them. In an October 1990 survey of 1,201 men and women by *New Woman*, 75 percent of women said they felt that the women's movement has made men more nurturing.[41] Such results suggest that men may be becoming more interested in being friends with their wives, rather than in having relationships that are heavily role-oriented, that they are growing more supportive of their wives' interests and career, and that they are developing more concern about parenting. Men's stereotypes are indeed changing, it seems, from "macho" to "sensitive," and this change can only be helpful for both men and women.

Tolerance would include a greater sensitivity toward masculine behaviors that do not fit current stereotypes about what appropriate behavior should be. In this context, males who pursue relationship- or nurturance-oriented employment would not face criticism for pursuing "women's work." Similarly, all of us would also show more respect and appreciation for women who become involved with positions traditionally considered to be "male."

Flexibility would, first of all, include the wisdom to appreciate the problematic aspects of the traditional male upbringing and the willingness to try to modify in oneself the effects of some of those influences. It would include a willingness to pursue deeper friendships with some of one's "buddies" and female friends. It would additionally involve a willingness to support female friends, and women in general, as they explore new roles of their own.

Flexibility would also include a willingness to be more involved in child rearing. Perhaps, by being willing to assume more domestic responsibilities, *flexibility* may include for husbands the willingness to support a wife's interests in further professional training or involvement. *Flexibility* would certainly mean a willingness to be more aware of ways to contribute to the Christian community through developing broader and deeper relationships.

For men to move from an identity-fixed to an *identity-flexible* gender-role model, from macho to sensitive, from a career-centered to holistic self-definition, from "safe" to sharing friendships, from "give 'em hell" to nurturance and caring is not easy. The realization that God calls us into relationship with one another, however, should challenge Christian men to try.

Questions for Reflection:

1. If you are male or have brothers: what did your family teach you about being male? What, for example, did your family allow males to do that females were not allowed? If you have a family (or hope to have a family), how do (or might) you treat boys and girls differently?

2. How have male stereotypes changed? How would you like to see them change further?

3. Why is it difficult to encourage males to be more active with affairs at home, from cleaning up to child rearing?

4. In what ways can males be encouraged to be more open with other males? With females? Why is it so hard for some men to have close relationships?

5. If you are male, when your wife or girlfriend thinks you work too much, what do you say? How do you attempt to integrate work and interpersonal demands?

6. If you are male, did your father openly show you affection when you were young? Did he ever hug you? Did he have long talks with you? How did he express his caring for you? If he was relatively inexpressive, how have you tried to develop your own sense of warmth and affection?

7. The Bible often talks of God and Jesus in mother-like terms (Hosea 11:1, 3; Isa. 66:13; Matt. 23:37). What applications do these verses have for men in terms of their relationships with others?

8. How do females help perpetuate unhealthy male stereotypes? How might they help men change in healthy ways?

For Further Reading:

Balswick, Jack, and Judith Balswick. *The Family: A Christian Perspective on the Contemporary Home.* Grand Rapids: Baker Book House, 1990. This book provides a thorough and scholarly discussion of family relations and problems from a Christian perspective. It proposes sound child-rearing practices that encourage the development of mature, responsible boys and girls.

Dalbey, Gordon. *Healing the Masculine Soul.* Waco, Texas: Word Inc., 1988. Dalbey discusses how Christian males should recognize that they can be strong enough in Christ so that they can be honest about their weaknesses.

Lynn, David. *The Father: His Role in Child Development.* Monterey, Calif.: Brooks/Cole Publishing, 1974. This book provides a psychological assessment of the many ways fathers influence male and female children, both in U.S. society and in other cultures.

McGinnis, Alan Loy. *The Friendship Factor*. Minneapolis: Augsburg, 1979. This is a well-known Christian book on developing healthy, meaningful friendships.

Olson, Richard. *Changing Male Roles in Today's World*. Valley Forge, Pa.: Judson Press, 1982. This is a short but sensitive and insightful book on current misconceptions men have about roles as friends, parents, husbands, etc. Olson provides good scriptural analyses of these misconceptions.

Osherson, Samuel. *Finding Our Fathers*. New York: Fawcett Columbine, 1986. Osherson provides an excellent discussion of missing components in the father-son relationship and how these gaps effect a man's adult life. He discusses how to improve connectedness with one's father.

Smith, David. *The Friendless American Male*. Ventura, Calif.: Regal Books, 1985. Smith discusses many of the difficulties males have in developing close friendships. From a Christian perspective, he suggests why and how males should have more meaningful friendships.

van Leeuwen, Mary Stewart. *Gender and Grace: Love, Work and Parenting in a Changing World*. Downer's Grove, Ill.: InterVarsity Press, 1990. The author, a Christian psychologist, examines physiological, psychological, and sociological reasons how people grow up as masculine and feminine human beings. She examines biblical passages that lead her to a reinterpretation of traditional views of women's roles in society and the church.

The New Male and Female: Great Expectations and Their Stresses

It's easy to explain (and explain away) struggles by stereotyping: "They're single—no wonder they are irresponsible," or "Married people never have time to think about these things anyway," or "Men don't notice everyday details like birthdays and anniversaries; you're expecting too much." We argue, however, particularly in our discussion of The Myth of Gender Differences in chapter 4, that, despite obvious differences among us — between women and men, between singles and marrieds — problems and struggles are more often shared among us than we expect.

Persons with various biblical perspectives described in chapter 3 (neo-traditionalists or biblical feminists) are just as prone to division: "I don't want to talk with them; they're so liberal" or "It's easy for that group of Christian women. They just have to submit." Biblical feminists sometimes assume neo-traditionalists are unfeeling authoritarians who believe that roles matter more than trust and caring. Neo-traditionalists, in turn, sometimes assume biblical feminists are self-centered and independent. Rights matter more than responsibilities. Neo-traditionalists find it hard to imagine that biblical feminists can understand their concerns and vice versa. Our stereotypes inhibit mutual understanding and sharing.

The Stresses of Modernity

Each of us shares cultural pressures toward egalitarian roles between women and men, economic pressures toward two-paycheck families, and technological pressures toward increasing education for men and women. Women in general, no longer so dependent on men, are freer now to make more independent and autonomous choices; and men, less constrained by rigid gender-role socialization, are freer, for example, to parent. Such changes have transformed modern life. But these pressures make our lives more complex than they used to be, so complex that we may feel as if we are constantly juggling responsibilities and relationships. We have more demands placed on us than we are able to meet, and we are aware of too many needs that we seem compelled to ignore. This is particularly true of urban Christians, where relationships are often segmented and difficult to maintain as people go their separate ways to work or to live, and the paths of friends or potential mates don't automatically cross.

This complexity is made more difficult by changing male and female roles. New gender roles bring unfulfilled expectations and frustrating contradictions between our past and these new expectations, or even among our expectations of ourselves, that we never anticipated. In the last two chapters we examined problems the two sexes have individually faced in developing their conception of appropriate gender roles. In this chapter, we'll discuss how pressures, especially pronounced in the past decade or two, affect the two genders as actors in a larger society. Women, for example, face "superwoman burnout," pressure toward work-centeredness, and the feeling that "you can't have it all" — expectations that the media and our societal dichotomy between their work and home lives introduced. Men face greater job competition, "gender-role strain" and fallout from the disintegration of the "macho image."

The Superwoman Image

"Superwoman burnout" was the buzzword of the '80s and is a continuing struggle as women, led to believe they can "have it all," find their work or personal lives suffer from the effort. Women cannot be first-class career women and, at the same time, first-class homemakers. There are not enough hours in the day nor enough energy to do both. As Sharon recently said:

> I feel like I'm supposed to spring out of bed, looking like Joan Lunden, eager for a day of handling corporate crises — telling the people I manage: "You're doing a great job" or "Consider doing this instead"; always on top of new products, never making a mistake. At 5:01 p.m., I become consummate Mother: infinitely patient and wise. Meanwhile, my house is supposed to be spotlessly clean and my children always dressed in the latest fashion. I'm not done yet! At bedtime, I'm supposed to spring into bed for passionate, perfect lovemaking in our designer bedroom.

The reality is strikingly different, and women are frustrated and exhausted by their efforts to do everything well.

Other women are caught between their expectations of themselves and other's expectations of them. Janis, six months pregnant with her second child and struggling to work full time as an assistant rector laments:

> What am I supposed to do? I get up in the morning and feel like throwing up — still. I take a pill to stop it . . . what else

can I do? I drop the toddler off at day care and drive to work, feeling carsick all the way. Once I'm there, I may be able to work for an hour or two, on good days, three or four. Then I throw up. I have to lie down then for an hour or so to stop the chills, then I may be okay for the rest of the day. Or maybe it starts over again. I feel like my body is betraying me. And now my boss wants me to account for every hour I spend on the job. I never expected to have so much trouble; I get so frustrated. Why can't a man be more like a woman? Then maybe he'd understand.

Too often, women ignore — or fail to satisfy — their own needs, sometimes because interpersonal and work pressures force them to. As one wag wryly said, "Women have to be twice as good as men. Good thing that's not hard." Robin, a computer programmer for a major computer company, began managing her division in her boss' absence, struggling to keep on deadline for a project even though half her division was out sick or traveling. Soon thereafter she became pregnant, and her maternity leave of absence was approved. She overheard a coworker explaining why the project was behind schedule: "Robin's pregnant." "That statement just wasn't true," Robin fumed to her husband that night after work. "There are far more significant reasons for the delay." She sighed, "I knew this would happen, but I'm thirty-eight — if I want children, what other option do I have?"

Singles, wives, mothers, part-time and full-time workers: all can experience the "Superwoman burnout" phenomenon. Robin's manager Angie, also in her late thirties, is similarly experiencing a desire to slow down:

I've traveled all over the country, and progressed in my job more rapidly than I ever thought I would. Now, with the recent reorganization in the company and layoffs, I have the chance to move up a tier in management. But I'm not sure I want to. I want a richer life: time to spend with my cats, to stay home for a change, to participate in all the Christmas and Easter activities at church, to go skiing and see plays. And I know, if I take the job, I'll have to spend more hours at the office and more hours on the road. It isn't worth it.

The "Superwoman" model of modern femininity is a composite created by contemporary movies and advertising, as well as by women's and men's experiences and knowledge of full-time mothering. The reality of the movies is not the everyday reality of most women. Melanie Griffith's character in the movie *Working Girl* is attractive, competent, and professional. She started out with few skills, working with a temporary agency. In a fairy-tale, romantic ending typical of modern Hollywood, she soon displaced her female boss—also attractive, competent, and professional—taking her job and her man. In the Hollywood world, women of note are necessarily professionals, and both women in this movie end up as high-powered professionals. In reality, of course, many women feel nonprofessional, less glamorous and powerful, and work in lower-paying jobs.

Another well-known woman of Hollywood, the Claire Huxtable character in *The Cosby Show*, manages to be a high-class lawyer, married to a high-class doctor (Bill Cosby), living in a spotless house, yet she never has to fold laundry or take care of sick children. The unreality of Hollywood too often shapes women's self-expectations.

Magazines are just as misleading, selling a plethora of products: makeup, shampoo, feminine hygiene sprays, all of which seem designed to make women perfectly beautiful and thoroughly employable. The high-achieving women of Hollywood and the flawless models of women's magazines seem never to lack high-level jobs, or time, or energy. Yet their very human counterparts clearly do. Women cannot "have it all."

Women's expectations of themselves as mothers and career women seem to meld together the models of the full-time mother and full-time career man. Women strive to embody—not their mothers or grandmothers—but both their mothers and fathers, or grandmothers and grandfathers. Their mothers or grandmothers—full-time parents—taught them to set high standards of parenting. Similarly, their fathers and grandfathers—full-time career men—taught them high standards of professionalism. The two sets of expectations come in conflict, however, in the everyday lives of hundreds of women who try to fulfill them.

These mothers or grandmothers were parenting in the '50s and '60s, when fewer women worked, particularly mothers of young children. Mothers stayed home full time because middle-class families could afford it. Except for the Depression, when wives often had to work to support the family, and World War II, when many women had to work to support their country while the men fought, the first sixty years of the century were for middle-class America a period of generally increasing affluence. The U.S. had a fairly strong economy, and there was little competition from other countries for U.S. markets. By the second half of the century, the increasing availability of labor-saving devices meant that mothers had less to do to maintain the household, and many used their energies to make the household better and the family stronger. Now, in the '90s, most women work. Yet they often try to maintain the same kinds of families, households, and relationships as they— or their parents—grew up to expect.

Many of these women find themselves saying, "You can't have it all," over and over, in response to situation after situation where they know they'd like to do more but can't. Most of these working women clean house or sew perhaps less often than their mothers did; they travel or eat out more often, and make a wide range of other compromises as they manage their home and work lives. They have to make choices, perhaps between work demands and friendships, home demands and church responsibilities, day care and home care. There are many configurations to holistic living— singleness or marriage, full-time or part-time work, working mothers or homemakers, professionals or piece workers—each of which can be marked by the signs of holiness: love for God, service to God and one another, and rich Christ-centered relationships.

The Pressure to Work-Centeredness

The pressure to be Superwomen, to "have it all," brings with it a pressure to work-centeredness rather than relationship orientation. Linda, administrative secretary for a vice-president of a Fortune 500 company, says:

> I'd like to work part-time or even not work at all, but we can't afford it. I enjoy being home. I have time for my crafts, my friends, making my home lovely. But my salary each month barely covers the mortgage, and we need Tom's salary

to pay all our other expenses. If I quit work, we would have nowhere to live. So I spend hours working each week when I'd rather be doing other things. I enjoy my job and know I'm good at it, but I really feel God wants me to spend more time with my family.

The stresses of modern life, while giving women more choices, also sometimes seem to limit them and pressure women to live lives different than those they would choose to live. The frustration of living with pressure toward a more work-centered life than one desires — and the burnout that occurs — is just as insidious as — and receives much less attention than — "Superwoman burnout." Indeed, although "Superwoman burnout" may result from well-meaning efforts to achieve in several areas, work-centeredness tends to exalt work as an ideal and is therefore clearly unbiblical.

Joanie, carpenter for a local contractor, feels caught in the pressure to make work more central than she feels comfortable:

> I make $25 an hour, and pay $5 an hour for childcare. Some jobs, I make $100 an hour. Given our mortgage, what sense does it make for me to stay home with the children except that I'd like to? They're three and five now [her voice softens and her eyes smile as she talks of them] and growing up so fast. So we compromise. I work full-time, my husband cares for them half-time, and I have two days of childcare. We usually pay our bills, but I regret their every hour of child care. I resent that I have to work and can't be with them.

Women need to learn to make decisions from a more holistic perspective, to replace work-centeredness with God-centeredness, to make choices that recognize the centrality of holiness in their lives. Joanie, evaluating her choices, may decide to stay home and make the financial sacrifices necessary to support their loss of her income, or she may work fewer hours than at present, allowing her more time to enjoy her children without the family losing all of her income. Financial issues are important, but secondary to Christian wholeness and relationship issues. When decision-making focuses on Christ, rather that on societal standards, cultural pressures for overachievement are lessened and women are freer to make choices that allow time for worship, relationship, and achievement. With such changes in decision-making, we may find ourselves freer from the pressures of success and power, and may even begin to transform the workplace, making it a more humane and personally satisfying place to be.

Male as Vulnerable Breadwinner

Men also feel conflict in the modern world. Our society's traditional image of men as "in charge" or our concept of husband-as-breadwinner has been eroded as the economy has changed. Men change jobs more often, or they may stay in school for longer periods of time, delaying their ability to be financially responsible for a family or even carry half of the household expenses. Women in relationships with these men find themselves questioning whether and how their partner, still in school or moving from job to job, can share in supporting a household. Although increasing work-related stresses men face are more a function of tightening job markets demanding greater and more specific skills than in earlier times, and of a weaker economy, than of changing gender roles, men find themselves struggling to feel good about themselves when they are unable to provide for their families as they would like.

Tim, in his mid-twenties, recently delayed his marriage "for at least a year and possibly indefinitely" because he was having difficulty finding a job in his desired location and, rather than take the job, he preferred not to marry right away if he did not have a means of financial support. His friend Stan, who went to work soon after finishing college and has now been out of college several years, has held four jobs in the last three and one-half years, all jobs that pay less than his fiancée's job. He seems responsible and capable of supporting a family, but at present, although thirty-one years of age, he does not have the track record to prove it. He and his fiancée struggle together, not with the romantic issue of "Do we love one another?" but "Can we together support the kind of family we'd like to have?"

Men may find themselves, of necessity or by choice, home with the children, while their wives work. The wife may make more money, or find it easier to get a job, or be working as the husband goes to school. Despite the rewards of child care, many men who choose to stay home find they miss the challenge of the workplace and that they are subject to the criticisms of others who consider child care demeaning and unmanly. All such problems are stresses of modernity.

Gender-Role Strain

Other pressures on men are the result of changing gender roles. The "macho male" is certainly not sensitive, and many people's image of the successful man is uncomfortably close to the Rambo character popularized by Sylvester Stallone. Men "make it" in business, often because they are willing to work long hours, as well as to be aggressive and insensitive, if they think the situation demands. "Sensitive" men find themselves criticized or teased because of their unwillingness to be "macho," and they may find it more difficult to succeed in some business settings. Many businesses today are beginning to realize the value of good human resources management, so advancing in such firms may not involve the sort of aggressiveness and insensitivity often associated with being successful in business. Still, the driven, hard-nosed executive is usually the image that most frequently comes to mind when we think of the term "successful businessman."

The new image of men includes sensitivity, as well as success. In the classic film, *Kramer vs. Kramer*, the husband, upon separating from his wife, finds it difficult to care for their son while working at the same frenetic pace as earlier, a dramatic example of the potential conflicts between our twin expectations of the modern man: sensitivity and success.

Sensitivity and success, as defined societally, are difficult to integrate into one's personhood, creating confusion and conflict that Joseph Pleck has described using the "sex-role strain paradigm."[1] (By our current definitions of sex and gender, it is more appropriately called "gender-role strain paradigm.") Before reading on, ask yourself the eleven questions in the Gender Roles Quiz on the following page. The more statements with which you agree, the more likely it is that you support Pleck's concept of gender-role strain. In other words, the more likely it is that you agree there are problems with our society's traditional definitions of masculinity and femininity.

Gender Roles Quiz[2]

	True	False
1. Society has very definite ideas about what men and women should be like.	___	___
2. There is no way that people can do all the things expected of them as men and women.	___	___
3. People who flaunt society's expectations about how men and women should act are usually ostracized.	___	___
4. There is greater tolerance of tomboys than sissies.	___	___
5. Many masculine and feminine traits we've learned from our society are undesirable.	___	___
6. Many people have ideas about masculinity or femininity that they cannot live up to.	___	___
7. Many men who seem too masculine are concerned about living up to society's expectations.	___	___
8. Probably most people fail to live up to society's expectations for men and women.	___	___
9. Masculinity need not exclude emotionality.	___	___
10. Masculinity and femininity would be less stressful if less stereotyped.	___	___
11. Masculinity need not include aggressiveness.	___	___

Doyle describes Pleck's concept of gender-role strain using five principles: (1) masculinity and femininity are not innate concepts, but rather learned during one's socialization experiences; (2) when a male feels guilty about or inadequate in his masculinity, he is recognizing the confused societal messages he has received, not showing inadequate gender-role development; (3) as men attempt to achieve masculinity as defined by society, they may develop unhealthy or dysfunctional behaviors such as extreme aggression or difficulty with intimacy; (4) many men find it difficult to be both successful in their work roles and sensitive, competent husbands and fathers and, as a result, feel conflict in attempting to accomplish the unrealistic demands placed on them by societal standards; (5) because society is changing rapidly, men feel less masculine, less competent than men in earlier generations in achieving the characteristics which society has taught them define mature manhood.[3]

Although there is much talk about the desirability of men developing their sensitivity, in fact, women and men are quite ambivalent about men becoming sensitive. Sensitive males run the risk of being called "weak," or "wimps," terms that indicate men better not fail, even at being appropriately sensitive. It is no wonder that some men decide it is better not to cultivate sensitivity at all.

Gender-role strain follows from societal definitions of success and sensitivity. By these definitions, men are to be aggressive, powerful, and achievement oriented. Sensitivity, on the other hand, connotes nurturance, dependency, and weakness. More biblically oriented definitions, however, allow the joint development of these two desirable qualities.

Biblically, success can be defined as optimizing one's talents and abilities in the context of God's calling for the individual. The world often defines success in terms of net worth, status, possessions, but the Christian must renounce these as bases for his or her evaluation of success. Net worth, status, and possessions are not bad in and of themselves, but they are entirely inappropriate criteria for Christians to use to evaluate success.

It is one's attitude toward things like net worth, status, and possessions that is the key factor here. If you are doing what God calls you to do in life, are in communion with Him, and are caring for your family and community, but you have little or no net worth, status or possessions, are you still successful? Yes! Success, in biblical terms, can coexist with sensitivity, or mutual caring and responsiveness. The biblical man embodies both qualities, while eschewing success at another's expense or sensitivity that would leave him weak and incompetent.

Although success and sensitivity, when appropriately defined, are not inherently in conflict, some jobs demand sixty-hour or more work weeks, making it difficult to find time to spend with family and friends. If this demand is for a limited period— a "season"—of your life, it may be okay. However, if this demand is continual, God may be calling you to settle for less societally-defined success in order to be able to live more caringly.

Furthermore, parenting is a demanding task. Children need fathers to participate in their care, and fathers need to make choices to be with their children, whether in the evening before bedtime, or in the morning before going to work, or one day during the week. Today, some jobs allow flexibility in work schedules. At least while their children are young, and at appropriate times as their children age, fathers may need to accept limitations on their work-related success and commitments.

Societal resistance to men developing greater sensitivity may come from our widely shared definition of maleness as "not female": men can be sensitive but not feminine.[4] Hence we develop the ideas that men can care for others but shouldn't care too much, that they can be sensitive but shouldn't cry, that they can take care of children but may avoid infants, and that they must not be stay-at-home parents. This definition of maleness also includes the thinking that men need to value friendships and support one another, but not at the expense of success and competition in the workplace.

Society, having defined men as "not female" may also pressure men to be successfully nurturant without being sensitive. Lillian Rubin, in her book *Intimate Strangers*,[5] concludes that nurturance and intimacy, which accompanies sensitivity, are different and that many men are nurturant without being intimate.

> Nurturance is caretaking. Intimacy is some kind of reciprocal expression of feeling and thought, not out of fear or dependent need, but out of a wish to know another's inner life and to be able to share one's own. Nurturance can be used as a defense against intimacy in a relationship—a cover to confuse both self and other, to screen the fact that it doesn't exist. It can be used manipulatively—as a way to stay in control, as a way to bind another and ensure against the pain of loneliness.[6]

Rubin acknowledges that women sometimes abuse nurturance to avoid intimacy, but argues that men do too; perhaps even more often. She quotes a male friend who confesses:

> The kind of nurturance I offer to women makes them very dependent on me. After all, how many guys are good at caretaking or at listening? And, as a result, a woman will reveal her soul to me and will tell me she's never had such an intimate relationship. But the truth is that they're so seduced by my nurturant style that they don't notice that I'm pretty careful about revealing my own vulnerabilities. It all seems very benign, but I'm quite aware that it's one of the ways a man can retain power over a woman; he doesn't have to dominate her in any oppressive way, he can dominate by giving her so much that he ties her to him for as long as he wants. She becomes emotionally dependent, then he's safe.[7]

Societal definitions of success trap men in autonomous, independent worlds, making sensitivity difficult. A biblical definition of success frees men up for sensitivity and holistic living. No longer subject to unreasonable demands on their time and personhood and no longer abusive of others, they find themselves able to be more responsible for others, more tolerant of differences, and more flexible in their lifestyles.

Double Binds

Many of these stresses, for men and women, are the result of "double binds." Double binds describe situations in which either choice brings costs. Some double binds are the result of a shortage of time. Helen recalls:

> I grew up in the South, where, in the summertime, people sat out on their screened porches and visited with the neighbors, shelling peas or shucking corn together as they talked, or just sittin'. I find it frustrating that I do not have the days, or even the evenings my parents had. I'd like people to feel free to "just drop in," but then I know that I'd feel the crunch of time and other commitments. My husband and I treasure those rare nights when we don't have other obligations, and

try to take time together. Even that sometimes seems a luxury.

Double binds also result from changing gender-role definitions. For women, now expected both to have a job and to parent, trying to "have it all" is a "double bind." Success at work may mean diminished success at home. For men, now expected to be both successful by cultural standards and sensitive, integrating both aspects into a holistic image of personhood proves difficult because the culturally accepted definition of success is often antithetical to sensitivity. Not until people grapple with the impossibility of meeting our society's demands on both personal and professional lives will we see workplaces being transformed and the potential met for less stress and greater satisfaction in our daily lives.

Women too find that nurturing their sensitivity and furthering their success in the workplace sometimes seem incompatible. As women take on increasing responsibility, they may feel themselves less responsive and nurturant. Karin, a female college professor and Christian in her early forties, laments:

> I know some students seek me out because I am female and "motherly." They want to talk. But I can rarely take the time, at least as much as I'd like to. I have to prepare tomorrow's lecture, or work on research, or rush to pick up the baby at the day-care center. I miss the days of graduate school, when I felt I could take the time I needed with students in the classes I taught. Maybe once I get tenure, my job will be less demanding.

Some women may resist increasing their responsibility because of its costs in "people time." This may, however, bring a lower salary, as it did for Valerie, a competent but poorly paid secretary at a beverage delivery firm:

> I don't mind my job. I never take it home, and I have time at work to talk to all the guys out in the trucks. My boss asked me to consider being her secretary, but I like answering the phone and managing "my guys." If I worked for her, I would work twice as hard, and I'd never see anyone but her. Of

course, it would pay more. But I can't see spending eight hours a day, fifty-two weeks a year, doing something I dislike. And I'd never have time for choir or Bible study.

Some women may resist power, choosing instead to empower others, perhaps feeling that their success, should they become powerful, would bring loss to another. Amy, a lower-level manager at a computer company, talks of her problems living with this choice:

> I sit in meetings as the only female, and find myself constantly nurturing and supporting others, without pushing my own ideas. I help Don finish his program, and Steve plan his, and don't get my own work done. Well, a lot of good it does me! When we had our year-end review, I was severely reprimanded for my unfinished work, in spite of all the help I had given to my colleagues. I was hoping for a raise. I'll be lucky to keep my job!

Women also experience the success/sensitivity double bind in child care. As one Christian counselor and author found:

> When our child was born, I naively assumed I would be back at work at three weeks of age, and I was, seeing clients in therapy. Meanwhile, this child was breast-feeding, but not on any schedule, and refusing to take a bottle. Needless to say, I and the baby had a few difficult hours. Once she settled into a schedule, I expected to be able to get an hour or two's worth of work done during the day, around her naps and playing. Instead, at six months, she slept no more than four hours at a time at night and cat napped (maximum twenty minutes) during the day. When she's asleep, I find myself washing clothes or cleaning up the messes we together make while she's awake, when I'd rather be writing. She's a priority for me, but sometimes I'd like to have some time for secondary priorities, particularly when I have a client to see or a writing deadline.

Male/Female Parallels

The double binds that society imposes upon women and men, primarily as a result of changing gender roles, seem in a sense flip sides of the same coin. While men fear sensitivity and true intimacy, believing that such tendencies challenge the basic definition of masculinity as successful, women fear success and the greater personal responsibility and status it often brings, feeling that such developments challenge the basic definition of femininity as relational. Men may resist sensitivity, choosing a wife or girlfriend who is capable of intimacy, yet fearing that acknowledging their vulnerabilities will undercut their male sense of success and stability. Women may resist success, choosing instead a successful husband. They may also resist success by avoiding it altogether, fearing that their power — although modified by sensitivity — undercuts their caring.

These are not really double binds in the classic sense, although they often feel as if they are. Stresses come as women and men broaden their self-definitions in violation of traditional societal definitions: women, to expand their experience of success, and men to strengthen their skill in interpersonal relationships. A woman can be nurturant and powerful, and a man successful and sensitive, but we need mentors and models who can help show us how to deal with such problems.

We also need to replace societal definitions of power and success with biblical ones. Women need to feel free to make choices that are biblically rather than societally driven, and men need to recognize that their choices are just as complex and important. Just as women are vulnerable to "Superwoman Burnout," men too are vulnerable to a parallel syndrome, "Superman Burnout." Their choices are equally complicated, centering on the needs of both the family and the workplace, their calling and their spouse's calling. But if we focus on God and make more biblical choices, then we can assert ourselves and maximize our potential while also being nurturant and sensitive to others.

Minimizing the Stress: Toward Identity, Stability, and Flexibility

Societal pressures toward maleness and femaleness have, in some senses, misled us as males and females. A brief reconsideration of ideas on the development of gender identity can help us re-formulate our understanding of maleness and femaleness. The psychological literature indicates that people are most content when they participate in a variety of roles: parent, friend, worker, and lover.[8] Stable identity for both sexes normally depends upon pursuing a balanced set of roles, whether in the home, volunteer work, or job. We need adequate time for work and play, for relationships and personal growth. Despite the demands of family and work, we particularly need to provide adequate time for personal and spiritual growth.

Developing a stable identity also depends upon the availability of both mother *and* father during the early child-rearing process. Children develop a stable sense of themselves by having warm parents who discipline appropriately and who provide consistent, stable guidelines for behavior and appropriate consequences for violations of these guidelines.

The Scriptures add to these guidelines for establishing a stable identity by requiring that we trust in God rather than societal standards for our identity (Prov. 3:3-6; Rom. 12:2). Our identity is better defined by the interpersonal qualities we develop—doing justice, loving mercy, walking humbly with God—than by worldly success (Micah 6:8; 1 Cor. 13:4-7). Indeed, the Great Commandment and its corollary are to love God and your neighbor (Matt. 22:36-40). Success is not mentioned. Success as biblically defined—that is, optimizing our talents and abilities in the context of God's calling for the individual—can perhaps best be evaluated by examining the personal qualities we evidence in achieving success: How joyful are we in our work? How much are we at peace? How patient? How faithful? How much self-control do we show? (Gal. 5:22-23)

These recommendations for developing a stable gender identity apply to both sexes equally, not one more than the other. To progress toward a more stable identity, however, women need to work on some aspects more, men on others. Women seem to value nurturance and fear power, while men value power and fear vulnerability. We need to redefine each of these so they are not sex-typed or negative, but reflective of our relationship to God.

Women can value nurturance but not be dependent on others, thinking they have to "be everything to everybody." They can work toward a more holistic notion of being supportive to others while still taking adequate care of their own needs. They can maintain their disdain of power in a domineering and manipulative sense but recast their views on the healthy use of power. They can accomplish this by reevaluating the importance of accepting personal responsibility for their actions and by using power in healthy ways to assist others.

Deborah (Jud. 4–6) exemplified such a woman, as does the woman of Proverbs 31. Successful—one as a judge, the other in the marketplace—they managed to integrate their sense of themselves as women in relationship (both were married, both had extensive relationships with women and other men) with their competence and power.[9] Ruth too demonstrated her commitment to her mother-in-law and her abilities by following Naomi's suggestions and acquiring food for them both. Although the details of their lives differed greatly, each of these three women succeeded in integrating their abilities in relationship with their sense of themselves as competent people, expressing a whole personhood.

Men can redefine their concept of success, recognizing the importance of optimizing their potential for God's glory while valuing power and success for the ways in which they can use these qualities to further God's kingdom and their personal relationships. Biblical men can maintain their sense of healthy competition (to avoid sub-optimizing their abilities) and at the same time develop their capacity for sensitivity and intimacy. Boaz was such a person (Ruth 2:5-16). Even before he fell in love with Ruth, as successful as he was, he was sensitive to her, using his power to meet her needs. Similarly, the Good Samaritan stopped to help out a wounded traveler (Luke 10:30-37), showing his sensitivity, and Paul cared for Onesimus, a slave, in his own imprisonment (see Phile.).

With an *identity-flexible,* rather than identity-fixed, model of gender identity, we—male and female—can show *respect* and *tolerance* for those who violate traditional societal roles of maleness and femaleness. We can do this, for example, by refusing to label sensitive men attempting to live godly lives as "wimps" and successful, godly women as "aggressive." We can practice *tolerance* for ourselves: as males learning to experience wholeness, when we're apprehensive about showing vulnerability, or if we fail to be sensitive. As females, we can practice *tolerance* when we show strength that initially feels inappropriate or impersonal, or when we fail to meet our own high expectations of ourselves in both the family and in the workplace. We show *flexibility* as we attempt to become more godly and whole people, and *responsibility* as we participate with others and support them in their own struggles toward holiness and wholeness.

Strategic Action:
Twelve Steps to Dealing with Gender-Role Conflict

1. Check the source of your pain: Is it from behaviors you've been criticized for? Expectations you believe you must fulfill? Assumptions you have made regarding what it means to be a man or woman?

2. Ask yourself: Whom am I listening to with regard to whom I should be or how I should act? Society? My friends? My parents? My partner? Or God?

3. Seek feedback from a good friend whom you trust: Ask for help in measuring thoughts and evaluating your perceptions. Encourage your friend to be honest with you.

4. Pray for wisdom: Ask God to show His view for your identity as a man or woman. Ask Him to indicate where your present thinking may be lacking, inaccurate, or distorted.

5. Study Scripture: Let God reveal anew to you His truths about life—and specifically about your life. Take time to see how He has dealt with His children throughout history. He will do the same for you.

6. Join a group: Seek out friends or a support group where individuals are openly examining their own assumptions of what it means to be feminine or masculine. Share your concerns. Seek new perspectives and vantage points.

7. Try a "Re-Visioning" Experiment: Imagine yourself trying on a new behavior that you once thought was outside your range of activity because of your views of what a man or woman ought do. What does it feel like, in your mind, to be doing this behavior?

8. Pray for courage and the capability to change: Change takes courage and time. Not all of us are capable of it. But with God's help, all things are possible. Trust Him to empower you—especially where you are convinced He is leading you to fresh changes in your life.

9. Get brave: Try the something new you imagined. Change a long-held habit. Take on that new activity—even just once—you never thought you could handle.

10. If you're convinced you're not supposed to change anything, then pray for peace: If God wants you to accept your present position or situation, He will grant you an inner peace despite the turmoil you may sense on the surface. If, after a time, you experience little peace, go through the previous nine steps again.

11. Evaluate your efforts: After several days or weeks, ask yourself, "Is this working out for me? Does this feel like positive growth? Do I sense that I am glorifying God or becoming more the person He desires me to be?" If not, be willing to try steps 1-10 again.

12. Affirm yourself: Change is never easy; nor is it easy to live with a situation we're fairly certain cannot or should not be changed. Whether you've made a "brave new leap" or learned to see anew your present circumstances, remember that God honors your authentic efforts. He's proud of you; you deserve to be proud of yourself.

Conclusions

Modern societal pressures to maleness and femaleness complicate our lives, contributing to gender-role strain, double binds, and imbalances between our work and family lives. As Christians we are not free of these pressures, but together can explore ways of minimizing these pressures and transforming our lives. Jesus provides for us a model of personal wholeness, integrating success and sensitivity in male personhood. He was sensitive and caring, sensing that someone needy had touched His robe and moved to meet her needs. He was nurturant, lamenting for the unbelief of Jerusalem, saying "How often I wanted to gather your children together, the way a hen gathers her chicks under her wings, and you were unwilling" (Matt. 23:37). He wept over the unwillingness of many to repent. He was successful, but not in a short-term sense, or by the world's standards. He never made much money and never advanced up the company hierarchy, but He certainly had power and influence, and He always exercised these capabilities for the good of those whom He met. As we struggle, male and female, toward personal wholeness, we can emulate His example. We can strive to express those personal qualities which we as Christians value, while avoiding incompatible or unreasonable standards imposed by society. In doing so, we will find life to be less stressful and more satisfying, and the complicated, conflicting pressures of maleness and femaleness to lessen.

Questions for Reflection:

1. In what ways have you been aware of the stresses of modernity: "Superwoman Burnout," pressures toward work-centeredness, the vulnerability of the male breadwinner, or gender-role strain? How have you been dealing with these issues? What new ideas does the chapter propose for addressing them?

2. Does the biblical definition of success proposed in this chapter help you think differently about success? Do you think it describes "nonprofessional" as well as "professional" success?

3. In what ways have you been aware of the conflict between success and sensitivity for men? How might you address this issue in yourself or with the male friends you have?

4. In what ways have you been aware of the conflict among

spiritual, personal, and work demands in yourself or with your female friends? How might you resolve these conflicts?

5. Can Christians be competitive and powerful at work? What limits are there on this? Can you give some examples of difficult situations when competition and power is somewhat abusive but seems unavoidable? How would you deal with these?

For Further Reading:

Balswick, Jack, and Judy Balswick. *The Family: A Christian Perspective on the Contemporary Home*. Grand Rapids: Baker Book House, 1989. This book provides a thorough and scholarly discussion of family relations and problems from a Christian perspective. These authors summarize contemporary societal pressures on families, acknowledge the difficulty of opposing these struggles, and propose biblical approaches to these problems.

Carr, Jacquelyn B. *Crisis in Intimacy: When Expectations Don't Match Reality*. Pacific Grove, Calif.: Brooks/Cole Publishing Co. 1988. This secular text suggests that relationships are in crisis, primarily because our expectations of relationships are outdated, unrealistic, or shaped by our fears of change. The author suggests that the crisis can best be resolved by recognizing our choices in our own lives. We can then choose to become committed to another, to give up self-centeredness and power struggles, and to develop inter-dependent and loving relationships.

Doyle, James A. *The Male Experience*. 2nd ed. Dubuque, Iowa: Brown Publishers, 1989. This secular textbook, designed for a men's roles course, provides an excellent, highly readable survey of contemporary and earlier definitions of masculinity. He discusses such central issues as power, sexuality, and male-female relationships.

Gundry, Patricia. *The Complete Woman: Living beyond Total Womanhood at Home, on the Job, and All by Yourself*. Garden City, N.Y.: Garden City & Co., 1981. Gundry challenges women to wholeness. Using the woman in Proverbs 31 as a guide, she relates her own personal experience to basic issues for women today, giving the reader page after page of wise insights and good advice. Examples of the issues she addresses include women's attitudes toward work, health, personal appearance, and financial investment.

Pleck, Joseph. *The Myth of Masculinity.* Cambridge, Mass.: MIT Press, 1981. Pleck suggests that most of us believe that parents are responsible for their children's sex-role identity development, and that male sex-role identity is risky and failure-prone. In contrast, he proposes (in what he calls the "sex-role identity paradigm") that male identity problems are the result of socialization into a society which has expectations of males which are internally inconsistent, impossible to achieve, and harmful to men. His book has become a classic in understanding male gender-role development.

van Leeuwen, Mary Stewart. *Gender and Grace: Love, Work and Parenting in a Changing World.* Downers Grove, Ill.: InterVarsity Press, 1990. The author, a Christian psychologist, examines physiological, psychological, and sociological reasons that explain how people grow up as masculine and feminine human beings. She recognizes the stresses of these roles and examines biblical passages and secular literature that suggest minimizing these stresses by alternative, more egalitarian roles.

*Responding
to
Our Calling*

8 Relationships: Avoiding Stereotypes and Being a Friend

Men (Women)! I'll never understand them. Why do they have to be that way? Whether in friendships, work relationships, dating, or marriage, we sometimes find ourselves wondering about the other sex. What makes them act as they do? Try as we may, understanding and dealing with many of these behaviors can be frustrating and annoying.

Carol Gilligan has suggested that this problem reflects two contrasting world views.[1] Men and women inhabit the same world but, she says, bring different values and priorities to it, interpreting and reacting differently to it. Many of these differences may not be real, but rather may be stereotypes; these differences may result from our perceptions of behaviors of friends and acquaintances. In actuality, Tim and Susan may act as they do because of who they are, not because they are male or female. Medical doctors and psychologists have shown that the similarities between the sexes are greater than the differences. Still, discussing some commonly perceived differences in behaviors of males and females may help increase understanding between the sexes and clarify confusions.

In our relationships with one another, we are to be *responsible, respectful, tolerant,* and *flexible*—regardless of the extent of our differences. The Bible tells us our love should be long-suffering (1 Cor. 13:7) and our annoyances kept short (Eph. 4:26-27). As we keep these guidelines in mind, knowing why problems in our relationships occur can help us develop our capability for patience and tolerance.

The Value of Friendships

The Bible commends us to friendships (see John 15:13; Eph. 4:32; 1 John 4:7-8). The encouragement, nurturance, and accountability our friends provide us are key vehicles for our growth as people and as Christians (James 5:19-20; Heb. 3:13; 1 John 4:7-11; Eph. 4:1-3; 1 Thes. 2:7-8). In singleness, dating, marriage, and work—friendships sweeten every experience of life. Most of us, at one time or another, can relate to Calvin, as he rhapsodizes about the virtues of his tiger friend.

CALVIN AND HOBBES copyright 1989 UNIVERSAL PRESS SYNDICATE.

In earlier years, dating and mating received such emphasis that basic friendships between the sexes were devalued. Now there are increasing opportunities to develop friendships as men and women are marrying later, staying in school longer, and a greater number are getting divorced. Indeed, friendships have become so important today that, in contemplating marriage, some women and men worry that their friendships will suffer as the marriage relationship limits their time for more casual friendships.

Further, the emphasis in marriage is now on being friends rather than filling roles, a trend that makes premarital and extramarital friendships even more important. Nurturing friendships with a spouse is easier and healthier when the marital friendship can be shared with other friends. Finally, men and women, married or single, establish friendships at work, with same- and other-sex friends, and these relationships can be both nurturing and conducive to mutual growth.

Friendships are receiving increasingly more attention. Women's friendships have been the subject of increasing numbers of movies (e.g., *Beaches, Steel Magnolias*, and *The Lemon Sisters*), and even male friendships have made the big screen (e.g., *Ferris Bueller's Day Off, Chariots of Fire, Three Men and a Baby*). One recent film, *Driving Miss Daisy*, described the warm, loving, long-term friendship of an elderly white woman and her African-American chauffeur, lasting long after the work relationship had ended.

A Good Friend Is Hard to Find

Friendships are more important and yet more difficult today than ever before. Sara, a Christian in her mid-thirties and a college professor, comments:

> When I took my present job twelve years ago, I established close relationships with several single women friends that remain strong, although maintaining these friendships has not been easy. I have watched my relationships change as I have become more assured in my job; my academic friends have taken various positions, my business friends have been promoted into more demanding, better paying jobs, and we have all made decisions about marriage and children.
>
> Whereas once I saw these friends weekly and shared everything, now we see each other once a month or even less. Our relationship is broader and richer, in some ways, than

earlier. We know our relationship is strong and appreciate its longevity, and we can quickly reestablish intimacy. Yet I still miss the frequent sharing and regret that our careers and marriages have led us in such different ways.

These and other "life-stage" changes—moving from lower- to higher-paying jobs, from school to career, from singleness to marriage, and from childlessness to having children—can introduce distance into a friendship.

Friendships in our contemporary society require more flexibility than earlier because our society is increasingly mobile and technologically oriented. Some studies have indicated that, on the average, people in the United States move approximately every six to seven years (and people in their twenties once every three years!).[2] Maintaining friendships through those moves and developing new friends in new places over and over again can be stressful and difficult.

Our society has also been characterized by rapid growth in communication technologies. While these might seem to benefit friendships—we can now contact friends on their fax equipment, cellular phones, and answering machines—they also increase the pace at which we live our lives and introduce distance into relationships. After the fifth call to a friend, as you leave a message on the machine for her to call your machine, you experience frustration and sadness that finding time for relationships is so difficult.

Friendships take time, time that is hard to find in our increasingly rushed lives. Many jobs now demand more than a forty-hour-work week, and in two-paycheck families time is even more limited. As a single friend in her early thirties sadly commented, "Once I've been to work, called my friends, and gone to church, I have no time or energy left over for meeting people—much less dating!" Sometimes we feel the need to limit our work lives and our technology—and nurture unhurried, low-tech friendships.

A Good (Other-Sex) Friend May Be Hard to Nurture

Three of the most important areas where the sexes encounter difficulty in relationship are decision-making, competition, and conflict management. Males and females may have learned to behave somewhat differently in these areas — at least at times — making cross-gender relations in these areas more problematic. Many of our difficulties, however, may be — rather than real differences — the result of unhealthy stereotypes of the other sex.

Decision-Making

Stereotypically, women are intuitive and illogical, while men are rational and logical. "I can't believe Jen," says Bob. "She told me weeks ago that Joel and Laura had decided to date seriously. She knew it without their telling her. I had no clue!" Jen responds, "Don't tell me you had no idea! It was *so* obvious." Some suggest that these differences are real: women are better at "multi-dimensional," contextual thinking,[3] and perhaps at "reading" nonverbal cues, whereas men are more linear and rational.[4]

One woman, a manager of a corporation's executive training program, remembers a meeting she had with her male boss about how to design the process to select new trainees:

> Darryl and I needed to work out the details of how our office chose the participants for a new development program for our fast-track young executives. We had seventeen candidates for the program, and we needed eight. Darryl and I were planning the procedures for the selection committee. Darryl wanted to center the committee's decision process on the candidates' performance appraisals for the past several years. I thought the performance appraisals were valuable, but given the potential importance of the program for these young executives' lives, I felt they should have at least ten or fifteen minutes to make a presentation to the committee about how they saw themselves and the company developing and growing. Darryl just couldn't see why that part of the selection process was so important. I tried to explain my views, but he couldn't understand why I saw things the way I did.

Not always will a woman be more relationship-oriented in her decision-making than a man. One woman, recalling decision-making in her church's board meetings, identifies more with the "male" style:

Things were pretty interesting, the more I think back on how the board meetings operated. When the church board reviewed matters at its monthly meeting, the women often focused on how they understood developments in the spiritual and emotional lives of the congregation. They talked about individual people's needs and comments they would hear in Sunday School and Wednesday night fellowship. The men would normally talk about the programs the church was offering, the program budgets and objectives, and attendance at Sunday School and the Sunday morning services.

Granted, women talked sometimes about budgets and men sometimes about issues of emotional growth, but you often had the impression there were two different sets of conversations—and two views of church life—going on. Every once in a while, you'd even hear muttered comments among a few of the men about how much smoother things would go if it weren't for the women's "talkativeness" about this or that decision. Y'know . . . it was funny. I often felt more comfortable with the men.

What some may describe as "women's intuition" may actually be a heightened sensitivity to the personal and relationship-related aspects of the decision. Janis may be more aware than Tom of how their friend Cindy—African-American, single, and fifty—would be affected by the decision not to keep the black assistant pastor. Janis may more clearly realize that Cindy will feel less accepted at church if such a decision were made, and she will focus on these issues rather than on the cost efficiency of the decision, pro or con. The different conclusions some women—and some men—reach based on these subtle, personal considerations may seem "mysterious" to those who are not usually aware of such subtleties.

Women may also feel less powerful and thus may express their ideas and exercise their influence more gently and less directly. While many women have recently taken on positions of authority in many areas of public life from which they have long been excluded, discrimination still exists—for example, in hiring, promotions, and pay. Brenda, a marketing representative in her late twenties, recognized that young employees at her office could profit from a course on media relations and dropped a casual hint to her boss over dinner, rather than making it formally at an office meeting, knowing and accepting that he would initiate the course without giving her credit.

Sometimes, of course, this effort to influence people can lead to or be perceived as manipulation. Still, the basic ability has served women well in a society which constrains them from affecting their environment as much as men can. The decision-making process women use to come to such decisions may seem "mysterious," but in actuality it is often just a different mode of accomplishing similar goals.

Furthermore, labeling a woman's decision-making process as "mysterious" is trivializing and distancing, because this label exempts the user from trying to understand how the decision was made. The implication—that the decision was somehow conjured up or arrived at by magic—suggests little effort in trying to understand the actual dynamics of the decision.

For their part, women may find it difficult to explain their basis for decision-making. They may have learned to emphasize relationships so much or to devalue their own reasoning powers so that they reach conclusions almost subconsciously, without being able to explain why they think as they do.

Women who struggle for self-expression may find themselves criticized for meandering. "Just say it," says her male friend. Some men, who may limit their concern to the basic facts and logic of the issue, may only want to hear about the objective aspects of the issue and find the other aspects peripheral and not worth their time to try to understand. (There is no evidence women have more trouble reasoning analytically.) Neither the stereotypically male nor female approach is better, and relationships are better served if females who experience this gender difference are willing to struggle to express themselves concisely while their male friends struggle to be patient.

Sometimes this dismissal of women's opinions can manifest itself in remarks among males, such as "That's a silly idea; women just don't think logically" or "Well, you know [sigh], women always think with their hearts rather than their heads." Christy, a mid-level manager in a U.S. Government agency, recalls some treatment she received:

I was in this meeting where we were doing some brain-storming about directions for our department and some of the problems we faced. It was chaired by a well-known senior manager, but one whom I had heard was not all that encouraging to the women on his staff. Boy, did that ever turn out to be an understatement!

In the meeting, we were sharing our ideas on the key issues. George, the senior manager, would nod thoughtfully when the men shared their opinions and would note their views with his marker on the flip chart. When a woman would share her ideas, he would nod and seem to be affirming, but he would move on to the next person without writing down any of her comments on the chart. Every time he came to a woman, he'd do the same thing—this "Yes-uh-huh-I-see" number—then move on. Needless to say, I was smoldering.

Then—in an almost bizarre twist—Dave, one of my colleagues and a good friend, apparently picked up on what was happening. After I offered an opinion—which George, of course, didn't write down—Dave a minute or so later would paraphrase what I had said. George would then note Dave's comments on the chart, and in this way I'd get my opinions considered!

Can you believe that?!

This attention to men's opinions and ideas and the frequently concomitant disregard for women's, appears in a wide range of settings.[5] Women are frequently observed to adapt their conversation styles to men's when in mixed company, but men virtually never adapt their conversation styles to women's.[6] Patrice, a bright, articulate woman in her mid-thirties with two graduate degrees, recognized this bias against women and compensated:

The opinions and observations I provided at work used to have a more intuitive or emotional cast, but I got murdered in the office for these. Over time I've changed my thinking—or at least my expression of my thinking—to have a more "rational" and "linear" dimension.

As a female business consultant once said, "I have been paid handsomely to go into an organization and teach its top management what they could be learning for free from the women around them!"[7]

Men and women, as indeed any two people, may also see different emphases in Scripture or hear different themes in the Sunday sermon. Jim laughed as he told the story:

> At Sunday brunch, Joan commented how much she enjoyed the sermon, and I looked at her in shock. "How could you?" I asked. "He's talking about tithing again, and you said you were tired of talking about it." "He was?" Joan said. "I loved his stories about struggling to be a good father. I never thought of parenting as tithing."

Both men and women can enrich their personal understanding of Scripture and support one another by appreciating distinctives in the personal values and backgrounds people bring to moral judgments.

Competition

Males seem socialized to competition, whereas females sometimes avoid it. "Competition" to many connotes taking advantage of or abusing another, activities that Christians eschew, and thus it may seem that not even males should be competitive. Healthy competition, however, means challenging one another to God's glory and so can be a necessary and rewarding part of one's personal and work life, whether male or female. As women take more positions of leadership and management, their competitive edge may be honed, creating transitional stress for them and their male friends.

Tom, a Christian male and a businessman in his early thirties, describes his experience observing women's struggles with competition:

> I've heard of women who don't push themselves in professional settings to avoid appearing competitive and threatening to their male colleagues. Maybe they also fear they won't be attractive socially. To be effective employees, these women need to change their attitudes.

He goes on to comment that males may need to change as well:

> If guys traditionally have become used to females not being competitive, meeting and working with women who are

professionally competitive may cause some difficulty. Maybe in such cases the guy perceives a competitive woman as a threat to his ego—maybe even to his job. If this is the case, the guy needs to readjust his ideas on what success and competition mean and why he thinks that women shouldn't be as competitive. Sometimes, it's even the case that the behaviors a guy would consider simply healthy competition from another man, he would label as "aggressive" if he saw them in a female.

Even relatively competitive women may compete for different reasons than men. Competition in work situations provides both men and women fulfillment and creativity, but men may use competition more to achieve power and prestige, while women may be more concerned about the potential richness of their relationships. One woman comments that for women, work generally

> becomes more than something one does to earn money; it becomes a "life work". . . . It means making a contribution which complements the other aspects of our life. It is not profit- and power-oriented; instead, it takes its meaning from creativity, bonding, humaneness, and service. . . .
>
> [A woman may say that when she concludes her life], it will be the relationships I have had . . . [that] are most important. It will not matter whether I have built a bridge, or written a book, or had a university named after me. I will cherish the lives I have touched and those persons whose lives have touched mine.[8]

Women may desire to be as competitive as men, but sometimes may be less effective for reasons outside their control. One Christian woman, a research chemist in her early thirties, commented:

> In professional meetings at my lab, we would go around the room in a circle, sharing our research findings. Men—usually repeat visitors to our research section—would often criticize the presentations by women in the group in an apparent effort

to make themselves look good by making the women appear less competent. You could tell this was what was going on because the criticisms were usually about pretty minor stuff. Sometimes the women in our group would respond by making light of such criticism, while other women would tacitly accept it, even though they knew their research procedures were solid and well-executed. The only way I found I could effectively squelch this criticism during my presentations was to lower the pitch of my voice and politely but firmly refute point-by-point all the negative comments that were raised. Once these visitors realized I would always give them a firm, reasoned response, they would stop trying to score points off me. I finally learned how to handle these guys, but it was pretty annoying and frustrating in the process.

Reporting a similar problem, a Christian male—a sales representative in his late twenties—gave one possible explanation of how "glass ceilings" and other elements of the business world often hinder women's advancement:

At a firm where I used to work, I'm sorry to say that the informal "rules" were sometimes weighted against women. A few of the managers who were not supportive of women making progress in the firm would set up a set of objectives and guidelines for a female employee. When she achieved those objectives, she would be given additional goals, with the remark that the satisfactory completion of the earlier ones was not entirely sufficient for advancement at the firm. As much as I didn't like this situation, there wasn't much someone in my position could do about it.

One difference between the genders bearing on competition involves contributions to group conversations. Sometimes a woman may hesitate to contribute to a discussion because of her desire to keep the conversation balanced by leaving the opportunity for everyone to participate more or less equally. Men, who usually will not hesitate to share opinions they think are important and germane to the topic, may view this quietness as reflecting a lack of initiative or a lack of competence with the subject matter. A man may think, "If she has anything interesting to say, she'd say it," and therefore draw the conclusion that the woman isn't an effective colleague or employee. Both men and women need to recognize such differences in attitudes toward participating in group conversations. Men need to encourage quieter group members to speak up, and women need to be aware that their quietness may be perceived as an inability to make an effective contribution to a group effort.[9]

Another competition problem, noted by a female social psychologist, is that women in the labor force are often still treated as tokens and are isolated from key events in the daily life of the firm. She describes a "good-old-boy" network, from which women are subtly excluded:

> Many business and professional decisions are made over coffee, lunch, or cocktails. Important contacts are established and maintained on the golf course, on the squash court, and in other traditionally male settings. Being excluded from these informal social occasions does not just make the female professional feel lonely; it can seriously interfere with her ability to do her job. . . .
>
> Promotions, job openings, and professional referrals are also discussed informally; by the time the female professional finds out about them, they have often been filled by that promising young man who plays squash so well.[10]

Partly as a result of such problems, females sometimes report they feel almost as if society requires they be two separate people — an assertive, competent person at work and a non-assertive, perhaps even dependent, person in one-on-one social situations. Kim remarks:

> Oh, yeh . . . this quasi-schizophrenic attitude our society sometimes expects of women is a problem I've run into often. You need to be assertive, perhaps even aggressive, in the business world to get the job done. On a date, though, some guys want you to act like a marshmallow. I know you shouldn't have one persona to use at work and another to use socially, but I can tell you for sure that a lot of guys don't like dating assertive women, even if the women are cordial and

gracious. What's a woman supposed to do? Do guys want to date wimps?

Whether friendships are between coworkers or church members, whether they are intimate or distant, we need to integrate our sense of ourselves as competitive people in a wholesome way into these relationships. Both men and women have every right to be competitive, but they need to be so in a fair and mutually supportive way. Especially as Christians, we're called to eschew unfair and unedifying behaviors and to treat people with charity and evenhandedness, following Christ's example and biblical admonitions (Rom. 2:11; James 2:9). Negatively stereotypical thinking, prejudice, subtle discrimination, and the like have no place in a Christian's thoughts or behaviors at work.

Conflict Resolution

Women, socialized to value relationships, may often seek to avoid conflict.[11] They do so on the assumption that open airing of conflict would be injurious to the relationship, which needs to be maintained at all costs. What usually happens in such situations is that the relationship suffers, in part because important disagreements are repressed, possibly leading to a more serious dispute later.

Additionally, healthy conflict is necessary for personal authenticity and validation of the self.[12] When people avoid conflict, they tacitly accept — and their acquaintances or colleagues support — a lower status for themselves. These people, as they avoid conflict, begin to perceive their feelings and needs as less important than those of others. In a close friendship, avoiding conflict by not sharing such differences of opinion also does a disservice to the other person, who may sense that something is amiss but not know what to do about it.

Many women — as well as men — need to practice healthy expression of disagreements and healthy conflict resolution:

> Conflict has been a taboo area for women and for key reasons. Women were supposed to be the quintessential accommodators, mediators, the adapters, and soothers. Yet conflict is a necessity if women are to build for the future.[13]

A truly authentic person is one who is true to oneself and can use conflict to grow:

> All of us, but women especially, are taught to see conflict as something frightening and evil. These connotations . . . have obscured the necessity for conflict. Even more crucially, they obscure the fundamental nature of reality—the fact that, in its most basic sense, conflict is inevitable, the source of all growth, and an absolute necessity if one is to be alive.[14]

With an adequate support network, one can overcome the fear of being isolated by conflict.

Once a conflict has arisen, many men may proceed to resolve conflict primarily by attending to its objective dimensions, while women focus on its subjective elements. Richard, a Christian man in his early thirties, reported an experience he had with a Christian woman he had been seeing:

> Nancy had attended a party with some casual friends and during the evening happened to comment about several aspects of our relationship that most people would probably consider private. I found out about this discussion a few weeks later and gently explained to her the problem I had with what she had done. I asked her about her interpretation of the events behind the problem to make sure that we saw things basically the same way.
>
> Nancy did agree that the events that caused the problem had occurred as I had suggested, but she seemed incapable of discussing the problem in terms of what actually had happened, as opposed to how she and I felt about what had happened. While I was willing to talk about this emotional dimension, I thought the problem could be far more easily managed without delving into the emotions that may have surrounded it. We eventually resolved the disagreement, but it was a very unpleasant and uncomfortable experience.
>
> Later, someone I shared this story with suggested that Nancy may have been focusing on the emotional dimension of the conflict as a buffer for our egos. Boy, if that were the case, her effort was certainly counterproductive!

Women, having resolved an issue or decided it is unresolvable, may want to "talk a problem through" while their partners may feel that it is time to "let it go." Men may find such talk tiresome and useless, since it seems unlikely to generate other solutions. On the other hand, women may find that talking further helps them feel better about it, perhaps because they're using the problem for relationship-building. Claire, a Christian business executive, relates an example:

> We were going to be shorthanded for a half-year or so in my office. Doug, my boss, gave me some accounts to cover that a former employee had managed. I didn't know how I was going to get this additional work done on top of all my regular work, but I agreed to try. My boss and I talked about my new workload briefly, but it would have been nice if he had expressed more concern for how much I was taking on and perhaps how some of my other responsibilities could have been adjusted.
>
> I shared these developments with Rick, my husband, and told him how I thought Doug and I should talk about things further. "Do you think you or Doug could come up with any other ways to deal with the work than what you have already?" Rick asked.
>
> "Not really," I said.
>
> "Then why talk about it?" he asked. "That seems pretty pointless."
>
> "I guess I felt Doug and I were friends. I wanted to connect with him personally and make sure we really understood one another's viewpoints on this problem."

Christians, called to serve the needs of the whole person, must recognize that problems have both objective and subjective, emotional and pragmatic aspects. Thinking of both aspects may particularly help resolve unexpected or especially difficult conflicts. Andrew, a physical therapist at a retirement home, reported a scene he observed at his institution:

> I once saw two older women arguing over the use of an exercise bike we had. One woman complained to another that

the second was using this equipment that actually belonged to the first. However, the only claim the first woman could assert was frequent use of the bike. The argument became very heated until a female supervisor arrived and stopped the argument by demanding that the women separate facts from feelings.

It was obvious as the supervisor helped the women resolve the conflict, that while the first woman had no claim to ownership, both women were equally guilty of precipitating the argument because of a long-standing dislike of one another. I doubt the women's more basic dislike of one another would have surfaced if facts and feelings had not been addressed.

Andrew wisely comments here that both facts *and* feelings need to be addressed in a conflict. Problems normally involve both facts and feelings, and the two are often so intertwined that it is unusual to resolve one without attending to the other. In serving the whole person in the context of conflict management, Christians can respond both to the emotional and the pragmatic aspects of conflicts, working for resolution and for mutually beneficial relationships.

A Good Friend Is More Valuable than Gold

Friendships need to be nurtured. Though friends don't usually make the vow spouses do—"for richer, for poorer, for better or worse, in sickness and in health"—some friendships are worth the effort to maintain them through life's stresses. Karen tells the story of a valuable friendship that survived several life stages:

When I left graduate school, an acquaintance asked me to keep in touch and visit when I could. I thought little of it, but, on my next trip, we had dinner—and found we had more in common than we thought. We planned a trip to England together and kept in touch. Thirteen years later, we married within six months of each other, and each had a child soon after. The relationship has been fun to share and more than worth the trouble!

Nurture same-sex friendships as well as cross-sex friendships. They are often stable and satisfying, and they enrich our lives. Henry remembers a birthday party at a friend's house:

> We had all gathered early at Lisa's for a surprise birthday party for someone in our church group. I was sitting on the couch, having a pleasant but serious chat with my friend Roger. A female friend of Roger's sat down on the couch on his other side. She was really good-looking, and Roger immediately dropped our conversation and turned to talk with her. I certainly don't mind my male friends noticing attractive women, but they don't need to ignore me to do it!

When our friends of the other (or even the same) sex start dating someone, or marry, our friendships with them may suffer. Some change in our relationships may be necessary, but important friendships are worth nurturing through these changes. Stu tells of a female friend at church who had a fairly narrow-minded attitude about male-female friendships and the changes that occur in them:

> Both Bonnie and I had been out of town for the summer on internships in different parts of the country. We had had a low-key but friendly relationship, so, early in the fall, I thought I'd see if she'd like to get together for lunch to talk about our summers. I mentioned the idea to Bonnie — but do you know what she said? Her response was, "Oh, I'm sorry. I'm dating someone now."
>
> I bit my tongue. "Who in the world said anything about a date?" I wanted to answer. Instead, I stammered something like "Oh, okay, I guess you're busy."
>
> To this day, I can't fathom her response. I had never given any indication of being interested in dating her, but still I got this "I'm-dating-somebody" business. Did she really consider our friendship that dispensable?

Claudia, a Christian woman in her mid-thirties, shares a similar story:

> While I was single, I had a good counseling relationship with my pastor, a nice guy several years older than I, happily

married with several kids. We would talk in his office or at a local restaurant about how we understood the Bible and pray together—basic stuff like that. Several months after I got married, I called up my pastor friend and suggested we get together for one of our chats. To my surprise, he agreed but suggested we meet at a restaurant in a suburb quite far from ours. I knew he would never be the sort to "play around" on his wife, so I asked him why he made the suggestion. He responded that he was concerned about people knowing he had been talking privately with a "married woman." I was astounded. Isn't talking to people something pastors are supposed to do? Was driving across town really necessary just for a friendly chat over lunch?

Ryan reports a more positive story:

During the months after I arrived in New York in September, I got to be really good friends with my new apartmentmate John. I also got to be good friends with his girlfriend Claire, who became his fiancée the following spring. During the time John and Claire were dating, Claire and I would occasionally get together for lunch or dinner, and John was pleased that Claire and I got along so well.

Sometimes when I would talk with Claire about my childhood in St. Louis and my family who still lived there, she would mention that she'd like to visit St. Louis if she should ever have an opportunity. Well, as things turned out, my high school reunion was coming up in the summer. Sometime after John's and Claire's engagement, I mentioned to Claire that if she would like to go home with me to St. Louis for the reunion, I'd be happy to have her company. She said she'd like to do that, and we both—independently—talked to John about the idea.

John thought the idea was fine, so—believe it or not—Claire went home with me to St. Louis. We had a great time together that weekend. Claire met my family, and we had fun touring around the city. John and Claire had a good summer themselves that year, and I was in their wedding the following fall. It just goes to show that in an atmosphere of trust and caring, friendships can really profit.

Cross-sex friendships are valuable. Some young adults feel so much pressure to be married that they cannot enjoy friendships. Cross-sex friendships may not—and need not—lead to marriage. Although some feel that relationships between men and women are necessarily romantic, one can have non-romantic but intimate relationships with members of the other sex. It may take some work to develop the proper personal boundaries and self-discipline, but such a relationship is often worth the trouble.

Conclusions

To nurture and enhance friendships, we need to *respect* the backgrounds and socialization experiences both sexes bring to relationships. We need to deal with one another *responsibly:* to avoid even subtle or unspoken discrimination and eschew harassment. We should listen carefully to one another's opinions and evaluate those opinions fairly. In our friendships, we also need to practice *tolerance* and *flexibility:* to be sensible and understanding in decision-making and conflict management situations and to appreciate views which at first might seem out of place or foreign to our own way of thinking. Although someone may not share the same values and assumptions in a work, family, or church situation, we should strive to acknowledge the value of what they have to say.

Friendships—with peers, potential partners, or spouses—provide the texture and richness in the quilt that becomes our lives. We hold one another in a web of caring, bound together in Christian community, sharing the colors of our diversity, and enriching ourselves in turn from these relationships. Together we shape the patterns that tell the stories of our shared lives—patterns which can be nurturing, rewarding, and complete, if we participate together in their weaving.

Questions for Reflection:

1. How much do you value friendships? To help you answer, consider how much time you spend with friends in comparison to time at work, or with dating or marriage partners.

2. Consider your closest friends. What kinds of friendships do you nurture? Do your friendships include singles and marrieds, older

and younger, childless and with child? Why do you choose to nurture these relationships, or why not?

3. Consider a recent disagreement between you and a friend of the other sex. Why did you differ? Do the ideas in this chapter help you resolve your disagreement? What ideas do you have for resolving disagreements, based on your experience?

4. What examples of subtle discrimination of one sex toward the other have you noticed?

5. What do you think about pursuing romantic relationships at work? Can this be done without causing problems?

6. How do you think it's best to handle keeping a relationship a friendship if you think the other person is interested in romance?

7. Review your life stages (e.g., going to college, first date, getting married, first job, having a child). How have these affected your sense of yourself as male or female?

For Further Reading:

Carli, Lina. "Gender Differences in Interaction Style and Influence." *Journal of Personality and Social Psychology* 56 (April 1989): 565-576. Carli discusses different strategies used by men to influence women and vice versa, as well as how successful these strategies are.

Davis, Keith. "Near and Dear: Friendship and Love Compared." *Psychology Today* 19 (Feb. 1985): 22-30. Davis discusses studies that try to define the different qualities and dynamics of friendship and love.

Houck, Catherine. "How To Defeat Loneliness." *Cosmopolitan* 207 (Sept. 1989): 263-65, 270. Houck discusses why people become lonely and offers suggestions of healthy ways to make friends.

McGinnis, Alan Loy. *The Friendship Factor*. Minneapolis: Augsburg,

1979. This is a well-known Christian book on developing healthy, meaningful friendships.

Schenkel, Susan. *Giving Away Success*. New York: McGraw-Hill, 1984. Schenkel analyzes women's interaction and work styles and suggests how they can participate in society and work more confidently and effectively. Much of her analysis is based on the "learned helplessness" she sees as hindering women's development.

Scott, Niki. *The Working Woman: A Handbook*. Kansas City, Mo.: Universal Press, 1977. Scott presents a broad-ranging discussion aimed at helping working women deal with the daily pressures they face at home and at work.

9

Singleness: Living in a Couples' World

I'm financially independent, own a home, and have a great social life. But I'm single. What's wrong with me?

© Rob Portlock

"We're an embarrassment, aren't we?" So begins a Christian book on singleness.[1] For many people today, singleness still feels like an embarrassment, a reason for apology, a motivation for therapy as shown in the above cartoon. We are asked if we are "called" to singleness; no one ever asks if one is "called" to marriage. We have to "deal with" singleness. No one ever talks about "dealing with" marriage, although all marriages are sometimes stressful experiences. Especially if we are single beyond a particular age—whether twenty-five, thirty, or thirty-five—singleness begins to dominate our worries and our friends' or family's conversations. After a certain age, though—forty or forty-five, maybe—people no longer dare mention it. We may be asked, "Why are you single?" But no one would ever think to ask, "Why are you married?" We begin to question God's provisions for us and to worry about our own attractiveness. Or we struggle to avoid thinking about the issue, putting on a brave and unconcerned front. "God will provide," we say, while secretly wondering if God will. For too many of us, ending our singleness becomes a mark of our happiness, of our mental health.

Singleness is *not* an embarrassment, nor necessarily God's "second best." Indeed for some, *marriage* may be "second best." Singleness is a cultural and economic phenomenon, characteristic of American society since the 1970s, that brings its own particular challenges and opportunities for ministry.

Why Are There So Many Singles?

People are marrying later than ever before.[2] One of the authors married at thirty-nine, certainly outside the norm today, but virtually unheard of even two decades ago. Whereas in 1970, 9 percent of men and 6 percent of women between the ages of thirty and thirty-four had never been married, by 1988, 25 percent of men and 16 percent of women between these ages had never been married, a striking increase.[3]

There are many reasons for the delay in marriage, one of which is that there is less pressure to marry now than earlier.[4] Earlier, one finished high school or college and got married. Few other lifestyles were prevalent. Today, when one finishes school, men and women often choose to live as a single. They find support groups, housing, consumer marketing targeted for older, affluent singles, and even church groups focusing on the interests of older singles.[5]

Today's singles—especially women—have much more freedom than in earlier generations. Ginger's mother is turning eighty. She was born in an era when there were few singles past their mid-twenties, and women were particularly protected. Ginger, a Christian woman in her mid-thirties, shares about her mother's views:

> Mom periodically writes me to suggest that I not venture out at night alone, even though I live in a quiet, safe suburb. Imagine what life would be like for single women if we could not go out at night alone! In *some* places, of course, women should *not* go out alone at night, and the problem that many places are not safe for women at night is obviously a discredit to our society. Still, it is interesting to note that now, as opposed to earlier, we are making the assumption that women *can* experience the evening—if they want to—as well as the day. Since women purchase many more goods than men, if we still worked under that earlier assumption, clothing and food stores would close, at least during the evening hours, and malls would empty. And, when would I see my friends? Yes, things have indeed changed.

Singles Are More Highly Educated than Earlier

As we have earlier suggested, greater education is needed to participate in an increasingly technologically oriented society.[6] This factor has greatly contributed to the higher incidence of singles. Men have always gone to school, but they are now in school longer. Additionally, women are pursuing college and graduate education in increasing numbers. In the late 1980s, in fact, women out-numbered men in high school, college, and master's level programs.[7] Going to school is stressful and increasingly expensive, so, although men and women do marry during their school years, many people prefer to delay marriage, hoping to reduce the stress of school and in their first few years of marriage.

Singles Are More Often Female

Think of the singles you know above the age of thirty. Most of them are probably women.[8] Another reason for the delay in marriage is the lack of suitable mates. Women outnumber men at every age above eighteen.[9]

The baby boom (the surge in births during the years 1948-1964) explains some of this gender inequity. Because of the tendency of men to marry younger women, men now in their early forties had a large selection of marriage possibilities, while women now turning forty — or soon to do so — have had a much smaller selection of older men. This difference continues through most years of the baby boom, evening out only in the population of young people now in their mid-twenties.[10]

This "marriage squeeze"[11] — with fewer men trying to select among more women, primarily because of the baby boom — has created a large population of singles whose character is markedly different from that of any other generation of singles. Many of these singles are women: educated, independent yet strongly connected to peer support groups, relatively affluent and mobile, and articulate.[12] Far from our image of single women as "old maids," these women are "hot tickets" — bright, articulate singles, often fully involved in their community or with friends in various activities. Many of these women are Christians who love God and actively serve Him in multiple relationships and activities.

"Hot tickets" they are. Carol, an attractive, competent, Christian businesswoman, is such a woman. Having known her through several relationships, we recognize with her that any marriage resulting from these relationships would have been "second best." A wise woman, she refuses to moan in her singleness. Instead, she loves God, lives fully, and shares of herself in many close relationships with women and men. Married friends, perhaps caught in less than fulfilling marriages, envy her clear vision and wise decision-making.

Although the highly educated, high-achieving women receive greater attention, many single "hot tickets" are male. A close friend of Carol's, an equally attractive Christian male who works with a large accounting firm, says:

> I have been matched up with every single woman I know — or any woman any of my friends knows, has met or even seen in a mall. . . . Somehow it doesn't work. Either she doesn't want the relationship to continue or I don't feel it is right. I was

sure my last relationship would work but it didn't. She had just come out of another relationship—through a painful breakup—and she was afraid of our relationship. "Give me time," she kept saying . . . and then she broke it off. I value my relationship with Carol because we can be friends. Neither of us expects or wants the relationship to be more. I know, when the time is right, I will marry—or come to feel comfortable with my singleness.

Singleness as a Desirable Lifestyle

The presence of this large group of single women and men has validated singleness in society's view to an unprecedented degree.[13] Many people now delay marriage by choice, choosing flexibility, autonomy, and job progress to early marriage and child care. Indeed, when some choose to marry, they may receive condolences from their single or married friends. As Mike said when his friend Bob recently married, "One more sells out!" He may mean it somewhat tongue-in-cheek, but the message is clear: singleness is more acceptable and desirable than ever before.

Does the Church Minister Effectively to Singles?

In the church, however, singleness may not have the same positive status. Most churches are strongly family-oriented, with programs focusing on every segment of the family, except the single person. A recent study of U.S. churches by Barna Research noted that

> [w]ith the recent upsurge in interest among church leaders in family-oriented ministry, it would be easy for many unmarried adults to receive the impression that they are the second-class citizens of the body. When we are asking these people to commit themselves to the church, it is imperative that the church itself return that kind of commitment to singles.[14]

When was the last time you heard a sermon with illustrations from the lives of singles over the age of twenty-five? Yet married people frequently populate our sermons. Singles, when they are addressed, are described as separate, as if they don't share the lives of the "rest of us." One recent sermon focused on "the needs of singles," as if singles share in common a large segment of their needs. Of course, the primary "need" discussed was for marriage, despite the multiple other everyday issues that many singles address.

A recent study of singles in America suggested that singles have two primary needs: belonging and having their individual needs and interests met. Half of the singles surveyed (53 percent) considered religion important in their lives. (The study included singles who attended church and those who did not, but the authors did not report how many singles were surveyed or how these singles were chosen.) These singles felt that the most important characteristics of a church were "making visitors feel welcome" and "having a strong youth program." Singles not in a church, when asked what would encourage them to attend, suggested sponsoring a musical concert or seminars open to the public.[15]

Loneliness may be the "bugaboo" of singles, a factor that churches should take into account as they seek to minister effectively to singles. Singles (particularly divorced ones) experience more loneliness than marrieds, particularly than married men, although marrieds too can experience significant amounts of loneliness.[16]

Too many churches, rather than attempting to meet the particular needs and interests of singles, ask singles—who are expected to have "lots of free time"—to run the church's nursery and Sunday School programs, on the assumption that singles wish they could spend more time with children. Some singles may want to spend time with children, but others don't. The needs and priorities of singles are frequently not recognized or met by traditional church programs.

Some churches have developed "singles programs" to minister specifically to the needs and interests of this group. These are often helpful, providing Bible studies, weekend retreats, and evening activities for their participants. Toni, however, finds herself frustrated with the generic nature of these programs and often does not attend. "What do singles have in common?" she rages. "You'd think that our lack of a mate makes us somehow similar. What a put-down! I am who I am because of my interests and abilities, not because I 'lack' something. If my church had a group of skiers, or of movie buffs, or even of social workers, I'd go in a minute!" Too often, these needs for sharing with people with similar interests—needs typical of young adults—get met outside the church setting.

Singles need churches which instill in them a sense of belonging, minister to their individual needs and interests, listen to the details of their everyday lives, and give them a sense that their lives have meaning (i.e., in serving God). The Barna Research concludes:

> In the final analysis, the keys to reaching singles are enabling people to forge meaningful relationships within the church structure, and feeling that the church is a haven from judgment and rejection, offering instead valid solutions and wisdom in response to expanding external pressures and confusion. Many single adults are interested in spiritual asylum, not a hostile challenge to their very existence. Any institution that can offer them a better perspective on how to live, and offer assistance implementing that perspective, will gain their attention, if not their loyalty.[17]

Singleness Is More Than Dating

Unfortunately, for many of us—married or single—the central issue of singleness is marriage. Browse through some of the books on singleness in your local Christian bookstore. Almost all deal extensively with dating and all but a few highlight dating in the title. Usually, many of us view singleness as a way-station, transitional to marriage. Once a single has passed the age of twenty-five, the shorter the time in this transition, we feel, the better.

Dating, when given too much priority, stunts the spiritual life and interpersonal relationships of the single person and may even interfere with the establishment of potential marital relationships. For some single people, the search for a mate may dominate the prayer life and conversational time with friends. It dominates their quiet time and personal reflection time. If the single has a "significant relationship," he or she may agonize: "Is this the one?" If there is no relationship in the offing, they may agonize over its absence. Such singles are obsessed. Unable and perhaps afraid to have fun, they fail to recognize their wholeness as human beings, and to live in full relationship with their same or other-sex friends. (We empathize with those of you caught in these obsessions and want you to know that healing is possible.)

Singles who are obsessed with dating relationships may be responding primarily to societal and church pressure. Singles who are not in a dating relationship—whether they actually crave such a relationship or don't seem to care—seem aberrant to many of us. We may question them ("Can't they get along with anyone?"), as if singleness is somehow *wrong* if it goes on too long, or question their male or female friends ("Can't they recognize a marriageable person?"). There is nothing wrong with desiring a relationship for oneself or for our close friends. But assuming that all singles hunger for relationship, and zeroing in on that one aspect of their personhood, is to stereotype them unfairly and limit their options for relationship.

Singleness as Connection
Many single men and women value their independence while equally valuing their connections with family, single friends, friends who are married without children, or friends married with children. One single Christian woman gave up an excellent job and a well-established niche with friends and in a church to move nearer her parents. "Since I have not established my own family yet," she says, "my connections with my parents and brother are really important to me. I want to know my nephew and niece, and participate in their rearing. I know I can establish new friendships—and find a new job—but I need this sense of rootedness." Married people can strengthen the sense of rootedness that many single people sometimes lack by remembering them on holidays, celebrating their birthdays, or simply offering them friendship.

Singleness Can and Should Be a Rich and Wholesome State

Singles are the result of recent cultural phenomena, with distinctive characteristics and interests far from the "bachelor"/

"old maid" stereotype. The feelings of embarrassment and despair that some singles experience—often the product of thoughtless remarks from friends or family who think of them as odd (and uncommon in our culture) or as "losers"—do not reflect reality. Singles are not a coherent group. For starters, the U.S. Census draws distinctions between the "never-marrieds," the divorced, and the widowed, aware that each group has distinctive characteristics. Some singles are young; some old. Some are "hot tickets," active and outgoing; some are "hobbits," preferring to stay home, wear comfortable clothes, and eat whenever and whatever they want. Some wear the latest fads; others prefer blue jeans. Some love children, while others love sports. For some, singleness has become a developmental phenomenon, soon to be terminated by marriage. For them, it is a stage of life which allows possibilities for growth and ministry that one will have at no other stage. For others, singleness is lifelong, providing exceptional potential for richness, personal growth, and service. Although all singles sometimes experience unique loneliness and frustrations, they can also experience the flexibility, freedom, and self-confidence that comes with healthy singleness.

Relationship Myths: Placing Dating in Proper Perspective

Singles hear certain messages about dating and marriage so repeatedly that these messages need discussion and clarification, and placement in the proper context of a full life. Each message carries some truth, but using them too blithely is harmful and misleading.

Pick a Date Fit for a Mate

This statement assumes that the primary purpose of relationships is marriage. On the contrary, healthy relationships focus on friend-ship building, not marriage. If marriage follows, fine. But if not, singles are richer for the friendships they have established. Perhaps the statement should be rephrased: Pick a date fit for a friend.

Many worry: Doesn't dating someone I would not consider marrying mean I might date a non-Christian, fall in love, and be "unequally yoked?" Marriage is a choice made by two people; one is not passively pulled into marriage. Responsible people can exercise discretion and self-control. At the same time, as Mark, who dated a non-Christian and struggled with wanting it to turn into marriage, advises, "If you think you won't be able to avoid falling in love, or you worry about your ability to make good decisions, limit the relationship before it becomes too much of a temptation. I wish I had."

Others defend their dating of non-Christians as "missionary dating." But Harold Ivan Smith warns:

> Yes, I have heard stories of believers who have helped to spark the faith of nonbelieving spouses . . . [This kind of dating] is motivated by the notion, "I can change him (or her). He'll come around." But too many of these missionaries have discovered after marriage that the interest in religious subjects has cooled considerably. One man played along with his fiancée's religious beliefs until the wedding ceremony and then announced to his new bride that he had no intention of being a Christian.
>
> Be careful. Dating exposes your heart and can leave you vulnerable to hearing what you want to hear.[18]

Many of our friends—by our choice or theirs—are not "marriageable" for us (although ideally we don't stop to evaluate this in most of our relationships!). Although some may say that a single person wastes time with non-marriageable friends, the reality for many of us today is that we have time for friendships and we should use this time to advantage—and, if we don't have time for friendships, we should make time. We may not have the opportunity to marry right out of college, or we may choose not to marry then. Many won't be married by thirty. Still, we have plenty of time to build friendships with different types of people and to be enriched by these relationships. Indeed, although friendships should never be established primarily for furthering our dating lives, many dating relationships develop from friendships or from meeting "a friend of a friend."

The saying "pick a date fit for a mate" dominated the dating lives of our parents and grandparents, when dating was a formalized activity in the process of mate selection and people married younger. Since the '70s, dating isn't what it used to be. Some singles say, "I don't date; what's wrong with me?" What's wrong? Nothing. People just don't date as much as they used to.[19] Many people think of dating as one-on-one activities, with a special someone. This assumption isn't as true now as earlier: When was the last time you heard of someone "going steady?"

As a woman in her mid-twenties said, "I have one friend who 'dates,' but mostly we just go out with a group of friends." Her friend Andy agrees, "I guess we guys used to have to ask someone out every Friday and Saturday night, but I don't have the money. So I meet women in other ways: at the exercise club or at the singles group. It works better that way. You can get to know someone without risking a lot."

Group activities and spontaneous get-togethers are much more the norm, and people who want to begin meeting others need to become involved in some group. Ideally, a group "just forms" for singles, a natural group that attends church together, goes to movies, and cares for one another. If not, singles need to search for a group whose activities they feel comfortable with and with whom they can establish good one-on-one as well as group relationships. When one is part of a group, the statement "Pick a date fit for a mate" becomes less pressing. Maybe it should be: Pick a *group* fit for a date?

The germ of truth in this statement "Pick a date fit for a mate" is: if one makes a commitment to date another exclusively, then he or she should make sure that the dating partner qualifies as a potential mate. Too many people settle into relationships that are comfortable, long-term, exclusive, but not acceptable for marriage. These relationships interfere with establishing more appropriate, long-term relationships and should be terminated if one eventually wishes to marry.

There's Only One Spouse for You

Also called the "one man-one woman" position or "right man-right woman"[20] position, this belief pressures the single person to find the "right" one. Assuming that there is only one possible spouse can make dating agony and decisions about marriage impossibly difficult. What if I don't recognize the spouse God means for me? Is that why I'm still single? What if I marry the wrong one? As one friend wryly observes, "Doesn't that throw off everyone else, condemning at least one other person and probably many others to marry the wrong person?"

If one is seeking God's guidance, it is irrelevant whether there is one or many potential spouses available. In fact, there are probably many people one could potentially marry. Individuals have many qualities which can complement another's qualities, as does any potential partner. Some relationships enhance some qualities; other relationships develop other qualities. Bill, having participated in several relationships simultaneously, felt it was time to make a choice:

> I had dated Linda seriously for a few weeks and had known Donna for a long time. Donna is loving and gentle, a real sweetheart. I love having dinner with her or going to the movies. Linda is stronger and less gentle, but more a friend. I don't have that same heart-stopping feeling I do with Donna. Our relationship is more independent, and more equal, and most of the time I like that. But we also seem to have more arguments. I agonized about it and prayed for guidance and finally decided to spend more time with Linda, and to let Donna know I wanted to be a friend but. . . . I know I could have gone either way, and they're both great people, but I can tell Linda anything, and I know she'll listen. Somehow that seems more what I need in marriage.

Recognizing that there are several potential spouses may help singles focus away from the question: "Does this person have the qualities I need?" and focus instead on: "What kind of relationship can we have? Is this relationship one which glorifies God and strengthens us together?"

The truth in the "one-mate" statement is largely after-the-fact. It is healthiest to approach dating as if there were many potential spouses until one marries. Once people marry, there is only one spouse for them, the one they have married. Then, the challenge is to continue to grow together and to complement one another.

God's Will for You Is Marriage

This may be the hardest to consider, because most of us would like to believe that God's will for us is marriage. We can do everything we can to prepare ourselves for marriage, but sometimes "God's best" for us—as shown by the choices we have made and continue to make, including the people we have chosen not to marry—is singleness.

No marriage is better than any marriage. Or, to put it more precisely, singleness is preferable to a bad marriage, particularly if God is calling one to singleness. Singleness is not a "consolation prize," something given when we can't seem to find a "better offer." Although it may *seem* that marriage is inherently better, particularly because marriage seems to bring a greater sense of belongingness to church or community, sometimes singleness is actually the better choice.

When one of the authors married, she recognized one of the hidden benefits of marriage:

> I married at thirty-nine and yet I felt that people finally viewed me as adult, as more mature, as somehow more legitimate when I married. I resented this implication that my life had just begun, that I had fulfilled my heart's deepest wish. I, in contrast, felt I had had a wonderfully rich and fulfilling life as a single.

In fact, marriage is supported by cultural and economic institutions and rituals that mark it as the norm, whereas singleness is not. Married people get a tax break over two single people sharing an apartment; they are offered honeymoon suites and coupons at hotels; they marry in a highly ritualized ceremony that is a big event for family and church members.

These institutional supports for marriage make life even more difficult and uncomfortable for singles, and ignore the complexity and individuality of single and married people. Maturity is marked by responsible decision-making and a willingness to care for others. Married people have no "corner" on these qualities. Indeed, marriage for many is a way of avoiding decisions, decisions which singles have more difficulty avoiding.

Harold Ivan Smith, recognizing the desire of singles to marry, offers the following advice:

> There's nothing wrong with wanting to be married. But there's also nothing wrong with being single. But here are

some things you should keep in mind:

—Your happiness should be based on who you are, not whether or not you are married. *Must*-centered relationships are destined for frustration and heartache. Instead, ask yourself how you can best use the gifts God has given you as a single person.

—Concentrate on being the person God intends you to be. Don't let all your time and effort be sidetracked into looking for a mate.

—Bitterness will only end up hurting you. It comes between you and God and keeps you from seeing the good things God has given you. Ask God to give you a positive, thankful attitude. It will do wonders for you.[21]

Singles, particularly in the church, need to be validated by all of us as mature individuals, with their own strengths and contributions to make. Instead of giving them the place of "not yet married," we should give them the recognition they deserve for their individual gifts and characteristics. Singles should be included in the church's life and activity because of who they are and what they can contribute.

These three myths: "pick a date fit for a mate," "there's only one spouse for you," and "God's best for you is marriage," are simplistic and misleading. They ignore the richness and complexity of the single's life, and of the relationships that one forms as a mature and responsible member of a church congregation.

Toward an *Identity-Flexible* Model of Singleness

Our model suggests that singles deserve *respect* and *tolerance*. Singles differ widely from one another, and each has their own abilities. Marrieds need to accept their diversity and get to know them as individuals well enough to recognize their strengths (see 1 Cor. 12:4-12).

Singles, on their part, need to be comfortable with *flexibility* and are called to *responsibility*. Based on our clinical practice, we know singles struggle with the following paradoxes: adaptability versus structure, independence versus dependence, and making commitments versus maintaining distance.

Adaptability versus Structure

Singles may need *flexibility* more than any other group of people, and many of those who end up in clinics and pastors' offices asking for counseling are struggling with the transition from the identity-fixed to an *identity-flexible* lifestyle. Healthy single lifestyles blend *flexibility* with a level of structure comfortable for the individual. Some people need more *flexibility* than others. Singles who prefer to structure their weekends may need to find a group of friends to do activities with or join an exercise class. They can make a list of people to call when they're eager to do something. Most singles find they need to plan some activities ahead, such as going to the movies, the theater, craft shows, or apple picking. If singles want to maintain relationships with married friends (and all singles *should* have some close married friends), they may need to structure time with them during the week, as weekends are more difficult for couples.

Of course, there is such a thing as being too flexible. Be dependable. Singles who commit to go out with someone, shouldn't back out because a better offer comes along. For one thing, they'll get labeled. That's "Susie I've-got-a-better-offer Smith. Every time she gets an invitation from a man, she drops her woman friends." People will see such a person as disloyal and desperate. Friends of the other sex may also look down on such an individual. It seems an extreme reaction and unfair, but single people have feelings too. Friends of a woman may not agree that the man of her dreams, whom she met on the ski slopes for ten minutes, is more important than they who have known her for ten years. Backing out on plans is okay once in a while, but people who cancel plans regularly, shouldn't schedule get-togethers—if they respect their friends and want to keep them.

Independence versus Dependence

Sandra, a Christian woman in her mid-thirties, reports a huge struggle with taking care of herself. She remembers:

> My first major trauma was buying my second car. The first car was easy. I bought it with someone else, named it "Bernadette," and she was as much a clunker as her name suggests. I'd stop at a gas station and, instead of the usual

"Please fill it up and check the oil," I'd embarrass myself
with, "Fill up the oil and check the gas please." Buying a new
car — alone — took me almost a year to do.

What are singles waiting for? For Sandra, it was buying a car; for
others, maybe it's moving out of the family home, or buying a
condominium. Sometimes singles fear these activities as a symbol
of independence, of beginning to "accept" singleness. Singles often
need to learn *responsibility.* It's as if they think that taking charge of
their own lives dooms them to singleness. Pay those bills; clean the
apartment; see the doctor; fix the lock on the door; take off those
jeans and put on more attractive clothes. Life generally becomes
more comfortable, satisfying, and rewarding when one begins to
take responsibility for it.

Another issue for singles may be going to parties alone. Some
singles never seem to need to do this. They have an active group
that meets all their social needs. But many people don't have such
a group. Unless we have a strong ego and a good sense of who we
are, most of us would rather not go alone. But go: find someone to
go with, or go alone — just go. Singles who do go will be surprised
that doing so is not as uncomfortable as first thought, and will find
that every time they go alone, they become more comfortable
about going the next time. No one respects someone who always
has to have a man in tow, or a woman on his arm, to feel self-
confident. Besides, the important aspect of going to a party is not
with whom one is seen — or whether one is alone or not — but the
relationships with friends that one enjoys at the gathering.

Many older singles struggle with the prospect of giving up
independence if they begin developing a more intense relationship
with another person. They have been on their own for a long time,
and they enjoy it, make money at it, and surprise themselves by
how well they can do. Giving all this up is not always easy, for any
of a number of reasons.

Singles don't have to give it all up. The key is mutual
responsibility. Replace independence with interdependence or
mutual *responsibility.* Each person in the relationship has something
to offer, and each has needs. In a relationship, each can be
dependent on the other, meeting their own needs and receiving
support. Healthy relationships also need space, particularly among

older singles. In this space, each can practice interests that the other may not share or simply have time to be alone.

Mutual *responsibility* demands a willingness to become inter-dependent. To develop this quality, both people must be willing to be vulnerable. Indeed, mutual vulnerability is an important vehicle for the edification of the community of Christ (Gal. 6:2).

At the same time, if they feel a relationship is not working out, healthy singles must be independent and willing to survive on their own. They should be willing to communicate this perception to their partners at the appropriate time and not be guilty of "stringing them along." For singles of any age, having too much dependence as an ideal makes it harder to cope with single-ness.

Mutual responsibility also requires honesty, and honesty demands that a person know his or her own feelings and be willing to talk about them. Some guys have problems with a simple "I enjoyed the evening—thank you" to a woman they're not interested in seeing further. Instead of leaving it at that, they confuse her with "I'll call you soon," never intending to do so. Many people fear the potential "He might want to sleep with me" so much that they communicate nervousness and dislike of the other person. Couples need to talk about their desires, for their own sakes and that of the relationship.

Of course, honesty also demands tact. We all like to feel desirable and wanted. Egos ride on such a simple event as the movie Friday night. The apostle's admonition is most appropriate here: be kind (see 1 Cor. 13:4).

Commitments versus Distance

It may seem odd, in discussing singleness, to talk about commitment. Yet singles—particularly women—seem determined to remain totally flexible, uncommitted to anything—house, car, or friendship—until they have the prospect of a marriage relationship. They seem determined to keep their lives on "hold," into their thirties and forties. It's as if they believe that commitment closes off options, and one wants to have as many options as possible.

Responsible Christian living, however, demands that we make commitments. Singles need to be open to relationships with both males and females. Don't assume that people who have a fantastic job are happy and have all the close friends they need, or that professionals have no social needs, or that those who are always cheerful and friendly actually feel that way. And don't assume that people who seem undesirable have nothing to offer you (note Paul's comment about this in Rom. 12:3).

Responsible Christian living normally calls us to be involved in our society. (Remember, even those called as monks or nuns are active participants in their communities!) Here are some suggestions for ways to pursue that involvement, involvement that will benefit both the single person *and* their community.

Cultivate interests. Don't study all the time, or work all the time, or even go to church all the time. Do something inter-esting—ski, swim, juggle, tap dance. . . . It is often easier to meet people through special interests or through friends than through groups designed for singles. Singles as a group of individuals are as diverse as the entire church population. When in a singles group, singles need to find others who share their interests. Every single one of us needs good friends more than we need dates.

Cultivate relationships with people of all ages. People limit the richness of life, and become prone to narcissism, when they limit their contacts.

There is nothing wrong with planning activities that are more likely to bring a person in contact with members of the other sex, but be sure such activities include both males and females. Sharon recently decided to go on a "manhunt." Literally. Several women met and talked about how to locate good quality, marriageable Christian men. That's a worthy goal but always the wrong tactic.

Live *toward* tomorrow, while living today. Each one of us may or may not be single as life unfolds. But if we live now as if we are marking time, we make for ourselves a prison, a prison that prevents our experiencing the richness God provides, that limits our potential for building relationships, and that restricts our opportunities for growth and service. Experience Paul's "freedom to . . . serve" (Gal. 5:13, NIV). Break free from this prison and move out into the light of day. Live *flexibly* and *responsibly*. By doing so, we draw others unto us and truly experience what life in God's service can offer.

Questions for Reflection:

If you are single:

1. Make a list of the things you enjoy about being single, and another list of things you do not enjoy. What can you do to ease the parts of singleness you find difficult? How do others deal with these issues?

2. Make a list of activities you enjoy doing. When have you last done one of those? Discuss what gets in your way. Plan an activity soon.

3. Go through your local newspaper's activity calendar and find activities you have never tried but think you might enjoy. Talk with a friend and propose trying one new thing now.

4. Consider whether you lack people to do things with. Why is it sometimes hard to find play partners? Some people feel comfortable calling others to suggest activities; others don't. If you're a caller, keep it up. If you're not, make a list of potential people to call. You might decide to call some people for some activities, others for other activities. Be sure to include some married people on the list.

5. Many singles find holidays difficult. Share your strategies for solving holiday struggles with a friend and consider what additional strategies you might use.

If you are married:

1. What did you appreciate about your own single years? In what ways does singleness encourage ministry?

2. What do you fear about singleness? How do singles that you know deal with these fears? How could you (tactfully) help or support them in these struggles?

3. What do you think your single friends wish couples knew about

them or their lives? What do you wish your single friends knew about your life? Invite some singles to dinner and chat about these ideas.

4. Consider activities that your family has recently engaged in. Do you include primarily couples? When might you include singles — not necessarily invited in pairs? Consider developing a close relationship with at least one single person. If you already have one, consider adding a relationship.

5. Consider your church's activities. Is it comfortable for singles to be there? (If you wonder, ask several singles.) If you have a singles group, do people act as if this group is enough to meet the needs of singles? Are church activities primarily couples-oriented? Are sermons and Sunday School lessons primarily for families?

For Further Reading:

Fields, Doug, and Todd Temple. *Creative Dating*. Nashville: Thomas Nelson, 1986. Humorous "do's and don'ts" of asking someone out, descriptions of the world's worst dates, and forty-nine ways to say "I love you."

Powell, John. *The Secret of Staying in Love*. Valencia, Calif.: Tabor, 1974. This book is a classic on love and self-esteem — loving others by loving ourselves.

Reed, Bobbie. *Learn to Risk: Finding Joy as a Single Adult*. Grand Rapids: Pyranee, 1990. "Forgive," "let go," and "reach out." She challenges singles, encouraging wholeness that depends on becoming more open, honest, and caring.

Smith, Harold Ivan. *Positively Single: Coming to Terms with the Single Life*. Wheaton, Ill.: Victor Books, 1986. Rather than singles feeling like losers because they can't find a mate, Smith provides practical advice for living positively. His guidelines include suggestions for handling anxiety, change, relationships, and ministry.

Stafford, Tim. *Worth the Wait: Love, Sex and Keeping the Dream.*

Grand Rapids: Zondervan, 1988. Stafford provides good advice for younger singles, discussing why sex is so attractive, how to handle pressure toward sex, and how to find and accept forgiveness.

Trobisch, Walter. *Love Is a Feeling to Be Learned*. Downers Grove, Ill.: InterVarsity, 1971. This classic poem/essay is wise and gentle, reminding us that love is both happiness and suffering, beauty and burden.

10 Successfully Negotiating the Dating Game

Dating—few other subjects evoke such mixed feelings of delight and despair. The world loves a lover, as the old saying goes. The fun of spending time with someone you like, the excitement and uncertainty of a new relationship, and the stress of working out differences when it seems you don't even speak the same language, all make up the roller-coaster of experiences that seem inevitably to accompany dating.

Dating has always been exciting and fun, but not nearly so problematic as it is today. As male and female roles have changed, dating has become more complex. Men seem less likely to plan a weekend date than ever before, and women worry more about their personal safety, even with men they know. The "operating rules" seem to have changed. Developing personal guidelines in the context of confusing and powerful societal pressures on relationships—that affect you and your partner—is difficult. No matter what you decide, it often seems that someone you like doesn't like your decision!

Although we assume that dating is the American way of meeting and has been around for most of our country's history, dating is actually a fairly recent phenomenon in American society, having begun in the first quarter of this century. Before the nineteenth century, men and women in our country got to know one another at the local community or church functions. Then after a young man petitioned a young woman's father for the privilege of visiting her, the two would spend a succession of chaperoned evenings in the family parlor at the young woman's home.

Greater mobility in our society changed that. With families and young people becoming increasingly mobile, with stable, long-term communities being transformed into social settings where families—or single adults on their own—didn't know one another, most of the old ways of meeting potential marriage partners seemed not to work anymore.

Growing numbers of automobiles, dating services, and singles living on their own began to add greater flexibility and mobility to the dating scene, but while these changes solved some problems, they created others. For example, couples could now meet almost anywhere—at the pizza parlor, a movie or a dance—but they also had to accept more responsibility for their own actions—their whereabouts, driving skill, and sexuality. "We're late because we had a flat tire" became an euphemism for "making out" that earlier generations would not have understood. Contemporary parents would quickly become suspicious of this excuse.

Dating: A Thing of the Past?

Dating has changed radically in recent years, and some have suggested that it is virtually passé. A recent poll published in a college magazine suggested that when students had gone out with someone on several different occasions, about 50 percent of women and men responded they would say they were "seeing someone," while only about a quarter would say they were "dating." Another tenth responded they would say they were "having a relationship," and about a fifth said they would "prefer not to define it." So, although the "getting-to-know-you" process may be more varied than before, the pairing seems to continue, with fewer people calling it "dating."[1]

Perhaps "dating" connotes for some a traditional process for establishing a traditional marital relationship. The search for new terms accompanies a sense that relationships are nontraditional, individual, or unlikely to lead to traditional marriage. We recognize the diversity of styles with which people develop relationships, and so we will use the terms "dating" and "establishing relationships" to refer to the process by which two people explore the possibility of an exclusive, long-term marital commitment.

Until recently, people initially got to know one another on the first date — perhaps after an introduction — but they now seem to be getting to know one another first in group activities or even at work. Occasionally two people these days will even become engaged after having spent a minimum of time alone together. Dating, therefore, is increasingly thought of as what one does in "serious" relationships. In our secular society, it has become increasingly sexualized, with both men and women often worrying about the sexual expectations or challenges they may face in relationships with others.

Both males and females recognize pitfalls and crises that must be negotiated for a relationship to develop. The values we present of *responsibility, respect, tolerance,* and *flexibility* provide guidelines for negotiating these pitfalls successfully. Although these stages are interconnected, we'll talk about these pitfalls in each of the three stages of a relationship: (1) initiation (or how to make it to the first date), (2) maintenance (or how to get past the first date), and (3) resolution (or how to resolve the marriage dilemma).

Making It to the First Date

Diane drops the receiver down on the phone and scowls — another dating catastrophe. Her apartmentmate Carolyn knows something is amiss.

> "What's up, Di?" Carolyn asks cautiously.
>
> "Philip has a lot of gall," Diane retorts. "He called me every week for two months. We went out, and he dined and romanced me — then nothing — for six weeks. He finally called and we went out, but then I heard nothing again for another two months. Now he's called once more and wants me to go out. We have a great time when we're together, and he always promises to call again 'soon.' But then he doesn't. *Enough* of this! I'm not wasting any more time with *that* joker!"

Gary is talking with his friend Doug about Celeste, a woman they both met at a church retreat a few months ago. Gary has seen Doug and Celeste talking at the young adults' group meetings since then.

> "How does it look, Doug? Think you might give her a call? I sure see you two chatting a lot," says Gary.
>
> "I dunno," responds Doug. "That's just the problem. I know she wants to go out, but she makes such a point of it. She watches me all during church and 'just happens' to run into me at school, at the mall. . . . You know . . . like it's pretty obvious she wants me to call her. She's a little too clingy, and I don't want to start anything and have trouble getting out of it if we don't get along."

Beginning a relationship is difficult. How does one appear interested yet not desperate? How do you get to know someone well enough to know whether you'd like to go out with them? This "The Far Side" cartoon illustrates some of the apprehensions we all feel about initiating that first contact with a member of the other sex. Sometimes it does seem as if we're in different worlds.

Same planet, different worlds

What Do I Say?

One basic pitfall in most relationships is lack of communication. To relieve their own anxiety, potential partners want to know more about one another. Honest, direct conversation communicates respect and caring in relationships, particularly those as uncertain and frightening—yet potentially rewarding—as dating is. Singles who are dating must learn the art of vulnerability—revealing a part of themselves—so as to interest others, while at the same time expressing a genuine interest in getting to know their potential partners.

Potential partners need to communicate important, but not emotionally weighted information at the beginning of a relationship, and ask for the same kind in return. One can tell one's partner that he or she likes Spike Lee movies, or Christian rock music, not that he or she is in therapy or has been sexually abused. On the other hand, if one's partner says she has been raped, or he is seriously depressed and on medication, support is the rule. If one wants the relationship to become closer, he or she needs to share something private; if not, one shouldn't.

Communication needs to be appropriate. If one "dumps their guts," as Corinne recently said, the other wonders "What's wrong with her?" and "Why do I need to know this?" To move a relationship into a closer one, choose a level of communication that is more advanced than where it is now. If one's partner fails to reciprocate, the speaker has learned something. The partner is not ready to share openly or to desire a closer relationship.

Couples need a sense of humor. Dating is a humorous process, and interpersonal intensity can be threatening. Laugh together about the mistake in your restaurant order (You just said you hate fish, and they brought you salmon, not spaghetti), or laugh at your mother's ridiculous restrictions on you (Who but a mother would tell a thirty-five-year-old woman when she should comb her hair?), or your joint misunderstandings ("I thought you said you were a broker and you said you were a practical joker"). Seriousness, in small doses, can come later.

Who Initiates Getting Together?

It usually has been the male who extends the invitation for the two people to spend time together, and it has been the male who has usually borne the costs which that time together may involve. Not anymore. While women used to sit at home waiting for invitations, they no longer see themselves as essentially helpless to develop their social lives. Fewer women than earlier are content to wait by the phone for a male to call about plans for the weekend. If the phone rings, fine. If not—and the week has already begun—they are nowadays just as likely to have already made their own plans.

Many males are pleased if women ask them out or make suggestions for joint activities. Roy, a Christian male in his late twenties, commented:

> I haven't been asked out too many times by women, but when I have, I've been flattered that the person would want to spend time with me, especially given the courage they probably had to work up to make the phone call. I found that the evenings themselves really weren't a problem. If the woman drove, it felt a little unusual to be the passenger instead of the driver, but we just laughed about it. I'll have to admit that we did have a good time. Those evenings were a lot of fun.

Other males are threatened by women who take the lead. There is a need to develop stronger men, who feel comfortable developing equal relationships with strong women.

Even though women asking men out might seem an easy resolution to the fear of male rejection, getting invitations from women is not received well by many males, so most females don't try. To make such invitations easier on their female friends, males could drop occasional hints to their female friends such as "Give me a call sometime and we'll get together."

Women have found that it frequently works to ask out guys they're interested in as part of a group or small dinner party and hope that something develops. Cindy admits, "I've asked a guy over several times, saying 'Lynn and I would love to have you come to dinner.'" She laughs. "Lynn, of course, would know nothing about it at the time."

Males are also sometimes receptive to one-on-one invitations if these invitations are low-key. Rachel, a Christian women in her early twenties, comments:

> If I've had a difficult week, I'll sometimes call one of my male friends and say, "Hey, Bruce (or Bob or Jim), could we get together for coffee or lunch Tuesday? I'd like to get your opinion on what I should do about some things that have come up at the office." That approach usually works pretty well. There's not much money or structure involved in the get-together, and the guy doesn't get the impression that he needs to put on some kind of performance to impress me.

If one has met someone he or she would like to get to know better, there is no reason not to express this interest — sensitively, and with openness to the other person's desires. After all, there's no verse in the Bible that says that only men can extend invitations for dates. If a man says "no," a woman has learned something about him and his interest in a relationship.

Game-Playing and Flirting

Don't. Right? Wrong! Game-playing sounds negative because it suggests being manipulative and deceitful. In this sense, game-playing *is* inappropriate and unhealthy. Yet, flirting, teasing, and practical jokes can be healthy games people play as they interact with and "test" one another to see how compatible their interests and personalities are.

Robin Williams has a routine in his ever-changing stand-up comedy act which begins something like, "I groove to your tune. I crave your fave!" If we tried opening lines like that, we'd get laughed at. But good relationships are playful, and responsible game-playing is often useful for their development.

As one Christian man said, "Flirting that says 'I'm interested in you. Are you interested in me?' is fine. Flirting that says 'I'm not interested in you, but I want you to think I am' is annoying and a real turn-off."

Some types of games appear in biblical dress, yet interfere with the establishment of relationships and are unchristian. The game of "I'm just seeking God's perfect will for a mate, so I don't need to show any commitment to dating relationships until God tells me to" is one that some people—usually males—play. This game ignores the contributions of the woman to the relationship, including her openness to God's guidance in her life.

Also to be avoided is the game of "I'm looking for a really spiritual Christian, so I won't let myself get involved with anyone who seems to be less spiritually mature than I am." This closes off relationships that are potentially life-changing and leaves one open to the sin of pride. None of us can really judge the quality of another's faith.

Just as problematic is the game of "I'm looking for someone who can really meet my needs, so I'm going to try out a lot of people and not get involved until I find *the one*." In this case, "trying out" can mean dating "seriously" two people at once without their both knowing you go out with other people, dating one person exclusively ("to get to know her better") for so long that the person is justified in believing that the relationship is serious, or making promises to call members of the opposite sex without ever intending to follow up ("unless nothing better comes along"). Too often, these games really consist of: "I'm evaluating whether you can meet my needs," not "Is our relationship a healthy and God-centered one for us both?"

Friendship before Romance?

Friends don't play games as easily as people who don't know one another well, and a healthy friendship can be a well-grounded basis for romance. Friendships that later become romantic often have a different tenor—a greater element of candor—than couples whose relationship starts solely on romantic terms. Besides, building friendships, whether or not they become romances, is a good idea (and certainly a Christian one)!

People who panic at the possibility of relationship—or who don't know how to start relationships—should consider joining a club or group of people with common interests. One Christian man noted: "I'm fine when I'm with my male friends, but the minute I get interested in someone, I'm a basket case: tongue-tied, blushing, clumsy. You'd think I was mute and stupid." A single who feels like this should consider meeting people by joining a group. Also, when their minds are on friendship or some activity, rather than romance, most people find themselves less anxious and more interesting as individuals.

Getting Past the First Date

"I have a series of one-nighters," moans Richard. "I ask a woman out, spend a lot of money on her, and she never goes out with me again. What am I doing wrong?"

Sharon feels her record is little better. "I date someone several times—maybe," she says, "we have a huge crisis, and the relationship ends traumatically. I wonder why I keep trying."

So much is invested in that first date that it's no wonder people are dating less and worrying more about it. How much money should I spend? Who pays? What do I do about the "S" word (sex)? Inevitably, when something goes wrong, we blame ourselves: asking, what's wrong with me?

Who Pays?

This hardly seems a major issue, yet it may be more problematic today than ever before. "Do I ask her to pay?" thinks Stephen, while his friend Grace wonders, "Do I dare offer?" Too often, couples don't have that first date because dating is expensive and the man doesn't have the money to pay for it. As relationships continue, even in relationships in which finances were not an issue, having enough money can easily become problematic.

Perhaps the initiator of the idea pays. If I ask a friend to a concert, shouldn't I pay? Yet, if the male always asks out the female, as is true in many relationships, he quickly finds himself weighing the cost of dates against the value of the relationship. No wonder dating is less frequent than earlier.

Women report that men sometimes view the issue of "who pays?" as a "power play." Ginger, a young adult Christian professional, comments:

> Some guys I've been out with seem to want to use the issue of money as a way to exert control in the relationship. It's almost like he's saying, "If I'm paying, I should be able to make the decisions about what we do together, and you should go along with them." I'm uncomfortable in this kind of relationship, so if it becomes clear that that's what he's doing, I'll bring it up after we've been together a few times so that we can get it straightened out. He may not be looking for physical activity—like petting or sex—from me in return for taking care of our expenses, but this approach can still be a problem. Generosity is one thing; exerting control is something different.

Her friend Sherrie reports a related problem:

> You might think that in the 1990s, the old saying of "He provides dinner; she provides dessert" is out-of-date. But let me tell you, I've known men who *still* think that if they buy you dinner, you owe them a one-night stand. And you know what? I've even gotten that line from *Christian* men I've been out with! [Sigh] It's certainly clear to me that this money-power connection remains pretty strong with some males.

Some women even see date rape as more "justifiable" if the man paid all, rather than some, of the evening's expenses.[2] Clearly, the issue of "who pays?" is an important one, with direct implications for the development of the relationship. If money is power, then, women — to protect themselves — need to get into the act.

The specifics of volunteering to pay are often difficult. Women many times don't ask if they can contribute to the evening's activities, perhaps because "it's easier not to," or "he might be hurt if he figures I think he's poor," or "I don't have the money." However, it's better for a woman to err on the side of generosity and make other plans — if neither can afford the present ones — than not offer at all and appear to take male's generosity for granted — and perhaps even certain assumptions he may have about returning the financial favor sexually. Some males may anticipate taking care of all the expenses on the first date, with more equitable sharing later on, and this is certainly an acceptable compromise.

While some women are willing but hesitant to help pay, others may think that contributing financially is inappropriate. Bob comments:

> I know this one Christian woman — a really sweet, thoughtful, humble person — who believes that women just should not contribute financially to dates. I asked her once what she thought the man received in return for paying for her dinner and entertainment time after time. She responded, "He gets a friendly 'thank you' plus the opportunity to ask me out again." Can you believe that? I've tried to tell her how unpopular her view would be with many guys, and I think her opinion may be changing, but what an attitude!

Jim, a Christian and a student in his late twenties, reports:

> Y'know, I often go out with Christian women who are earning an income, and their financial resources are much more than what I have. I find it frustrating that these women never offer to contribute financially to our dates, even though they know I'm a student with limited means. I'd ask for a contribution, but I don't want to appear to be begging. Besides, I know from things these women have said at various times that they

think it's more appropriate for a guy to pay for dates. I'd like to continue going out with these women — they're interesting and friendly people — but it's really stretching my budget.

Perhaps women want to perpetuate the old traditions, but only when it's convenient. As another male bitterly complained, "She wants me to treat her equally, until it costs *her* something."

As was the case with extending invitations, a little grace and flexibility can go a long way in the area of finances. If a man asks his date to help out financially, she should be willing and prepared to do so, or not accept his invitation. Of course, if he expects her to pay, he should make this clear in his invitation. If he doesn't, it won't kill her (or upset him) if she gently offers to contribute. He can always (politely) decline, if he wants to treat.

Finances on the first date is generally a less important issue than on subsequent dates, unless that first date "breaks the bank." In most relationships, as they progress, both male and female soon begin proposing ideas for activities, or the female takes over this role.

A couple should discuss finances together, and, if both partners care about the relationship, they should be willing to contribute financially to their time together and to live within their joint financial constraints.

How to Resolve the Marriage Dilemma

As relationships continue, one partner may conclude that the relationship is "marriage material" whereas the other would prefer to maintain the relationship as is, or end it. Dealing with those differing expectations can be painful.

Basic to their resolution is communication. One member of a couple cannot know the other's feelings and desires unless he or she is told. Often, this communication becomes "the talk" that seems to make or break the relationship.

The "Are We Getting Serious?" Talk

Some people prefer holding this serious conversation after four or five dates, some after eight or nine. The direction of the relationship must be discussed, however, at some point before one or both people develop clearly mistaken ideas about where things are going.

Often the best time to have the first stage of such a chat is when one of the partners begins to feel that the relationship is at a change point—that it may be ready to move into a romance or needs to be kept a friendship. While having such talks are helpful, one needs to realize that the mere act of discussing a relationship usually means it will change somehow. A person who wants such a chat but thinks he or she would be unready for the attendant change is probably better off delaying the discussion.

The principal problem if such discussions are not held is that one of the members of the couple may be under the impression that the relationship is developing as a romance, while the other continues to think of it as a friendship. One Christian woman comments:

> Although I'm sure it probably happens to guys too, I've had a number of women friends who've been victims of what I call "emotional defrauding." That's where one person intends all along for the relationship to be a friendship, though they don't communicate this to the person they're seeing. Without this information, the other person usually has no real reason to suspect the relationship isn't developing as a romance. Several of my women friends have been really hurt because the guy they were seeing would continue to ask them out, but not talk to them about where the relationship was heading.

The Marriage Talk

The partner who first wonders about the direction of the relationship usually brings up the topic of marriage. This is often the woman, as she may have spent more time thinking about the relationship. Also, men may be slow to discuss the dynamics of the relationship. Judy comments:

> I've had a number of female friends who've found it difficult to talk with their men friends about their relationships. It seems the guys get uptight about such discussions because they think they should be the ones basically deciding the direction of the relationship.

It's even more of a problem for these guys when they perceive the woman as more interested in the relationship than they. Then they get the idea the woman's hearing wedding bells, and that really scares them away from this conversation they both need to have. Why can't these guys get it through their heads that any relationship is a two-way street and can't function without good communication?

Women often hear, "You're analyzing the relationship to death. Don't be so neurotic." In fact, any good relationship in which the two members are committed to one another requires good communication about the relationship.

One may ask to talk about the relationship, not because this person is ready for marriage, but because he or she feels the relationship is confusing or stagnated. Witness the story of Stacey and Bob. They had been dating for several months. Both were friendly, outgoing Christians in their late twenties—she a graduate student in social work and he a ministerial student at a local seminary. Stacey recalls:

> As I had gotten to know Bob better, I began to wonder about the "hot and cold" signals he sometimes gave. Generally Bob seemed to enjoy the times we shared together, but I wasn't sure that was really how he felt.
>
> One incident in particular gave me pause. Bob and I were chatting with Steve and Jennifer about a weekend we four were planning to share a house at the beach. As we all were making the final arrangements, Bob turned to me and said, "Oh, by the way—would you mind if my friend Donna came along and joined us? She hasn't been to the beach in awhile, and we could just pick her up on our way there."
>
> I about choked on my dinner, but managed to comment politely that I didn't think Bob's suggestion was convenient at that time and that perhaps Donna could enjoy a trip to the beach with some friends at a later time.
>
> After that evening, I remained optimistic about things—I wanted to give Bob and our relationship the benefit of the doubt. I didn't want to be too critical of Bob just as the relationship seemed to be getting stronger. But then, lightning struck twice.

Several months later I was cleaning my apartment one day when Bob stopped by to talk about plans we were making to spend several days together at a cabin in the mountains. "Say, Stace," Bob inquired, "how 'bout if my friend Joan comes with us to the mountains? She's planning to be in town that weekend, and I'm sure she'd enjoy the scenery. We could all have a great time!"

I was furious! Right then and there I felt like lowering the howitzers and blasting that guy right out of my apartment! What nerve this guy had—and a Christian guy at that! But I kept my cool. I told him firmly but politely that his suggestion wouldn't work and that if he wasn't interested in my company, he could find someone else to be his date to the mountains. The problem blew over, but I ended the relationship soon afterward. You know, I heard several years later that he was married. All I can say is that I'm glad he's off the streets!

Needless to say, Bob was being incredibly rude and insensitive with his comments about inviting other women along on his dates with Stacey. If he wasn't interested in Stacey, he should have just told her so and not "strung her along." This is a classic example of inadequate communication.

Some people don't want to hurt another person's feelings by telling them they are not interested in marriage. Gayle comments:

I know that some of my female friends avoid being straight-forward with men about where the relationship stands because they think the Bible says we should nurture and care for one another. They don't want to hurt their male friends' feelings, but—it's unfortunate—they actually end up hurting them more by waiting so long to tell them how they really feel.

Those people who are not inclined to be "up front" about relationships end up hurting people, often unintentionally.

The Sexual Struggle

Emotional intimacy and the physical expression of affection are of significant concern in modern premarital and dating relationships, as the following "Left of Center" comic shows.

A 1988 poll of approximately 1,500 teenagers in conservative churches indicated that by age eighteen, 65 percent of youth had had sexual contact of some kind and 43 percent had sexual intercourse.[3] Older singles are subject to the same pressure to progress too fast sexually in a relationship.

The Bible proscribes against premarital intercourse. Too often, young people are given this injunction, without further advice. Every relationship is somewhat physical, and, as Lewis Smedes argues in his useful book *Sex for Christians*, Christians need better guidelines than "just say no," with the unspoken assumption that the issues are as simple as that.[4] Older singles are particularly in need of such guidelines that are more precise and less "black and white."

The physical aspects of a relationship need to be balanced with the psychological and spiritual ones. A couple needs to be familiar with how one another thinks and feels and how they see themselves and God in the context of their Christianity before furthering their intimacy and physical affection by touching, hugging, and kissing. Proceeding sexually before being emotionally and spiritually ready unbalances the relationship and leaves one vulnerable to hurt and unwanted sexual intimacies.[5] Even premature emotional intimacy—inappropriate disclosure, strong signals about interdependence—are not particularly healthy if the psychological and spiritual foundations of the relationship have not been firmly established. Stephen, a Christian man in his late twenties, voices this sentiment well: "Both partners need to be aware of the power that physical affection has in a relationship and introduce it only with much care."

Cindy emphasizes that both persons need to agree upon their level of intimacy and physical affection:

Sometimes, physical affection has a far more significant effect on women than guys actually realize. A certain amount of physical affection can be of only moderate importance to a guy, in terms of the commitment and romantic interest it implies, but of much greater importance to a woman. Guys really need to watch out for the messages they send with physical affection.

Rick agrees that a balanced view of intimacy and physical affection—rather than avoidance or excess—and one that is comfortable for both partners is best:

Rigid rules about physical affection—except about premarital intercourse—seem inappropriate for mature Christian adults. One of the problems I notice often among Christians is that their needs for touch aren't met. It's like there's this palpable tension between the desire to have this need met and the fear of having it met. It's almost as if it's unchristian for friends of the opposite sex to touch. This seems true both for Christians in groups as well as Christian couples starting out in a relationship.

A dating couple must keep in mind the primary importance of the spiritual and psychological dimensions of the relationship, be sensitive to the other person's preferences, and, most of all, pursue intimacy only in ways that honor God and edify the Christian community.

With the changing gender roles in our society, some people seem to feel that anything goes. However, while there may be fewer moral reference points in society than before, the reference points in Scripture remain firm. One can—indeed, *should*—readjust perspectives on gender roles, but only in the context of God's basic moral guidelines for human interaction. Particularly in the area of intimacy is this moral constancy a reflection of our mutual responsibility and respect as we seek to edify one another and glorify God in our relationships.

The Marriage Decision

There are a lot of pressures on individuals—both from society and the church—to marry. Society—and our churches—tell us we're incomplete as a single person. One Christian woman remembers:

> I had been married for several months when I had lunch with
> Jeannie, one of my friends from church. We began to talk
> about what we'd been doing recently and she commented—in
> all seriousness—that she imagined things must be going
> pretty well for me, since I was married now and had all of my
> problems solved. I was a little surprised—Jeannie is a pretty
> sensible person, and I wouldn't have thought she'd have come
> up with an idea like that.

The widely shared belief that marriage is a panacea for one's
problems makes us idealize married life and ignore the
complexities of the decision to marry. Marriage can indeed be a
rewarding and fulfilling relationship, but it is not one to be entered
into without serious thought.

Our churches further collude in the pressure toward marriage by
suggesting that it is the biblical model for Christians. Singleness is
considered a less desirable option. In contrast, however, Paul
describes singleness as the holier calling and suggests that marriage
is for weaker members (1 Cor. 7:7-9).

What kind of attitude should we have about finding a mate? The
Bible provides us with at least three possible models.

(1) *Wait and God Will Deliver:* As exemplified by Adam and Eve, if
one is patient and long-suffering enough, God may eventually
provide a spouse. This works for some, but, in this time of cultural
anomie and individual isolation, others need to act to bring
themselves in contact with potential spouses. Further, for others,
blindness comes along with waiting, so some Christians begin not
to notice good, single, potential Christian spouses.

(2) *Work and Prepare:* Jacob worked for seven years to gain the
hand of Rachel, then for seven more years after that (Gen. 29).
One good way to prepare for marriage is by developing one's own
spiritual maturity: working to conquer bad habits or to develop
one's prayer life and ministry.

This is the calling for every Christian, married or single, to grow
spiritually. However, those who work toward spiritual maturity may
be fixated on the belief that God will provide a mate and, when He
does not, may be vulnerable to self-doubt and questioning God.

God may not provide a mate, despite their continued maturation, and individuals may blame themselves and God for personal deficiencies which seem to be preventing marriage. But, in reality, people let themselves get sidetracked from what really is God's best plan for them—serving Him as a single adult.

(3) *Seek and Ye Shall Find:* As was true of Isaac and Rebecca (Gen. 24), a person desiring marriage remains alert to possible prospects for a mate and takes an active role in searching for them. Searching may consist of joining singles groups in larger churches, getting involved in community activities, or letting friends know of your interest in marriage.

The best model for marriage is probably a composite of all three models. If we're concentrating on doing God's will, He will supply our needs, whether it's a mate or the ability to be happy without one. As Steve Haynor, a nationally respected Christian leader of young adults and current head of InterVarsity has said, "Remember—when you get to heaven, the key question God's going to ask you is not 'Were you married,' but 'How did you respond to My Son?'"

In pursuing a romance, particularly one with the potential for marriage, persons need to move ahead with persistence, specificity, and comprehensiveness in the same way that God pursues humans (Eph. 4:2, 32). God has never given up with humans, in spite of their wanderings. God provides not only for humanity as a whole but also for the needs of individuals. Furthermore, God takes care of us in a broad range of ways, meeting our needs on many dimensions. In similar ways should we try to pursue persons we love, being patient when they do things that don't please us, being attentive to their specific needs, and caring for them as whole persons.

The following values are important for any friendship: *respect* for the other person, mutual *tolerance* and a sense of *responsibility* when differences arise, and *flexibility* to adapt to one another when necessary, together with a mutual commitment by the two people of their relationship to God. These values are even more important when a man and woman consider moving their romance to marriage.

Should a romance move to marriage? John Holzmann suggests two sets of questions a couple considering marriage should ask themselves. First, are you two, as partners, the best friends either of you have ever had? As friends would, do you enjoy doing the same kinds of things, do you trust one another implicitly and completely, and do you know each other thoroughly? Second, have you discussed your general goals and objectives for your lives? Careers? Children?[6] Marriage is a yoking—a tying together of two people—and common goals and objectives are necessary for a successful marriage. Unless these areas have been discussed in detail, a romantic relationship is probably not ready for marriage. *Respect*, *responsibility*, *tolerance*, and *flexibility* are fundamental components of these questions.

The Decision not to Marry

What if the individuals decide their romance, while strong, isn't the sort that should evolve into marriage? Should they remain friends? Given the importance the Bible assigns to the community of believers (e.g., Rom. 14:13, 15:5; 1 Peter 4:8), the value of keeping one another as friends should be given serious consideration. Couples invest a great deal in one another, and their mutual feelings of affection and respect can be a strong basis for friendship.

Yet, sometimes two people struggle to retain a friendship when their relationship has been too hurtful to one or the other. The intimacy demanded in the relationship leaves one open to potential hurt and scarring. Sometimes there simply is too much pain involved. In these cases, recognizing our imperfections and vulnerabilities, one member of the relationship should feel free to end the friendship, at least for the present.

Conclusion

In few other areas of relations between women and men than dating are *identity-flexible* and identity-fixed concerns more germane. Both sexes need to realize that their healthy functioning in a personal relationship is far more dependent on the substance of their relationship than on the form. In a period of changing gender roles, one can expect to find a range of ideas among Christians (and people in general) as to what constitutes the most appropriate etiquette in dating and romantic relationships. In Christian charity, we need to value one another's opinions about such issues. Some men and women telephone their partners frequently; others do not. Some prefer group activities; others enjoy dating. Some talk easily about their relationships; others do not. In dealing with these differences, a good amount of grace, patience, and Christian charity are necessary.

Responsibility includes making effective, biblically based decisions as we deal with the changes in our society and assisting others to do the same. One should pursue holiness in one's own life and help foster it in others (2 Cor. 7:1; 1 Peter 1:15; 1 Thes. 5:11, 14), but not in a way that is domineering. After all, Christianity is a personal, as well as a corporate, calling.

Tolerance means bearing with another even when he or she does problematic or displeasing things. Indeed, the agape love (1 Cor. 13) and grace Paul discusses in his epistles provide the basis for the active acceptance of another that *tolerance* requires of partners. *Tolerance* also involves helping one another to grow in the Lord and deal effectively with the changes in gender roles we currently face in our society.

Flexibility means appreciating someone with differing ideas about male-female relationships (especially in dating situations) and encouraging others to be tolerant (Rom. 12:18; 14:4-5; 15:2). It also means changing oneself if it becomes apparent that such changes facilitate better, more ethical, or more moral relationships with our friends and acquaintances (1 Cor. 10:31, 16:14; 2 John 6; Matt. 5:16).

Respect means valuing one another even when we disagree. It implies a recognition of our diversity as Christians and of the multiple contributions each one of us brings to relationships (Rom. 14:5-8). It means treating one another well whatever the stage of our relationship, particularly when a relationship does not meet the needs of the two participants equally and is therefore in transition (Eph. 4:29-32).

In our society, dating can be complicated and anxiety-provoking, but at the same time, it's a fun and useful transition process for marriage. With God's grace, we can participate in this process as Christians, more ethically than abusively, with more *agape* than narcissistic love. We can establish strong friendships that sustain us for life and possibly one unbreakable friendship that forms the basis of a healthy, God-centered marriage.

Questions for Reflection:

If you are single:

1. How do you think dating has changed since you've been dating? How have you adjusted to these changes?

2. What factors affect how frequently you date?

3. How do you meet people to date?

4. In what ways have you found changing gender roles — for example (if you're male), concern about finances or sensitivity, or (if you're female) concern about career or independence — affecting your dating relationships? How have you managed these?

5. In what ways is dating a relationship between "pursuer" and "pursued"? Should it be? How does thinking of dating as between friends — rather than between pursuer and pursued — change the nature of the dating relationship for you?

If you are married:

1. How important do you think it is for two people to be friends before they start dating? What problems, if any, does a couple have to deal with if the relationship from the start is a romantic one?

2. How have you managed the issue of the transition from friendship to romance in your relationships? How have you managed the issue of sexuality?

3. What model (or combination of models) of marriage do you espouse: wait and God will deliver, work and prepare, seek and you shall find? What ideas can you glean from the model(s) you did not choose?

For Further Reading:

Hershey, Terry. *Clear-Headed Choices in a Sexually Confused World*. Loveland, Colo.: Group Books, 1989. Hershey offers a thorough discussion of Christian ethics in personal relationships. He argues for a "life-giving" approach to sexuality and other relationship issues and tries to develop an analytical framework to examine the most relevant issues.

Holzmann, John. *Dating with Integrity*. Brentwood, Tenn.: Wolgemuth and Hyatt, 1990. This book presents a good examination of the differences between friendships and romances. The author discusses how each of these types of relationship can be developed and maintained.

McDowell, Josh. *The Art of Loving*. Wheaton, Ill.: Tyndale House, 1989. This book presents a series of useful steps designed to help people improve close relationships.

McGinnis, Alan Loy. *The Friendship Factor*. Minneapolis: Augsburg, 1979. This is a well-known Christian book on developing healthy, meaningful friendships.

Rinehart, Stacy, and Paula Rinehart. *Choices*. Colorado Springs, Colo.: NavPress, 1982. This husband and wife team provide a nice examination of the importance of discretion, wisdom, and a sense of responsibility in dating relationships, well supported by Scripture.

Marriage: Old Dance, New Steps

Marriage — an art form, a dance as wonderfully poetic as any ballet. It's a dance that can look easy to those in the audience, but the performers know how much work it takes. Refining the moves, developing the poetry of the motion is a long and intense labor of love.

Choreographing this dance has been a challenge over the centuries, a challenge not without its controversies about how partners are chosen, what the best steps are, and what stories to present. The dancers, who create their own choreography, may refuse to perform if their movements don't flow together smoothly or if the dancers disagree on how to interpret the piece. Still, the most unexpressive among us is moved to joy and inspiration by a *pas de deux* where the partners demonstrate a near-perfect synergy. . . .

Marriage in History

Marriage is one of the most important and meaningful relationships we can have as human beings. Marriage enriches our lives and provides the fulfillment and companionship many of us seek. At the same time, just as beautiful performances are not danced without first a lot of hard work to make the presentation flow smoothly, even good marriages — as husband and wife will readily admit — are not without conflict. While the key characteristics of marriage have remained consistent over time, some aspects have changed, and these changes have usually brought conflict of some sort with them.

The "key characteristics" of marriage — the foundations of the dance — are that it is a relationship designed by God and, in a Christian marriage, the couple's commitment of their lives and marriage to God is the central focus of their relationship.

The "other aspects" — the steps of the dance — are issues such as why people get married, how two people find and wed one another, and how the wife and husband relate to one another and to their children. As a society changes, some aspects of marriage change as well. Sometimes these societal changes are positive and healthy; other times, less so, as in the "Kudzu" comic below. Sometimes we can ignore the effect a changing society has on marriage. At other times, these changes and their effects on marriage can be so massive that we ignore them at our peril.

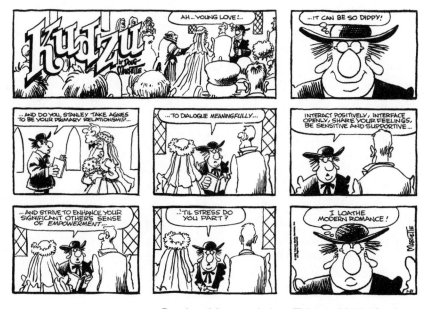

Reprinted by permission: Tribune Media Services.

Even a brief look at the history of marriage illustrates the diversity of approaches to marriage people have used over the centuries. We will briefly discuss attitudes toward marriage in the medieval period and changes in American marriage in the nineteenth and twentieth century, letting these serve as examples of the many changes in marriage throughout history. We can continue our dance metaphor: These changes in marriage parallel changes in the kinds of dances popular throughout history (e.g., pavanne, waltz, jitterbug, bus stop, disco) — each a different style, a different rhythm, with different steps, but in each case execution of the dance takes place in partnership with another.

Change in marriage (unlike most changes in dance forms) often accompanies deeper societal changes. Boys and girls learn the steps to dances that are popular as they are growing up. These dances change, of course, and in similar, though much more complicated ways, so also do changes in society and marriage affect the experiences boys and girls have growing up as they learn about marriage. As we learn new dances, we modify our expectations of our partner's dance steps. Similarly, early experiences learning about marriage are important, since they modify people's expectations of their own marital commitments. Some dances are easier to learn than others; some require more improvisation; and some are more showy than others. We choose our preferred dance form for many reasons: how adept we are at dancing, how much we care about other people's opinions, how well we communicate with our partner. Most of us, however, choose the dance form that is popular when we are dancing. Marriage forms too reflect the nature of society and the growing-up experiences of boys and girls within the society. A few brief glimpses at history make this clear.

Medieval Marriage

There was a strong surge of asceticism in the medieval church. Jerome (an early church father) contended that "he who too ardently loves his wife is an adulterer," and this view became the general ecclesiastical opinion during the medieval period. Since sexuality was viewed as the principal means by which Satan exerted his control over human beings, marriage was basically tolerated as a remedy against lust. Indeed, church confessors' manuals stated that sexual intercourse was to be performed in only one position, not during penance, and not on Sundays, Wednesdays, Fridays, and some holidays. Intercourse, except when specifically undertaken to beget a child, was often considered a spiritual offense.[1]

Also through the Middle Ages grew the idea that everything had its place in God's creation, a system known as the Divine Order. According to this system of thought, some people were born to serve (slaves), while others were born to rule (kings). Adherents to this system held that the rain was regulated by angels who opened literal windows in heaven, and the sun revolved around the earth.[2] According to this system, women also needed to be ruled by men in order to prevent evil and chaos. After all, these scholars and church officials thought, someone must rule in marriage, and that God-ordained someone was the husband.[3] The medieval church did help shape marriage in healthy ways, such as by disapproving divorce and instituting some property rights for women. In terms of an overall positive influence in marriage, though, the medieval church had a mixed record.

Victorian Marriage

As European and American society moved through the Industrial Revolution into the nineteenth century and the Victorian period, a wealthy middle class developed, as did a new concept of womanhood and femininity. In contrast to earlier periods, when women were often seen as base, sensual, and licentious, they were now seen as morally superior to men, delicate, and asexual. Women became symbols of truth and purity, to be protected from the "real world" of business and commerce where their less-than-pure husbands worked (as did the women of the lower classes). Part of being this symbol of truth and purity was the notion that sexual intercourse was not something for a woman to enjoy. Rather, she was to tolerate it to make her husband happy. Additionally during this period, not working outside the home became the mark of a refined, upper-class wife, one who was appropriately sensitive to values of family and home.[4]

This concept—that the home was the proper place for the refined and cultured woman—was heightened in the U.S. in the post-World War II period. Although women had participated in large numbers in the labor force in World War II, women after the war were again encouraged to consider life at home as their sole proper fulfillment. As the GIs returned to the States to take jobs and pursue college on the GI Bill, women were told it was their patriotic duty to return home so that men could take an active role in the civilian economy. Incentives, such as the GI Bill and low-interest mortagages, were offered to offset the decrease in family income as the wife left her employment.[5]

Dealing with Change

Just as cultures and people change over time, so does marriage, and people adapt. Remember that most people in those earlier societies (selected among many we could have discussed) thought they fully understood what was "appropriate" male or female behavior in marriage. Some of those concepts may seem quaint or harsh to us today, but they were usually thoroughly accepted by people in their respective societies. In many cases, those "quaint" ideas were backed by the authority of the society's religious leaders. Adapting to changes in concepts of marriage is to learn "new steps for the old dance."

The changes in marriage we have noted in this brief historical discussion probably necessitated a significant amount of adjustment on the part of the partners. Consider how different daily life might be depending on whether a woman thought (and her husband agreed) that she was pure or base, wise or in need of correction, sexual or asexual. Consider as well how different life might be depending also on whether men worked as hunter-gatherers, or downtown in large offices; or whether they spent most of their time away from home, or made it a priority to spend time with the family; or whether they served as "head" of the household and ultimate decision-maker, or as coparent and coequal decision-maker. Knowing about the arrangements and assumptions that characterized marriage in the past helps us to appreciate how much marriage has changed over the centuries. It also helps us put in perspective our concern about adjustments to contemporary changes in marriage!

One key theme that winds its way through the history of marriage is the growing sense of spiritual and legal partnership of the two people. To return to our dance metaphor, the dancers in a marriage were increasingly turned toward one another and their choreographed steps were increasingly intertwined. In spiritual and psychological terms, seeing one another as whole persons — each wonderfully made by God — and seeing the relationship with one another as less and less hierarchical, has been increasingly important. As women began to play more active roles in public life, instead of just being involved with the home, so also did their rights in marriage improve: to own and bequeath property, to experience physical and sexual safety in the home, and to be protected from capricious divorce by their husbands.

Marriage continues to change. As we focus on responding to contemporary change in marriage, we want to emphasize that a central response for both partners will be to adapt to change in ways that both edify their relationship with their spouse and glorify God.

Why Have We Needed New Dance Steps?

Marriage Is Political
In the political realm, the developments of the women's movement in the early 1960s have helped make people aware of conscious and unconscious stereotypes they had about men's and women's roles at home and at work, the inequity in pay scales, and the importance of personal and intellectual growth of all the members of society. Although some developments in the women's movement have not been healthy, the movement as a whole has been a positive and important motivating factor for women. It has encouraged them to pursue education and to enter the labor force, politics, and other areas of public life. With these political and societal changes, the nature of marriage has also necessarily changed.

Marriage Is Economic
Economics has also been an important factor because after the late 1950s, European nations and Japan developed as competitors with the U.S. in world markets, in addition to being our customers. Markets for our goods weren't as easy to obtain as earlier, which increased unemployment and led to women entering the labor force (although often in lower-paying jobs), because their husbands couldn't earn as much money as before or were laid off. Further, the U.S. government provided extensive economic and military aid in various parts of the world during the 1950s and 1960s as well as embarking on major social programs at home. Expenditures for

these programs, though in many cases worthwhile, contributed to inflation and the national debt. The resulting slower rate of U.S. economic growth led, for many families, to a situation where both spouses needed to work to make ends meet.

Marriage Is Technological

Greater labor-saving devices provided women who worked as homemakers more time and energy to pursue other interests. The increasing availability of effective birth control provided couples more control over when they had children. Women were then better able to plan their educational, professional, and social lives. Women became more involved in activities outside the home, and men and women had more time available for their interests and careers.

Increasing technology and specialization within our society has led to greater emphasis on education as a means of job advancement. This is probably the greatest contributor to delayed marriages now in comparison to earlier years.

To Summarize

In reviewing these trends, one is reminded of the multiple changes that have affected our society in the past quarter century. It's easy to imagine the many ways these changes have affected the roles that we earlier assigned to one sex or the other, whether married or single.

Awareness of these changes helps us understand whether it makes more sense to support the change, to try to modify the change and its effects, or try to modify our attitudes toward change. In some cases, we can shape these changes to lessen their impact on us. In other cases, though, we may respond to change in ways that seem ineffective and frustrating, perhaps because we underestimate the strength of the factors that have brought about societal change in the first place.

One change with which many families struggle is the increase in two-income families: Can a woman choose to be a full-time wife and mother? If she chooses to work, how can she manage family and work responsibilities? Shifts in the country's economy in the past few decades have increasingly favored two-income families creating pressure on single-income families to have another wage earner. Many wives, particularly young mothers, would rather not work outside the home, yet experience great financial stress and often some loneliness when they do stay home. Other wives and mothers feel they cannot economically choose *not* to work. The decision to work or not to work is more complex than before, for reasons often outside an individual couple's control. Those who feel, against their wishes, that they must work can minimize their frustration and self-blame—or understand the causes of their problems more appropriately—if they realize that societal changes in the past few decades in the U.S. have been dramatic and heavily biased toward families with two incomes.

Are You Sure the Dance Has Really Changed?

Given the general societal trends we've mentioned, what are some specific indicators of these developments? One example is that, in contrast with earlier years, over half of women with children under six years of age now work (18 percent in 1960, 56 percent in 1988).[6] In over half of families, husbands are not the sole wage earner (41 percent in 1958, 66 percent in 1982).[7]

A recent telephone survey by *New Woman* of 1,201 adults indicated that roles of husband and wife, and husbands' and wives' expectations of marriage, have changed dramatically in recent years.[8] The authors of the survey found couples to fit primarily into one of three categories. The first category—the *traditional* couple—was primarily descriptive of those couples over forty-five years of age. In the traditional couple, the wife derives her identity through the family and her role as wife and mother, and the husband defines himself through his work and his role as breadwinner, and is the "king of the castle." In the *egalitarian* couple, primarily found in that part of the population under forty-five, husband and wife view their union as an equal partnership. The two share their roles as parents and breadwinners, and both gain their identity from both roles.

In between are the *transitional* couples, in which the partners struggle to integrate aspects of the old with the new. The survey reported that more husbands than ever before desire to spend more time at home with their children. More wives are working, and more husbands expect them to work. Transitional marriages, the study's authors speculate, may be "hotbeds of conflict," as both spouses find it difficult to change their expectations and desires. Husbands may feel they are less than adequate in providing for the household, and wives may find themselves struggling to be both full-time mothers and full-time career women, while keeping the house clean at the same time. The marital dance, therefore, has changed dramatically in the past few decades, and we all find ourselves having to adapt.

Changes in the stability of marriage are as striking as changes in its nature. Between 1960 and 1989, for example, the annual rate of people marrying stayed about the same, but the divorce rate more than doubled. About one out of every three new marriages in the late 1980s and the 1990s is expected to end in divorce.[9]

Modifying the Dance: What Steps Have We Learned?

How do we best deal with the effects of social change on gender roles in marriage? A response to this question needs to focus on the assumptions a man and woman make about one another's roles and behavior and the ways the two seek to resolve disagreement in these areas.

One woman, married several years, said she found her marriage enjoyable and meaningful. It hadn't always been easy for her, however. Marriage, she said,

> is like taking an airplane to Florida for a relaxing vacation in January, and when you get off the plane you find you're in the Swiss Alps. There is cold and snow instead of swimming and sunshine. Well, after you buy winter clothes and learn how to ski and learn to talk a new foreign language, I guess you can have as good a vacation in the Swiss Alps as you can in Florida. But . . . it's one hell of a surprise when you get off that marital airplane and find that everything is far different from what one had assumed.[10]

Partners in a marriage usually come to that relationship with a rich set of ideas about what marriage should be like and how it should work. Our image of marriage is probably somewhere between the near perfect, comic model provided by the Huxtables ("The Cosby Show") and "The Waltons," and the zany, irreverent model provided by the couples on "Rosanne" and "The Simpsons."

When a marriage doesn't turn out exactly the way each of the partners hoped, we are disappointed and troubled. We may wonder if we have misunderstood God's guidance and chosen the wrong person. Or we may question God because the marriage seemed to work well for awhile, then turned sour. Has God mislead us? Rather than a flaw in God's leadership, the real problems are more likely our lack of faith in God's guidance and our lack of flexibility.

As soon as any preconceptions about a relationship or marriage are recognized, it is important that couples examine these together. As 1 Corinthians 13 suggests, the love that husband and wife share should enable them to work together to surmount these obstacles.

There are several common misconceptions about marriage. Here are a couple:

If my spouse really loved me, he or she wouldn't act that way. When our expectations are violated, we are quick to feel the spouse has betrayed a basic trust. Sometimes, of course, the partner's behavior may be inconsiderate or unthoughtful, but quite often, it's just a different way of doing things. This differences can be as simple as being a "station grazer"—rapidly moving through the television channels with the remote control—rather than staying on one station; or choosing a parking place close to the door rather than one "a mile away"; or reading the mail first at the end of the day, then relaxing with one's spouse, instead of relaxing first then reading the mail; or being silent rather than a talker when facing a tough decision or conflict with one's spouse.

George, happily married for ten years to Cheryl, remembers:

> I recall our early disagreements concerned how we got things done around the house. In Cheryl's family, you see, everybody was expected to pitch in when something needed doing—like cleaning the house or straightening up after dinner. If you didn't immediately hop up and volunteer, you weren't being a "loyal" member of the household.
>
> In my family, things were a little different. With us, if a family member needed help with some job, they'd ask. The rest of us just assumed that things were fine and that you

could keep doing what you were doing unless the busy person asked for assistance.

Well, you can imagine how Cheryl took to my going about my business when there was something she wanted done. We finally got that one straightened out — but not without a few bumps along the way.

Another difference may involve setting schedules and priorities for tasks, or being spontaneous versus making careful plans for joint activities. Corinne recalls:

I'm one of those types that likes to set deadlines for myself. If I don't set deadlines, I'm likely to let things fall through the cracks, particularly if they're just minor chores. It helps sometimes if people remind me of my commitment. As long as they do it politely, it's fine.

Well, Dan doesn't work that way, so I found out after we'd been married a few months. There was some paperwork he needed to take care of for some consulting he did, and I wanted him to finish with it, because we needed the money. Trying to be helpful, I set a deadline for Dan — I told him I'd give him two weeks to wrap things up. That was probably my first mistake.

Several days before the two-week period was over, I asked how things were going with the paperwork and then got this "Why-did-you-have-to-bring-this-up-again" kind of look.

It turns out he had just sent off the letter with the forms a few hours earlier, and he was pretty annoyed about my "being on his back." So, I've needed to adjust. I haven't quite got this one figured out yet, but I'm working on it.

_____ *is your responsibility. You figure it out.* As years go by, the life changes we experience — a move to another city, the birth of a child, aging — can bring changes that may not always be desirable or easily negotiated.

For example, a child's changing schools or making the soccer team will mean that the wife and husband should talk about how to get the child to and fro. A husband who simply assumes that the wife should adjust her schedule because the children are primarily "her" responsibility is focusing too heavily on stereotyped roles, rather than on shared responsibility. Or, if the husband has had to spend some additional time at work each day in order to learn a new job, the wife shouldn't get upset because he hasn't gotten the new battery for the car (unless he promised to do it). If the extra demands of work go on a long time, both members of the couple need to problem solve about the expectations and adjustments needed.

The children often become the wife's responsibility (along with her job), while the husband's responsibility remains only his job. This rigidifying of roles is often unhealthy, for the children as well as the parents. For example, one recent study concluded that, when fathers are involved in care of the children, children become more empathic, more often expressing care for other children.[11]

Another example can be taken from the early 1980s, when many areas of the U.S. faced a major economic recession. Blue and white collar workers in the "Rust Belt" and elsewhere frequently found themselves out of work, a misfortune that often placed the responsibility for a family's financial welfare solely on the wives' shoulders. These developments frequently led to great marital tension: not only were families' economic resources less, but couples who continued trying to relate to one another in traditional ways (e.g., the husband as the primary breadwinner) only made their problems worse. One unemployed man described his feelings about his wife, who had taken a job after he was laid off: "You better believe I feel badly about her being out there [on an assembly line] on her feet all those hours. It's supposed to be the other way around. I don't like taking her money."[12] In future periods of significant economic difficulty, we predict similar tensions for traditional couples in which the husband experiences job instability.

Flexibility is clearly important for healthy, edifying marital and family development, sticking to firm notions about what are "appropriate" roles for husband or wife is not. Recognize that changes will occur in marriage and require joint problem-solving. These are *family* issues, not his or hers to deal with alone.

Does the Dance Have a Leader?

Sometimes these preconceived notions about marriage and the spouse's behavior are tied to views about submission in marriage. Traditionally, most Christians have perceived the husband as the unquestioned head of the household—the key decision-maker—even though the reality may be quite different. In the past century or so, views of marriage have changed, as earlier discussed, and many Christians have come to believe that the wife and husband are equal before God, as individuals but not as spouses. While they share family decision-making, they may have different functions, with the husband described as the spiritual head of the household and the principal decision-maker. For thorough analyses by Christian writers who support this viewpoint, see Hurley,[13] Piper and Grudem,[14] and Foh.[15]

A growing number of Christians these days, however, believe that Scripture affirms that wife and husband are equal before God not only as believers, but as partners in marriage as well. In this view, the two may perform different tasks as individual people in the marriage, but they contribute more or less equally to the spiritual direction of the household. They share responsibility in major family decisions, in somewhat the way that partners in a business relationship might conduct their business affairs. This solidly evangelical understanding of Scripture calls wife and husband to relate as spiritual equals in their marriage. Useful books espousing this view include Bilezikian,[16] Hull[17], and Wright.[18]

We assert that our discussion of roles in marriage is relevant and useful for couples, *regardless* of whether the spouses perceive the husband and wife to be spiritually equal or see the husband as the spiritual head. We believe this because most of the observations and analyses we offer concern how couples can better understand and appreciate the different behaviors of their spouses, rather than which person holds the spiritual authority at home.

We continue to encourage people to reexamine their notions about "appropriate" female and male behaviors. We advise people to be *tolerant*, *responsible*, and *flexible* in their attitudes on these matters, and to consider modifying attitudes which create problems for themselves or others.

Dancing on—Nurturing Love

Don't Be Seduced by Flashy Dance Partners
Our society tends to confuse flashiness with long-lasting quality:

Flashy	*Long-Lasting*
Passion	Peace
Ecstasy	Joy
Consummation	Commitment
Fun	Fulfillment
Temporary	Ultimate

One Christian counselor tells the story of an orchestral conductor married to a woman who became severely depressed. This depression continued for seven years, during which time the husband lovingly took care of her and their three children, with little outside help. The woman finally came out of her depression and, when asked what was most important for her recovery, responded that it was her husband's unselfish care for her while she was ill.

A Christian author relates the story of a husband who had a terrible accident and became impotent as a result. Although the couple was no longer able to have sexual intercourse, the wife willingly stood by her husband, citing the importance of the covenant she had made with him "for better or worse, in sickness and in health." She said she planned to continue the fulfilling marriage they had had, in spite of the setbacks caused by her husband's accident.

Learn to Dance with Another Rather Than Alone
The primary requirement for interdependence is communication. The "Arlo and Janis" comic strip on the next page illustrates classic miscommunications in marriage.

Christians—especially husbands and wives—should bear with one another's shortcomings and weaknesses (see 1 Cor. 13:7; Eph. 4:32). Don't broadcast your spouse's weaknesses on every street corner! Keep open minds on points of difference, and learn where and when to talk about troublesome issues.

Ed and Jan struggle with decision-making. Ed has strong opinions, about just about everything, and Jan is much more soft-spoken. For years, she let Ed make all the decisions, believing that her choices were not as wise. As she watched his decisions, however, she came to realize that her opinions were also valuable and sometimes even better than Ed's. She is working on expressing herself better, and Ed is working on listening to her.

ARLO & JANIS reprinted by permission of NEA, Inc.

Recently, when the couple faced decisions about decorating their new house, Ed made his decisions then asked Jan to go with him to get her opinion about the line of furniture he had selected. Jan felt he wanted her to rubberstamp his opinions and refused to do so. She convinced Ed that she needed to go to furniture stores with him. As a result, they left their children with Jan's mother on Saturday mornings and had breakfast together in their favorite place, then visited various furniture stores. Although their mornings were not without conflict, they selected most of their furniture, much of it quite different from what Ed had originally chosen. Moreover, they enjoyed their Saturday mornings together so much that they planned to continue their outings on a biweekly basis.

Sexually dancing together may be the most difficult of all. Good sex depends upon having a good overall relationship and particularly upon good communication. Many couples find communication about sex difficult; yet partners usually appreciate knowing what the other likes and knowing that the other person enjoys having sex. The first step — learning to communicate — is the hardest. Once communication is established, both partners generally enjoy sex more, and find themselves being more vocal during sex, expressing their desires and their appreciation.

Recognize the Dualities in the Dance

As they develop their marital relationship, a couple needs to be able to move back and forth smoothly across four dualities:

(1) Seriousness and light-heartedness,
(2) Self-control and spontaneity,
(3) Independence and interdependence, and
(4) Objectivity and subjectivity.

Couples that have a harmonious relationship display a capability to move along these continua with little difficulty. They can move the tone of their relationship across the balance point of seriousness to light-heartedness or vice versa when the situation calls for it, or if they just on a whim want to change the tone for a while (see Rom. 15:2). *Flexible* partners can accept their spouse's being at a different place on a continuum than they are, even on those occasions when the partner is at one end of a continuum and the spouse is at the other end. Each partner has his or her own style and preferences, and the *flexible* spouse can appreciate and understand such a repertoire.

Dance without Seeking Perfection

Seek to have a good marriage, rather than a perfect one, understanding that seeking perfection in marriage is an ultimately frustrating goal. No marriage is perfect, even those that appear so. Ask the participants in what you feel is the "perfect marriage" whether they have tough points. Most likely, they'll laugh at your question.

Dance without Seeking Completion

Couples too often seek to find in their partner the values they lack, or fear they lack, in themselves. In getting to know a spouse, one quickly learns that he or she also has weaknesses in these areas. The person who struggles to feel comfortable in groups may marry someone who seems supremely self-confident, but later feel betrayed when that partner confesses to feeling anxious or when its revealed that he or she has a tendency to offend certain of their friends.

The person who has trouble making decisions may marry someone who seems a consummate decision-maker, only to find that the partner makes ill-considered decisions and refuses to consider alternative choices, even in the face of financial ruin or potential loss of friendships. The problem in such cases is not with the partner, but with the one who feels incomplete in his or herself. A healthy relationship depends on ending the search for a partner who completes one's self and becoming comfortable with one's own gifts and abilities.

Dance without Overvaluing Youth

Couples prosper when they can stand firm with their partners through the seasons of life, changing with their partners as their partners change with them. The movie *On Golden Pond* quickly became a classic because of Henry Fonda and Katherine Hepburn's loving portrayal of an aging couple who had come to know each other well enough to laugh together at their shared weaknesses and still preserve their love and caring for one another. Aging is difficult. Maintaining love while aging is worth the challenge.

Dance Even When Offended

Practice continual forgiveness, knowing nursed hurts and resentments only create more problems the longer they're held (see Matt. 5:41; Col. 3:13; 1 Peter 4:8). One couple, Don and Anita, in their late fifties, came in for therapy at their children's request. Don and Anita had fought for years, with Don yelling at Anita and Anita walking away. Anita would nurse her hurts in silence for days, as the whole family suffered, until she decided to talk again. As a result of participating together in counseling, the couple came to see that their joint style of confronting conflict was both self-destructive and destructive to their children. They then struggled to dance together: Don tried to express his anger civilly, and Anita tried to talk the issue through. When he yelled, she still walked away, but only for a short time. Their children are pleased to see their renewed love for one another and wish that they had modified their dance years ago.

Psychological research has shown that poor interaction patterns can be detected early in a couple's relationship (even before marriage) and that the longer these unhealthy patterns persist, the harder they are to change.[19] The sooner a couple corrects problems they may have in healthy conflict management, the better off their marriage will be.

It Takes Two to Tango: Conflict and Communication

As two Christian specialists on the family recently noted, if couples say they never have any conflict, either

> they have not been married very long, they don't know each other very well, they don't talk to each other very much, or they are lying. Conflict is a normal part of intimate relationships. Simply put, a conflict is a difference in opinion.[20]

Another Christian writer adds that couples who experience few problems are rare. Using the metaphors of house maintenance and of machinery for marriage, rather than the metaphor of the dance, Gundry writes,

> Most of us . . . must work at our marriages constantly to build up broken places, remodel the rooms, sand off the rough spots, and plump out the cushions. When you think of it, it is really amazing that we treat the most important alliance in our lives as though it must maintain itself without our wholehearted effort. . . .
> The problem in marriage is not the love. The problem is that love cannot carry the burden alone. Love is the oil that makes the machinery of marriage run smoothly and hum with satisfaction. But we must tend the machine. We must repair, and adjust, and maintain it. Love cannot do it all.[21]

Change and conflict are inevitable in relationship. Failing to recognize the inevitability of change and the significance of conflict, and failing to learn how to "fight fair," contributes to dysfunctional and divorcing families. Psychological research has shown that the couples that can settle disagreement with candid, respectful arguments report greater marital satisfaction than those couples who rarely disagree with one another.[22] Such couples have developed a "relational efficacy"—a confidence that they can successfully weather conflict together.[23]

So, what steps does one take if one has a healthy view of conflict? Be respectful, candid, and hospitable; stay focused on the specific issue at hand; and make the effort to see the issue from the other person's perspective. Determine how principal household tasks will be done, such as cooking, finances, and child care and review these periodically (see 1 John 4:7-8; 1 Thes. 3:12).[24]

Also, work on communication. One counselor, reported that as a rule, she had to ask men to be consciously aware of their feelings before they could actually respond to questions about their emotions. One man, relating to the counselor his frustrations about his wife's asking him for information about his emotions and about his activities, commented:

> She objects because I do a lot of reading, and she keeps hassling me that I don't talk to her enough. She tells me all the time we can't be really close if we're not talking to each other. It's hard for me to understand what she means. Doesn't she know that it feels close to me just to be in the same room with her? I tell her, but all I get back is more of her talk. I get so tired of hearing words all the time. I don't understand how women can nag a subject to death.

His wife responds:

> He says I need to live every experience at least twice—once in the living and then in the talking about it. And I think he's right. [with mounting irritation] But what's wrong with that? Why can't I get him to share the reliving of it, or examination, or whatever you want to call it, like I can do with any of my women friends?[25]

The wife in another couple offers similar comments:

> But . . . how can I say it's the real stuff that goes on in him I want to know about. I mean, I want him to be able to say

something hurts or scares him, not just to barricade himself off behind the paper or something.[26]

Helen, a Christian wife, notes the struggles she had with a certain issue she and her husband faced in their marriage:

> My prime problem was that I hated conflict. I had learned early in marriage that, if I did not go along with Jake, he brought it up to me time and time again, always accusing me of not being a submissive wife. I had learned to cower under this treatment. What was most difficult was facing up to the fact that my commitment to Christ left something to be desired. The truth was that I would rather have peace in my home (though not a godly peace) than pay a price to serve Christ. . . .
>
> My pastor helped me to see that what I was wanting to call submission was nothing more than a lack of courage.[27]

Another woman offers a slightly different perspective:

> It's hard to explain, but sometimes I feel a real safe feeling in the fact that he doesn't notice what's happening with me. That way what I'm feeling and thinking is only up for notice and discussion if I bring it up. There's a way it feels safer even though there's also a kind of loneliness about it. It means it's all up me to have it on the agenda. If I don't bring it up, forget it, Lloyd's certainly not going to. So, like I said, it works both ways; it's got its good points and its bad ones.[28]

Everything a person does in relation to another is communication. Even silence is communication. Since silence can so easily be (mis)read as indifference, apathy, or even anger, spouses (and, it seems, especially men) need to be aware not only of the value of spoken communication, but also of how their not talking is likely to be understood.

A key aspect of communicating, particularly if problems are developing between wife and husband, is candor and respect. Communication must not be manipulative. It must be forthright, even confrontational at times, positively and respectfully reminding one's spouse of the mutual accountability the partners have to one another (see Matt. 18:15; Rom. 14:14; Gal. 6:3). Caring and confrontational communication must be infused with respect and love.

Conclusion

The *identity-flexible* model is consistent with the suggestions we have made throughout this chapter. Rigid notions about what one's spouse should be or do is not a healthy or edifying way to approach marital responsibilities and problem solving. Such identity-fixed notions can cause disappointment and frustration for oneself and make life unpleasant for one's spouse, especially in light of our society's broad changes in the last half century. It is much better to have a range of preferences about what the other spouse should do or be than a fixed model of how one's spouse should act in the marriage. *Flexibility* increases one's ability to adapt to one's spouse in the early stages of marriage and increases the likelihood that two partners can adapt together as the marriage evolves.

Partners should *respect* one another (Eph. 5:21) and be *tolerant*. Indeed, the Bible calls Christians — and especially spouses — to love, patience, and mutual edification. Believers are to seek ways in which both partners can effectively serve God as individuals and as partners in a marriage, and encourage strengths while being patient with weaknesses. Partners should be *responsible* to one another: each should own his or her emotions, preferences, and life changes, and each should be supportive of the other partner. Rather than trying to suppress or cover up feelings, preferences, and reactions to life's changes, the two partners should try to understand and accept each other forthrightly and charitably — in ways that edify their relationship and glorify God.

Children in a marriage bring added demands for mutual *respect, tolerance, responsibility*, and *flexibility*. Partners, planning together for child*bearing*, need also to plan together for child *rearing*: respect one another's interests and callings as you discuss dividing up the child care responsibilities; tolerate the other's concerns about childbirth and child rearing and be willing to discuss these in detail; responsibly share in caregiving (however you divide the tasks); and recognize that, with children, demands for role flexibility and flexibility in meeting the day-to-day demands of living bring real challenges—and real opportunities—for growing in your relationship to one another and serving God.

As one grows in marriage and seeks to edify his or her spouse and glorify God, healthy adaptation to the challenges that life and marriage bring are important to a well-functioning marriage. The more flexible the spouses are, while standing firm on those things that should not change, the more effectively they can shape themselves and their marriage in healthy, edifying ways.

Questions for Discussion:

If you are single:

1. What expectations do you have of your future husband or wife? Where are you willing to be flexible?

2. How do you expect marriage to change your life? Discuss these expectations with married friends. Do they think your expectations are realistic?

3. What are the advantages of marriage? How does it help further your ministry? Disadvantages?

4. What fears do you have of marriage? How realistic are those fears? Discuss them with some married friends to see how they handle their difficulties.

If you are married:

1. What expectations did you have of marriage? How have these changed? How have you and your spouse dealt with these changed expectations?

2. How do you and your spouse express disagreements? How do you resolve them? What are some negative ways you have for resolving conflict? Positive ways? How can you deal with disagreements more often in positive ways?

3. Think of a recent discussion you had with your spouse. How

well did you communicate? Were you tolerant? flexible? respectful? responsible?

4. If you have children, how have children changed your relationship to one another? Have you become more *identity-flexible* or identity-fixed? In what ways would you like your present child-care arrangements and responsibility sharing to change?

5. In what ways are you and your spouse presently struggling with integrating work and family roles? What alternatives are there? Can you problem-solve to a solution that benefits you both equally? In what ways can you better serve God in your relationship with your spouse?

For Further Reading:

Alsdurf, James, and Phyllis Alsdurf. *Battered into Submission: The Tragedy of Wife Abuse in the Christian Home.* Downers Grove, Ill.: InterVarsity Press, 1989. This is a short volume that discusses the psychological, theological, and ministry problems involving wife-beating in Christian homes.

Balswick, Jack, and Judith Balswick. *The Family: A Christian Perspective on the Contemporary Home.* Grand Rapids: Baker Book House, 1990. This book provides a thorough and scholarly discussion of family relations and problems from a Christian perspective. It advances some theoretical frameworks of family management that take into account both the Bible and contemporary psychology and sociology.

Fairfield, James. *When You Don't Agree.* Scottsdale, Pa.: Herald Press, 1977. This is a handy volume in workbook style that provides many good suggestions on conflict resolution.

Gundry, Patricia. *Heirs Together: Mutual Submission in Marriage.* Grand Rapids: Zondervan, 1980. A short but thoughtful volume that examines traditional views about marriage and suggests some of the relationship problems generated by this approach.

Mason, Mike. *The Mystery of Marriage: As Iron Sharpens Iron.* Portland: Multnomah, 1985. Insightful, wise, both idealistic and realistic, this book should be read, again and again, by those who desire marriage and those who are already married.

Piper, John, and Wayne Grudem, eds. *Recovering Biblical Manhood and Womanhood.* Wheaton, Ill.: Crossway Books, 1991. The contributors to this volume offer arguments from a broad range of disciplines (theology, history, psychology) why men should have the principal leadership role at home and in the church. This is a sensitive and thorough explication of the neo-traditionalist position.

Rubin, Lillian. *Intimate Strangers: Men and Women Together.* New York: Harper and Row, 1983. This book is one of the most interesting volumes in the secular literature on why individualism is so important to men, while relationships are so important to women.

Stafford, Tim. *As Our Years Increase.* Grand Rapids: Zondervan, 1989. This practical guide is unusual in its emphasis on aging. Written for families struggling with aging parents or other family members, it provides answers to questions about retirement, finances, health care, changing relationships, death, etc.

Wright, Linda Raney. *A Cord of Three Strands.* Old Tappan, N.J.: Fleming H. Revell, 1987. Wright examines some of the personal and theological problems associated with traditional views on husband-wife relations. She argues marriage should be a team effort.

1 2 *Toward the Future: Redeeming Man and Woman in Community and the Church*

Societal pressures have led to changing gender roles, modifying our sense of our selves and shaping our options. Women and men today perceive themselves as having more options than their parents did, and despite the stresses, most of us would rather not go back.

Changing gender roles have also altered our churches. We've seen more egalitarian roles in marriage, fathers becoming more involved with their children, women becoming more powerful and more prominent as leaders, and more people in the paid work force and therefore fewer volunteers available for church activities. Probably every church has recently discussed at least one of these issues. Consider the last church supper. Someone may have commented: "I don't have enough time for everything I have to do;" "John tries so hard to be home before the children go to bed;" or "My daughter is interviewing at Price Waterhouse." All these comments reflect our changing options and lifestyles.

As Christians, we are called to be part of a *redemptive revolution.* Change inevitably introduces the potential of deterioration and loss, of increasing anomie and distance from Christ, of loss of personal identity and individual integrity. We, however, with foresight and motivation—and with God's guidance—have the potential to transform society, to "re-vision" ourselves as individuals and as partners in relationships, participants together in Christ's kingdom. Change can bring for us the potential of growth and gain, of increasing our sense of community with one another and our relatedness to God, of strengthening our sense of who we are and of what God calls us to do.

As Christians, we are called to bring the redemptive revolution to others. Changing gender roles have created divisions in the church and society, leaving many of us confused and isolated, quick to label others and in turn to be labeled ourselves, and uncertain of what to do next about these problems or whose advice on them to take. With greater understanding of the changes affecting these roles and with clarity as to our calling, grounded in the love and caring of Christ, we can move forward, "re-visioning" ourselves and our society and communicating this vision to others.

This redemptive revolution should be compassionate and humane, one which ministers to the needs of others rather than exalting our own, one which bestows upon both men and women a position of worth, dignity, and equality. This redemptive revolution is founded in the essential integrity granted us as creations born and blessed in the image of God. It is this integrity—our specific preciousness before God—that insures our identities as women and men, not the specific roles each of us may play.

How Does Change Take Place?

In our attempt to call the church and ourselves as Christians to a redemptive revolution, we have returned again and again to certain themes, which we believe form the basis for an edifying and well-grounded understanding of changing gender roles.

We Need to Recognize and Understand the Issues Raised by Changing Gender Roles

Gender roles have changed, whether we like it or not. Yet many of us resist this fact, acting as if it were possible to return to an earlier, easier, less anxious time, but one which also provided fewer opportunities. We unnecessarily complicate our lives and increase our anxiety by refusing to address the issues ("What, me change?"), by remaining invested in concerns that are no longer the central concerns of modern living ("Maybe as a woman I really shouldn't consider going on to college, since I won't find a husband if I do."), or by failing to recognize recent demographic and societal trends ("I'm single, and I didn't know that there are more unmarried men than women in their twenties now.").[1]

By failing to address these issues and recognizing their complexity and pervasiveness in our lives, we leave ourselves "behind the eight ball," reacting when we should be initiating, responding when we can and should be setting the agendas for cultural and societal change, ignoring bits of information that can clarify our calling and better equip us for service to church and community.

Churches too find themselves responding piecemeal to the pressures of change: what is an appropriate Christian response to the increasing numbers of divorced people in our churches? The increasing numbers of single people? The fewer numbers of members in our churches? Their tendency to give less and less money to the church? The difficulty of finding volunteers to carry out church projects? The reality in too many churches of "burnout" among the "regulars," because there are too few recruits? Surely the causes of these factors are complex, yet intimately wrapped up in these causes are the dynamics of changing gender roles and increasing numbers of two-career families. For example, if both parents work, many couples consider Sunday morning as the only time for the family to be together and hesitate to spend this time in church. Understanding problems such as these, and how to address them, can provide a coordinated, proactive response to a range of problems.

Knowledge protects us from "present shock." Toffler called his book *Future Shock*,[2] but the shock is no longer in the future. We are in the midst of it. Shock brings confusion, chaos, anxiety, and often a desire for entrenchment. With appropriate knowledge about ourselves, our experiences, and our society, we can replace confusion about our calling with clarity, chaos with order, anxiety with peace, and a desire for entrenchment with excitement about meeting the challenges of change. "Re-visioning" ourselves and our community provides us "shock protection": we can move forward on the promises of God, knowing that to which we have been called.

Changing Gender Roles Create Benefits and Problems Shared by Both Men and Women

Societal changes and the new expectations that accompany them lead to more alternatives than earlier, and men and women have greater options than before: singleness or marriage, childlessness or childbearing, career or job. These options benefit all of us, whether we are women who would like to establish a career or men in relationship to these women, whether we are men who enjoy having a child greet us with delight as we come home from work, or women who enjoy sharing the joy of child care—and the work.

Men and women struggle together, however, with the transition. What's next? Will I be married after graduation from college? Will I be able to find the job I want? Will I be able to afford a house? Should we have children? If so, when? These questions, so many of which feel isolating and lonely, are instead common questions which young people share. Modern gender roles, rather than creating barriers between men and women, have begun to break these down, freeing men and women to become better friends and to share their concerns and their problem-solving abilities.

Just as their struggles in this transition to modern gender roles are often similar, so also do men and women experience parallel crises and anxieties. Joseph Pleck, in his book *The Myth of Masculinity*, outlines the "sex (gender)- role strain paradigm," which suggests that men's struggles with masculinity are a result, not of their inability to learn their role, but of inconsistencies in societal definitions of masculinity.[3] Although Pleck used this paradigm to describe men's experience, a parallel analysis can be developed to describe women's experience. Societal expectations of both men and women are confusing and often contradictory, creating stress in our attempts to meet these expectations and a sense of failure when our attempts seem inadequate or imperfect.

Women experience these contradictions as they participate in the workplace. Societal pressures may encourage them to participate in the labor force, but women still often find that they are subject to pay differentials, the "glass ceiling" (the covert selection factors which make unlikely their progressing past a certain point in management), the "mommy track"[4] (promotion procedures which hinder a woman's progress up the ranks in business once she has had a child), and other biases against women.[5] Women experience similar contradictions as they attempt to be superwomen. Despite all their disavowing comments ("I'm no Superwoman!"), women often firmly believe they can have a rich and extensive life simultaneously with both family and full-time work. Their attempts to integrate work with personal life takes place in a society which makes achieving this integration difficult.

Men experience these contradictions as they attempt to be both successful and sensitive. They find they must negotiate between "macho" and "wimp," between career and fathering, between sensitivity in relationships and self-protection. The resulting gender-role strain that men encounter affects women as well as men.

Women cannot be superwomen, and men cannot be supermen. In our struggles to "have it all" (this term applies equally well to men and women), we have to make choices, and accept less than we might be capable of achieving in some areas in our lives for the sake of achieving more in areas of greater importance. As men and women, we need to convince our society, friends, and employers of the need for better approaches to building up the family and fostering the development of whole people.

Guidelines for Resolving These Conflicts
Are Similar for Women and Men

Women and men need to place the blame properly for the contradictions they face. Societal standards are inconsistent and unachievable (the "sex [gender]- role strain paradigm"), and women's and men's feelings of inadequacy and confusion are generally not their fault. These feelings are probably not the result of inadequate personality development, or insufficient Christian faith. These feelings cannot be primarily blamed on parents. Additionally, these feelings are appropriate in our present societal context and are experienced, to a greater or lesser degree, by every one of us, whatever our sex or age.

After recognizing that societal standards are internally inconsistent and difficult to achieve, women and men can begin to address these standards; to make life choices appropriate for their individual situation, relationship context, and Christian calling; and then to accept (rather than feel ambivalent about or continue to reevaluate) the choices they have made. These choices should be made, not in isolation, but in communion with other Christians and with the church. Individuals who continue to struggle with these issues should seek out others who have the same concerns, for mutual support and continuing discussion of these issues and communal prayer. If concerns still seem insurmountable, these individuals should consider seeing Christian counselors who understand the changes that have taken place and their implications for believers.

Our goal is to help persons toward balanced lives: spiritually, personally, and professionally. Particularly in this time of changing gender roles, lives are balanced when they center on Christ. He provides the fulcrum, around which we can sort out the conflicting messages and contradictory demands to which we are exposed.

Balanced lives need a measure of personal time, for relationships and for time alone. In our present work-centered culture we may devalue personal time, feeling that we have to fit it in among everything else, or we may feel that if we're not doing something actively with our time, we are wasting it. Particularly true of singles, this attitude is unhealthy and unbiblical. Balanced lives nurture mental and physical health and are necessary for our sustenance and personal growth. In our headlong rush to success, we may lose ourselves and our God.

Balanced lives need also professional time, by which we mean experiences which stimulate a sense of one's competence. These experiences need not be for pay, but people, to be content with themselves, seem to need a variety of roles: parent, friend, worker, and lover[6] and they need to feel competent in these roles.

The Struggle toward Balanced Roles Is Necessary for Both Sexes

Some women and men would like to ignore the changing gender roles in our society because these individuals subscribe to the Myth of Choice (we can choose whether roles change or not). In the confusion of changing roles, we may feel safer if we choose *not* to respond to these developments—rather than face the risks of change.

Women and men, however, who subscribe to the Myth of Choice delude themselves. Gender roles have changed, and no one in contemporary American society is exempt. Our self-identity, expectations of ourselves, and relationships with one another: all these areas bear the marks of the transition we have earlier discussed in detail.

Despite our lack of choice about societal change, we do have individual choice about our own response to society. Our challenge as responsible men and women is to make choices which acknowledge the complexities of modern society (e.g., the choice for a woman or man to be full- or part-time at home with the children).

Many men would perhaps like to say, "Women's roles have changed, so let them deal with the changes. That's not my problem!" Men's roles too have changed, whether one looks in the marketplace or at home. And men and women participate together in relationships, which have also changed. Moreover, many of the issues of gender roles our society cavalierly labels "women's issues" do not belong just to women. Any problem which affects the women men work with, become friends with, and marry affects men as well. After all, women are one-half of the U.S. population (actually more, at almost every age), and it would be hard to imagine that a problem that affected one-half of the population wouldn't in some way affect the other half as well.

"So," says our mythical skeptic male, "I'll just choose a wife who wants to be traditional." Yet, as we have already discussed in chapter 3, the traditional woman's role—a desirable one for many, particularly those with children—is more complicated than before. Despite its benefits, for many women it brings more costs and risks than it did in the past. Is it a good idea to seek out a woman to fill a set of roles that have clearly become more problematic in this day and age? Women and men need to work together to deal with these issues that affect them both in important ways. As the poet John Donne wrote, "No man is an island, entire unto himself."

Women too would sometimes like to pretend that gender roles have not changed. "I'll stay home when I have children," says one, stating the sentiments of many. Yet her realities when she actually has children may be very different: she may be in a job she likes or her husband may wish her to work. Or her choices may be more constrained than she expected: she may need to work for financial reasons. She may nevertheless choose to stay home—and, if she does, she makes a valid and worthy choice.

Risk-Taking and Crisis Are Inevitable for Producing Positive Change

One cannot mature without crisis. According to psychologist Erik Erikson, who bases his theory of development on the concept of

crises, one faces certain developmental challenges. These are resolved in adolescence by the development of identity or role
diffusion; in young adulthood, by the development of intimacy or
isolation; and in middle adulthood, by the development of genera-
tivity or stagnation. Development proceeds through the resolution
of crisis.

Many of us would prefer to be bystanders in this process,
comfortably watching from the sidelines as the changes take place,
reacting when we feel like it, not reacting when we don't. This is
not, however, an option. Consider the characteristics of your
present lifestyle. Your spiritual, personal, and professional lives
have undoubtedly been affected by the trends we have discussed.
Perhaps even without your awareness, you have compensated and
adjusted, making choices that are appropriate for you at this point
in time, place, and faith.

The risks of waiting for the crisis to end are greater than of
joining the melee. Disengaged, you risk increased anxiety,
frustration, isolation, and missed opportunities. Certainly, deciding
to address these issues brings risks as well: you may make wrong
decisions, or experience the anxiety of change. You will, however,
whatever your stance (waiting or joining) have to make decisions.
Forward-looking, proactive, engaged decisions will undoubtedly be
better informed, wiser, and more timely than the decisions of
avoidance and reaction.

Women and Men Need to Retain Their Openness to Spiritual Guidance

Central to wise decision-making is continual openness to God's
guidance. "The Lord is my shepherd, I shall not want," the
Scriptures say (Ps. 23:1), and God continues to protect us as we
seek His guidance.

Perhaps we think that God cares more for our spiritual lives than
our gender roles. In a sense, this is true. God is less concerned
about whether we wear dresses or pants than He is about our
relationship to Him. Yet, He cares about whatever is of concern to
us and provides guidance wherever we need it.

We exalt ourselves inappropriately to believe otherwise.
Discerning among societal pressures is a difficult task and
maintaining our stability is often even harder. Changing our gender

roles changes our identity. No wonder the struggle is so difficult! We cannot remain anchored in our selves, for they too are in transition. To negotiate these crises well and to resolve them, we need to remain anchored in Christ. It is He to whom we should turn first for help in dealing with these conflicts. It is He who helps us confront these issues, then move ahead. As the writer of Hebrews says: "Let us throw off everything that hinders and the sin that so easily entangles, and let us run with perseverance the race marked out for us. Let us fix our eyes on Jesus, the author and finisher of our faith" (12:1-2, NIV).

Women and men — and church leaders — need to recognize the centrality of the church in bringing about change. At the same time that we strengthen our individual relationship with God, we also need to strengthen our relationships with the community of Christ. "I feel I cannot be who I am at church," a single friend, manager of a small store, recently commented. "I feel I have to watch what I say, and that I always have to apologize when my kids won't behave." When the church accepts the diversity of its members, women and men can feel comfortable and accepted, and the church can more effectively become a central context for people's growth.

Women and men who do not feel comfortable in church, however, need to think carefully before they leave it. In no other context is the wholeness of their personhood and the centrality of spirituality nurtured. Persons who recognize the problems of changing gender roles and who experience personally the isolation that these can bring — even from other church members — should consider remaining in the congregation, hoping and praying that their insights can be helpful to those around them.

Barriers to Change

Why is change so difficult? Many of us have been struggling with these gender issues for a long time, and yet it seems that people continue to believe The Myths of Gender Difference, Gender Stereotypes, Constancy, and (perhaps particularly) Choice (see chapter 4). Churches too often seem to ignore the facts that men and women's roles have changed and that women and men view themselves differently than they did thirty years ago.

Many factors — individual and societal — inhibit such change in our Christian communities:

■ Our tendencies to stereotype, and our difficulties in letting go of these categories and recognizing individual differences.

■ Our difficulties with communicating feelings and vulnerabilities in relationship (and the resulting problems for the growth of the Christian community).

■ Our different perspectives on changing male/female roles, and the struggle of many of us to ignore these changes (one can't talk about a problem one pretends does not exist).

■ The frustrations of women who find that their opinions are not taken seriously in society in general or in the church.

■ The "burnout" among women who get too little help with the housework and children.

■ The lack of parental leave policies.

■ The problem of people (usually women) who are inappropriately excluded from certain jobs and are not reimbursed fairly for their work.

■ The problem created by a society that tells women they are to be appreciated primarily because of their body and by the church communities that subtly support this view.

■ Our ethnocentrism, which prevents our recognizing and appreciating international cultural diversity.

■ The difficulties of cross-gender communication.

■ The fear of rape, or other physical or sexual abuse, particularly by acquaintances.

■ Issues of money and power, particularly in marriage.

■ The difficulties of "re-visioning" one's self or one's relationships.

■ The difficulties of modifying unhealthy expectations that have developed as a result of socialization (even though we as Christians affirm we "should not be conformed to this world," we often—unthinkingly—treat members of the other sex in the same unedifying ways our non-Christian acquaintances do).

■ The difficulties of negotiating relationships which are unlike those with which one is familiar.

Given this list of factors (and there are many others), it is no wonder that societal changes are difficult and slow.

We should not be discouraged. Change *has* taken place, as anyone who was a teenager ten or more years ago can quickly tell you, and change will continue to occur. The speed and the compassion of healthy accommodation in our communities to gender role change is up to us—with God's guidance.

How Can I Change?

Awareness of the issues elicited by changing gender roles is the first step toward change. Having begun to understand some of these issues, we can then begin to make choices that are appropriate for us as individuals and as members of the Christian community and to act on those choices.

Change requires, in addition to making appropriate personal choices, making choices that support others in their change process and that support and sustain the church community. As we grow and change, we are in a better position to stimulate change in others.

As you work toward change, keep in mind the model that has informed our book. Your goal should be *identity-flexible*, not identity-fixed, gender roles marked by *tolerance*, *respect*, *responsibility*, and *flexibility*. Review again your Identity-Flexibility Quotient (chapter 3). How are you doing?

Perhaps the most difficult aspect of the transformation from an identity-fixed to an *identity-flexible* model of gender roles is decision-making. When faced with choices about gender roles, how does one decide what to tolerate and what to challenge? Where to be flexible and where not to change? What to respect and leave alone, and what to challenge respectfully? What to be responsible for and what to leave alone? Although there is no single easy way to make these decisions, some guidelines can help you choose among alternatives. In each choice you need to make, specify your options, then carefully consider the following questions.

Table 12-1
Should I Flex, or Should I Stand Firm?

1. Are any of the choices potentially harmful to my faith? My community? If so, specify how, to whom, and how great the harm is likely to be.

2. Are any of the choices clearly unbiblical? If so, specify what principles of Scripture, or what specific verses, these violate. Rank the positive alternatives also—how much do they benefit God, your Christian community, yourself (in that order)?

3. Do people whom you respect disagree on whether these choices are unbiblical? If so, evaluate the validity of their various claims.

4. What motivates people who have already made the choices you contemplate? What are the fruits of these choices as far as you can tell—good or bad? To what extent do these people generally put Christ and other people first in their lives?

5. With which options are you most comfortable? Evaluate why (i.e., consider factors such as theology, practicality, personal history, temperament, norms of your church community). Why are you uncomfortable with each of the other options? If you are uncomfortable in part because of theology, consider whether any other reasons make you uncomfortable as well.

---

6. Visualize what taking on each of the options would mean for you as an individual and for God's calling for you. If you have trouble with this part of the process, ask people who represent the positions of interest to you.

7. What is God saying to me: Am I to accommodate or stand firm? To question further or to decide?

8. Pray about God's leadership on these issues and ask the Holy Spirit to lead you to that decision which will best honor Him and edify your neighbor.

As you answer these questions and pray for guidance, your thinking about these issues will undoubtedly become more complex, more spiritual, and more personal. You may decide that you now have clear leading on which options to choose. If not, consider whether you are missing some central information that will help you make the decision. You can wait for further information, repeat the seven-question process, or ask for insight from others who represent each possible alternative.

If you have made a decision about how you would like to change, initiate changes immediately. Imagine the benefits of the change and how you might bring it about. Consider where to begin and what to do next. Consider who might help you as you progress. Let others know of your new goals and keep in contact with them, asking, "How am I doing?" Pray that God will help you become a new person, "transformed by the renewal of your mind, that you may prove what is the will of God, what is good and acceptable and perfect" (Rom. 12:2, RSV).

How Can the Church Change?

As individuals, we are to wait, pray, and work for wholesome change. As members of the church community, however, we need to evaluate, not just who we are as individuals, but who we are as a community. Consider the following questions about your church body:

Table 12-2
How *Identity-Flexible* or Identity-Fixed
Is Your Church?

1. Is your church theologically and/or ethnically diverse while at the same time affirming the basics of Christian beliefs? Identity-flexible churches encourage diversity. If your church is not very diverse (i.e., does not have many people with different biblical perspectives or from different races, church backgrounds, ethnic groups), it is probably identity-fixed as a church.

2. Do people who are "different" feel comfortable in your church (e.g., divorced, working mothers, stay-at-home mothers, singles, people from different church backgrounds)? Think of the people who stand out most to you. Ask them how comfortable they feel.

3. How are disagreements—particularly theological ones—handled in your church? Are they generally discussed openly and comfortably, and the people who raise them treated with responsibility and respect? (If you do not know of any disagreements, they are probably generally avoided.)

4. Do conspicuous males in the church exhibit success *and* sensitivity? What about power *and* intimacy? Do conspicuous females exhibit nurturance *and* competence?

5. Do sermons avoid using labels such as "traditionals," "liberals," or "feminists" to identify the "bad guys?"

6. Are sermons generally gender-typed, with males generally in business and females generally married mothers at home?

7. Are sermons generally oriented toward topics of interest to families, with few messages meant specifically for singles?

8. Do stewardship sermons encourage giving of yourself to

relationships and developing a balanced lifestyle, as well as giving of material things?

9. Are people who contribute to the church in supportive, relationship-building ways given as much recognition as those who are high-profile leaders?

10. Do men and women, boys and girls, help out in the nursery?

The more of these questions that you answered with "yes," the more identity-flexible your church is. If you gave ten "yeses," hold onto your church! You have an unusual one. If your church needs work in one of these areas, get involved. Talk to the pastor, priest, church board members, or friends. The following table gives some ideas to consider.

Table 12-3
One Dozen Things You Can Do to
Encourage Gender-Role *Flexibility*
in Your Church

Every church is different, and indeed, we would acknowledge that God is accomplishing His purposes through many different faith communities — both "conservative" and "liberal." Your church may or may not be ready for some of the following suggestions. Be sensitive. Pray for the Lord's leading. Seek His wisdom as you seek to employ these ideas. Remember that it is as important to be obedient as it is innovative; a searching faith may lead you to accept your church, change it, or leave it.

■ Sponsor a discussion group where members in your church can discuss the conflicts and opportunities they've experienced, as men and women, in the past decade.

■ As part of a prayer meeting, suggest that individuals

pray for members of the church who are challenged with gender-role conflict issues, (e.g., a working mother who is struggling to balance work and family).

■ Encourage your church to adopt a non-sexist policy in the hiring of support staff (e.g., the church secretary doesn't always have to be a woman).

■ Encourage your church to use non-sexist language in referring to Christians.

■ Nominate a pair—both a woman and a man—to head an important committee at your church.

■ Hold a session of an adult Sunday School class in which the merits and drawbacks of the four positions (traditional, neo-traditional, biblical feminist, and secularist, see chapter 2) can be discussed. Have members discuss the biblical basis, if any, for each.

■ Volunteer to teach a Sunday School class on "Men and Women of the Bible" where a strong emphasis is placed on showing the full range and diversity of professional and personal callings both sexes were given in Scripture.

■ Start a Bible study exploring biblical guidelines to gender-role behaviors.

■ Encourage your church to develop a partnership with a local minority church group, for example, a Korean or African-American church, recognizing that their experiences as males and females can inform yours.

■ Talk with members of your church who are single or single parents or from different religious, social, or ethnic back-grounds, asking them whether they feel accepted in the church and how they might feel more comfortable parti-cipating in the church. Work as an advocate for their needs.

■ Volunteer for non-traditional responsibilities in the church. For example, if you are male, volunteer for the nursery (if men don't generally help out); if you are female, volunteer to lead a Bible study (if women don't generally lead Bible studies).

■ Organize a group of people who are interested in gender-role issues in the church to help you generate ideas specific to the needs of your church and to help you carry them out.

Anchored and Actualized: Toward a Gender-Mature Spirituality

The latter half of the twentieth century demands that we not only examine how gender roles fit (or do not fit) within the cultural climate and societal milieu we inhabit, but that we explore just what it means that God created us as men and women, in His own image. With God's help, we can understand who we are, from where we come, and where we are going. By making positive choices that recognize the reality of change and our own calling, we can help shape the direction that change takes, nurture ourselves and one another, and build up the body of Christ.

If "imago Dei" is to be more than just religious rhetoric, then there must be a fresh understanding of the composite character-istics which the Creator granted His creation. There must be an understanding of the range of difference He imbued to His beings, woman and man: we must recognize not only their variability and diversity, but the complexity and richness of His own character as well. A gender-mature spirituality affirms the commonanlity of woman and man before God—as well as their differences as—in fact, part of the dynamic underlying reflection of His own being.

If men and women both are capable of being, by turns, sensitive and strong, tough and tender, gentle yet firm, warm or cool, active or passive, loving or detached, then there is much that we might affirm in a God who encompasses all these possibilities—yet who is, by His own sovereign nature, all good, all just, all righteous, all holy, and all grace. If woman and man are indeed the fullness of His creation, then they must express, in their hearts and by their lives, a worship of Him which brings forth the very substance that makes them men and women.

A gender-mature spirituality says that, in faith and in practice, we live lives which reflect the very best that God created in both a man and a woman. Wherefore it has been traditionally held that doctrine be "tough" and "strict," enforceable, and a man's terrain, we might well see in our theology and tenets, the openness and receptivity, the gentleness and purity traditionally designated as "feminine." Wherefore, in practice, we have observed the dominant presence of women in the Christian education of the young, we might well now applaud the place of men taking their part as spiritual mentors of their children.

In short, wherever God's Spirit empowers the lives of His people, there is the possibility of a dimension of richness, with men and women becoming all they can be as His creation: fully differentiated yet fully participative as joint and equal heirs of the kingdom.

As Christians we are called to be part of a "redemptive revolution," "to press on toward the goal . . . of the upward call of God in Christ Jesus" (Phil. 3:14). Rather than being "conformed to this world" we are called to be "transformed by the renewal of *our* minds that *we* may prove what is the will of God, what is good and acceptable and perfect" (Rom. 12:2, authors' paraphrase). In the midst of change, we are called to recognize the stability of God. In the midst of chaotic and confusing voices, we are called to hear and follow the leading of God. Change need not be frightening or overwhelming. With God's help, we can recognize who we are and who we are called to be. As individuals and members of community, we can be transformed to God's glory, that we may together reflect God's greatness.

Questions for Reflection:

1. Review your *identity-flexible* quotient (chapter 1). In which areas are you less flexible than others (relationships with others, self-honesty, sharing opinions, taking responsibility for others, labeling . . .)? What positive steps should you take to raise your quotient?

2. Take a recent situation in which you have struggled with an

appropriate gender-role response. How did you resolve it? Now answer the questions in Table 12-1. Is there a difference in how you would resolve the situation now?

3. Review your church's *identity-flexible* quotient (Table 12-2). Are you satisfied with this quotient? What suggestions could you make to the church to improve its flexibility?

4. What barriers to change have you personally experienced, either within yourself or outside yourself, in your church or the community. What fears do you have? How might you address the internal barriers? The external ones?

5. Evaluate your gender role now and five years ago. In what ways have you changed? Are you more tolerant now, more self-confident, better integrated into a support group?

6. Based on your self-evaluation, what goals would you like to set for the next five years? What areas continue to concern you? How can you address these?

For Further Reading:

Balswick, Jack, and Judy Balswick. *The Family: A Christian Perspective on the Contemporary Home*. Grand Rapids: Baker Book House, 1989. This book provides a thorough and scholarly discussion of family relations and problems from a Christian perspective. They summarize contemporary societal pressures on families, acknowledge the difficulty of opposing these struggles, and propose a biblical response. Their book ends with sections on "creating a positive environment for families," and "incorporating the biblical ideals of *koinonia* and *shalom* in community and society."

Olson, Richard P. *Changing Male Roles in Today's World*. Valley Forge, Pa.: Judson Press, 1982. Olson evaluates biblical guidelines for modern males, separates cultural guidelines from biblical teaching on the male-female relationship, and challenges men to experience relationships transformed by Christ. He ends by discussing the healing of women, men, and the church.

Payne, Leanne. *Crisis in Masculinity*. Westchester, Ill.: Crossway Books, 1985. Recognizing that society has made it difficult for many men to function competently in our society, Payne shows men how to overcome the problem biblically and challenges them to greater wholeness. Her final chapter is titled "A New Vision, A New Freedom: The Liberated Man from a Christian Perspective," with sections on "I am set free to experience life more fully . . . to experience the life of the Spirit . . . for others."

Rubin, Lillian B. *Intimate Strangers: Men and Women Together*. New York: Harper and Row, 1983. Rubin provides a superb analysis of male- female relationships and the difficulties of these relationships. She concludes by discussing "people in process," and why people find it so hard to change.

van Leeuwen, Mary Stewart. *Gender and Grace: Love, Work and Parenting in a Changing World*. Downers Grove, Ill.: InterVarsity Press, 1990. The author, a Christian psychologist, examines physiological, psychological, and sociological reasons that explain how people grow up as masculine and feminine human beings. She recognizes the stresses of these roles and examines biblical passages and secular literature that suggests minimizing these stresses by alternative, more egalitarian roles.

Notes

Chapter One: *Gender Roles: A Contemporary Crisis*

1. John Fischer, "A Single Person's Identity." From Discovery Papers, a transcript from a sermon delivered by John Fischer at Peninsula Bible Church, Palo Alto, Calif., 5 August 1973.

2. "The Marriage Crunch: If You're a Single Woman, Here Are Your Chances of Getting Married," *Newsweek*, 2 June 1986. The authors of this study have distanced themselves from the 5 percent figure, and Tom and Nancy Biracree note that the low projections in the Yale-Harvard study for older women marrying are based on the assumptions that women will continue to seek older, more highly educated men as spouses. The Biracrees argue that such assumptions may not be accurate and that the actual probability of a thirty-five-year-old college-educated woman marrying by age sixty-five is about 32 percent. See Tom and Nancy Biracree, *Almanac of the American People* (New York: Facts on File, 1988), 189-91.

3. Teresa Jump and Linda Haas, "Fathers in Transition: Dual-Career Fathers Participating in Child Care," in *Changing Men: New Directions in Research on Men and Masculinity*, ed. Michael S. Kimmel (Newbury Park, Calif.: Sage Publications, 1987), 98-114.

Chapter Two: *Identity and Interdependence: In Quest of a Biblical Model*

1. Gilbert Bilezikian, *Beyond Sex Roles: What the Bible Says about a Woman's Place in Church and Family*, 2nd ed. (Grand Rapids: Baker Book House, 1990).

2. James Hurley, *Man and Woman in Biblical Perspective* (Grand Rapids: Zondervan, 1981).

3. John Piper and Wayne A. Grudem, eds., *Recovering Biblical Manhood and Womanhood* (Wheaton, Ill.: Crossway, 1991).

4. Susan Foh, *Women and the Word of God* (Grand Rapids: Baker Book House, 1979).

5. Patricia Gundry, *Heirs Together: Mutual Submission in Marriage* (Grand Rapids: Zondervan, 1980).

6. Berkeley Mickelsen and Alvera Mickelsen, "What Does *Kephalē* Mean in the New Testament?" in *Women, Authority and the Bible*, ed. Alvera Mickelsen (Downers Grove, Ill.: InterVarsity Press, 1986).

7. Walter Kaiser, "Paul, Women, and the Church," *Worldwide Challenge,* (September 1976), 9-12.

8. We gratefully acknowledge, in this section of our discussion, the summary purview of the relevant passages of Scripture provided by Shirley Lees and Sanford Hull. We have borrowed a number of their exegetical observations for the outline below. See Shirley Lees, *The Role of Women* (Leicester, England: InterVarsity Press, 1984). 14-18; and Sanford Hull, "Exegetical Difficulties in the 'Hard Passages,' " Appendix 2 in *Equal to Serve,* Gretchen Gaebelein Hull (Old Tappan, N.J.: Fleming H. Revell, 1987), 251-66.

9. See Phyllis Trible, *God and the Rhetoric of Sexuality* (Philadelphia: Fortress Press, 1978), 90; Bilezikian, *Beyond Sex Roles,* 255; Aida Besancon Spencer, *Beyond the Curse: Women Called to Ministry* (Nashville, Tenn.: Thomas Nelson, 1985), 26-29.

10. See Hurley, *Man and Woman;* and F. LaGard Smith, *Men of Strength for Women of God: Has the Time Come for Shared Spiritual Leadership?* (Eugene, Ore.: Harvest House, 1989).

11. Michael Griffiths, "Husband/Wife Relationships: A Practical Christian Viewpoint," in *The Role of Women,* ed. Shirley Lees (Leicester, England: InterVarsity Press, 1984), 64.

12. Cf. Mickelsen & Mickelsen, "What Does *Kephalē* Mean?" Catherine Clark Kroeger, "The Classical Concept of *Head* as 'Source,' " in *Equal to Serve: Women and Men in the Church and Home,* Gretchen Gaebelein Hull (Old Tappan N.J.: Fleming H. Revell, 1987); and Bilezikian, *Beyond Sex Roles.*

13. For a defense of "headship as authority," see David Field, "Headship in Marriage: The Husband's View," in *The Role of Women,* ed. Shirley Lees (Leicester, England: InterVarsity Press, 1984), 53-58; for a more egalitarian defense, see Griffiths, "Husband/Wife Relationships," 106-112; Mickelsen & Mickelsen, "What Does *Kephalē* Mean?" 97-110.

14. Griffiths, "Husband/Wife Relationships," 64.

15. Cf. Kaiser, "Paul, Woman, and the Church."

16. Note comments on *authentein* "to hold authority" in Catherine Clark Kroeger, "1 Timothy 2:12 – A Classicist's View," in *Women, Authority and the Bible,* ed. Alvera Mickelsen (Downers Grove, Ill.: InterVarsity Press, 1986).

17. This problem is addressed in Linda Raney Wright, *A Cord of Three Strands: Exploring Women's and Men's Roles in Marriage, Family, and the Church* (Old Tappan,

N.J.: Fleming H. Revell, 1987), 90, 194-96. Some scholars note that the point about the absence of women elders is an argument from silence, e.g., there were apparently no black elders either.

18. Some translate this "deaconess," but one must note that the same basic word was used to refer to her as to men.

19. See Wright, *A Cord of Three Strands*, 190. The name, as spelled in contemporary documents, is used to refer only to a woman, not a man.

20. For a discussion of the lack of evidence for this contention and demonstration that the available evidence is confusing, see Wright, *A Cord of Three Strands*, 194-96. For evidence that women did exercise leadership roles in the early church, see Ben Witherington's scholarly study, *Women in the Earliest Churches* (Cambridge, England: Cambridge University Press, 1988), 194-202.

21. Paul Jewett, *Man As Male and Female* (Grand Rapids: Eerdmans, 1975); Gordon Fee and Douglas Stuart, *How to Read the Bible for All It's Worth: A Guide to Understanding the Bible* (Grand Rapids: Zondervan, 1981).

22. Wright, *A Cord of Three Strands*, 229.

23. Ibid., 37-38, 42-45.

24. Ibid., 81, 114.

25. David Augsburger, *Sustaining Love: Healing and Growth in the Passages of Marriage* (Ventura, Calif.: Regal Books, 1988), 136.

26. Quoted from Augsburger, *Sustaining Love*, 136.

27. Ibid., p. 155

Chapter Three: *A Developmental Model of Gender-Mature Spirituality*

1. Paul Tournier, *The Gift of Feeling* (Atlanta: John Knox Press, 1981), 102.

2. Ibid., 110.

3. Walter Trobisch, *All a Man Can Be: and What A Woman Should Know* (Downers Grove, Ill.: InterVarsity Press, 1983), 73.

4. Ibid., 89.

5. Bill Gothard, *Institute in Basic Youth Conflicts: Research in Principles of Life* (Oak Brook, Ill.: Institute in Basic Youth Conflicts, 1975); Wilfred Bockelman, *Gothard*

the Man and His Ministry: An Evaluation (Santa Barbara, Calif.: Quill Publications, 1976), 78.

6. See Field, "Headship in Marriage"; and Piper and Grudem, *Biblical Manhood and Womanhood*, especially pp. 35-52. (Neo-traditionalistis have used "complementarian" to describe themselves, although both those who espouse the neo-traditional and the egalitarian positions value male/female complementarity, recognizing that male/female relationships in many ways are—and should be—complementary.)

7. For biblical feminists who support male headship defined in this way, see, e.g., Mickelsen and Mickelsen. "What Does *Kephalē* Mean?"; Bilezikian, *Beyond Sex Roles*. For biblical feminists who deemphasize authority, emphasizing instead mutual submission and egalitarianism, see Jack Balswick and Judith Balswick, *The Family: A Christian Perspective on the Contemporary Home* (Grand Rapids: Baker Book House, 1989).

8. See Betty Friedan, *The Second Stage* (New York: Summit Books, 1981); Susan Miller Okin, *Justice, Gender, and the Family* (New York: Basic Books, 1989).

9. Carin Rubenstein, "The American Gender Evolution: Getting What We Want," *New Woman*, November 1990, 62-65.

10. Gretchen Gaebelein Hull, *Equal to Serve: Women and Men in the Church and Home* (Old Tappan, N.J.: Fleming H. Revell, 1987), 240-41.

Chapter Four: *Becoming Male and Female: Myths and Realities*

1. Diana Baumrind, "Current Patterns of Parental Authority," *Developmental Psychology Monographs* (1971): 1-103.

2. Rhoda Unger, "Toward a Redefinition of Sex and Gender," *American Psychologist* 34 (1979): 1085-1094.

3. Eleanor E. Maccoby and Carol N. Jacklin, *The Psychology of Sex Differences* (Stanford, Calif.: Stanford University Press, 1974).

4. When spatial ability is measured, one is asked, for example: What would this pattern look like from the other side? and, Is this a left foot or a right foot?

5. Anne Moir and David Jessel, *Brain Sex* (New York: Lyle Stuart, 1991), 17-19, 54-58.

6. Ibid., 48-49, 110.

7. Ibid., 16-19, 42-47, 91.

8. Beryl Lieff Benderly, *The Myth of Two Minds: What Gender Means and Doesn't Mean* (New York: Doubleday, 1987), 1.

9. Carol Gilligan, *In a Different Voice* (Cambridge, Mass.: Harvard University Press, 1982).

10. C. Stephen Evans, *Preserving the Person: A Look at the Human Sciences* (Downers Grove, Ill.: InterVarsity Press, 1977).

11. For a historical view of why this has happened, see the following authors: Richard Olson, *Changing Male Roles in Today's World* (Valley Forge, Pa.: Judson Press, 1982); Zillah Eisenstein, *The Radical Future of Liberal Feminism* (Boston: Northeastern University Press, 1981); Jewett, *Man As Male and Female.*

12. Moir and Jessel, *Brain Sex,* 78–85, 172–73.

13. We cannot, however, accept these standards as biblical guides to the appropriate use of power and appropriate success. See chapter 5.

14. J.S. Bruner, J.J. Goodnow, and G.A. Austin, *A Study of Thinking* (New York: Wiley, 1956).

15. Daniel Levinson, *The Seasons of a Man's Life* (New York: Ballantine, 1978), 17; and Moir and Jessel, *Brain Sex,* 86, 181.

16. See chapter 10.

Chapter Five: *The Total (and Totaled) Woman*

1. Betty Friedan, *The Feminine Mystique* (New York: Dell, 1963).

2. See Betty Friedan, *The Second Stage* (New York: Summit Books, 1981).

3. Described, e.g., in E. Mavis Hetherington and Ross D. Parke, *Child Psychology: A Contemporary Viewpoint,* 3rd ed. (New York: McGraw-Hill, 1986).

4. Ibid.

5. Anne Wilson Schaef, *Escape from Intimacy* (San Francisco: Harper & Row, 1989).

6. For discussion of the development of this problem, see Susan Schenkel, *Giving Away Success* (New York: McGraw-Hill, 1984).

7. See Deborah Tannen, *You Just Don't Understand: Women and Men in Conversation* (New York: McGraw-Hill, 1990).

8. Ibid.

9. "Average Pay for Women Is Reportedly Two-thirds That of Men," *Boston Globe*, 26 April 1990, 11.

10. Patricia Gundry, "Why We're Here," in *Women, Authority and the Bible*, Mickelsen.

11. See Carol Tavris and Carole Wade. *The Longest War: Sex Differences in Perspective*, 2nd ed. (San Diego: Harcourt Brace Jovanovich, 1984).

12. Brannon, cited in Edward Thompson and Joseph Pleck, "The Structure of Male Role Norms," in *Changing Men: New Directions in Research on Men and Masculinity*, ed. Michael Kimmel (Newbury Park, Calif.: Sage Publications, 1987).

13. Maccoby and Jacklin, *The Psychology of Sex Differences*.

14. I. Broverman, et al., "Sex-Role Stereotypes: A Current Appraisal," *Journal of Social Issues* 28 (1972): 59-78.

15. Anne Wilson Schaef, *Women's Reality* (Minneapolis: Winston Press, 1981), 100, 132-34, 138.

16. One specialist, interestingly, speculates that because male decision-making occurs in more specialized patterns in the brain than female decision-making, males sometimes make decisions faster because they sort through fewer aspects of the question at hand. See Moir and Jessel, *Brain Sex*, 169.

17. For discussion of the healthy ways in which women can use power and conflict, see Jean Baker Miller, *Toward a New Psychology of Women*, 2nd ed. (Boston: Beacon Press, 1986).

18. Janet Shibley Hyde, *Half the Human Experience: The Psychology of Women* (Lexington, Mass.: D.C. Heath, 1985), 160-62.

19. Francine Prose, "Confident at 11, Confused at 16," *New York Times Magazine*, 7 December 1990, 22-25, 37-38, 40, 45–46.

20. Ibid., 23.

21. Susan A. Basow, *Gender Stereotypes: Traditions and Alternatives*, 2nd ed. (Monterey, Calif.: Brooks/Cole, 1986).

22. Ibid.

23. Schenkel, *Giving Away Success.*

24. Pauline Rose Clance, *The Imposter Phenomenon: Overcoming the Fear That Haunts Your Success* (Atlanta: Peachtree Press, 1985).

25. Natalie Shainess, *Sweet Suffering* (Indianapolis: Bobbs-Merrill, 1984).

26. Items and scoring scale adapted from Ibid., 13-15.

27. Kaye V. Cook, "If Life's So Good, Why Do I Feel So Bad?" *Stillpoint* 3 (Summer 1988), 14-16.

28. D.S. Bailey provides this summary in his *Sexual Relation in Christian Thought* (New York: Harper & Bros., 1959), 63-64.

29. In her popular volume, Susan Brownmiller, *Femininity* (New York: Simon and Schuster, 1984), discusses a variety of ways in which Western women have been socialized to decorate or shape their bodies to meet their society's criteria of feminine attractiveness.

30. David M. Garner, et al., "Cultural Expectations of Thinness in Women," *Psychological Reports* 47 (1980): 483-91.

31. For an extended discussion of the biblical confusions around appearance, see Helen Bray Garretson and Kaye V. Cook, *Chaotic Eating: A Christian Guide to Recovery* (Grand Rapids: Zondervan, 1992).

Chapter Six: *Modern Masculinity: In Transition from Macho to Sensitive*

1. Adapted from Alan Loy McGinnis, *The Friendship Factor.*

2. This story is recounted in Herb Goldberg's *The New Male: From Macho to Sensitive But Still All Male* (New York: Signet, 1980), 29-30.

3. Brannon, cited in Thompson and Pleck, "Male Role Norms," in *Changing Men,* Kimmel.

4. McGinnis, *The Friendship Factor,* 20.

5. See Harold Robbins, "Must Men Be Friendless?" *Leadership* 5 (Fall 1984): 24-29.

6. Dan Benson, *The Total Man* (Wheaton, Ill.: Tyndale House, 1977), 75.

7. Lillian Rubin, *Intimate Strangers: Men and Women Together* (New York: Harper and Row, 1983), 161.

8. Quoted in David Smith, *The Friendless Amerian Male* (Ventura, Calif.: Regal Books, 1985), 14.

9. Ibid., 85.

10. James Alsdurf and Phyllis Alsdurf, *Battered into Submission: The Tragedy of Wife Abuse in the Christian Home* (Downers Grove, Ill.: InterVarsity Press, 1989).

11. Smith, *Friendless American Male,* 50.

12. Cited in Robbins, "Must Men Be Friendless?" 25.

13. Robbins, "Must Men Be Friendless?" 26-27.

14. Ibid.

15. Olson, *Changing Male Roles.*

16. Robbins, "Must Men Be Friendless?" 27.

17. Herbert Freudenberger, "Today's Troubled Men," *Psychology Today,* December 1987, 46-47.

18. Rubin, *Intimate Strangers,* 73.

19. Ibid., 74-75. See also Tannen, *You Don't Understand,* 80-83.

20. Gordon Dalbey, *Healing the Masculine Soul* (Waco, Texas: Word Inc., 1988), 64.

21. On problems men have with such sharing, see Anne Moir and David Jessel, *Brain Sex* (New York: Lyle Stuart, 1991), 135-37.

22. Benson, *Total Man,* 176.

23. Ted Dodson, cited in Dalbey, *Healing the Masculine Soul,* 13-14. There is also evidence that father-child bonding occurs more slowly than mother-child bonding. See Moir and Jessel, *Brain Sex,* pp. 141-45.

24. Cathy Skrzycki, "More Fathers Taking Up Their Paternity Benefits," *International Herald Tribune,* 27 December 1990, 9, 11.

25. Tavris and Wade, *The Longest War.*

26. For a review of this issue see, Robert A. Lewis, "Men's Changing Roles in Marriage and the Family," in *Men's Changing Roles in the Family,* ed. Robert A. Lewis and Marvin B. Sussman (New York: Haworth Press, 1986).

27. Samuel Osherson, *Finding Our Fathers* (New York: Fawcett Columbine, 1986),

28. Benson, *Total Man*, 178 (italics in original).

29. Dodson, cited in Dalbey, *Healing the Masculine Soul*, 13-14.

30. Ibid.

31. Dalbey, *Healing the Masculine Soul*.

32. Ibid.

33. Rubin, *Intimate Strangers*.

34. Mary Stewart van Leeuwen, *Gender and Grace: Love, Work, and Parenting in a Changing World*, (Downers Grove, Ill.: InterVarsity Press, 1990).

35. Moir and Jessel, *Brain Sex*, 55-56.

36. This observation refers to two-parent homes. In single-parent homes, children need close relationships with caring men, who can be either friends or family members.

37. Osherson, *Finding Our Fathers*, 6-7.

38. See Gregory Herek, "On Heterosexual Masculinity: Some Psychical Consequences of the Social Construction of Gender and Sexuality," in *Changing Men*, Kimmel, 69-70.

39. Balswick and Balswick, *The Family*, 157, van Leeuwen, *Gender and Grace*, 57. On males and aggression, see also Moir and Jessel, *Brain Sex*, 80-82.

40. Henry J.M. Nouwen, *The Road to Daybreak: A Spiritual Journey* (New York: Image Books/Doubleday, 1988), 30-31, 220-27.

41. Rubenstein, "The American Gender Evolution," 62-65.

Chapter Seven: *The New Male and Female: Great Expectations and Their Stresses*

1. Joseph Pleck, *The Myth of Masculinity* (Cambridge, Mass.: MIT Press, 1981).

2. Ibid., 133-34.

3. James Doyle, *The Male Experience*, 2nd ed. (Dubuque, Iowa: Brown Publishers, 1989).

4. Brannon, cited in Thompson and Pleck, "Male Role Norms," in *Changing Men*, Kimmel.

5. Rubin, *Intimate Strangers.*

6. Ibid., 90.

7. Ibid.

8. Tavris and Wade, *The Longest War.*

9. For a nice discussion of Miriam, Rahab, Jael, Huldah, and Abigail, in addition to Deborah and the Proverbs 31 woman, see Hull, *Equal to Serve*, 109-13.

Chapter Eight: *Relationships: Avoiding Stereotypes and Being a Friend*

1. Gilligan, *In a Different Voice.*

2. Tom Biracree and Nancy Biracree, *The Almanac of the American People* (New York: Facts on File, 1988), 75.

3. Schaef, *Women's Reality*, 130-31.

4. Gilligan, *In a Different Voice.*

5. See Edward Fiske, "Lessons: Even at a Former Women's College, Male Students Are Taken More Seriously, a Researcher Finds," *New York Times*, 11 April 1990, section B8; and Moir and Jessel, *Brain Sex*, 48, 170-73.

6. Tannen, *You Don't Understand*, 235-37.

7. Schaef, *Women's Reality*, 131.

8. Ibid., 113. See also Moir and Jessel, *Brain Sex*, 167-68 on women's perception of work.

9. Tannen, *You Don't Understand*, 144-45.

10. Joanna Bunker Rohrbaugh, *Women: Psychology's Puzzle* (New York: Basic Books, 1979), 229.

11. Jean Baker Miller, *Toward a New Psychology of Women*, 2nd ed. (Boston: Beacon Press, 1986).

12. Ibid.

13. Ibid., 125.

14. Ibid.

Chapter Nine: *Singleness: Living In A Couples' World*

1. Margaret Evening, *Who Walk Alone: A Consideration of the Single Life* (Downers Grove, Ill.: InterVarsity Press, 1974).

2. See Leonard Cargan and Matthew Melko, *Singles: Myths and Realities* (Beverly Hills: Sage Publications, 1982) for evidence that the number of singles is increasing and J. Peter Stein, ed., *Single Life: Unmarried Adults in Social Context* (New York: St. Martin's Press, 1981) for an explanation of why. See also William Novak, *The Great American Man Shortage—and Other Roadblocks to Romance* (New York: Rawson Associates, 1983) for a discussion of gender differences in singleness.

3. Bureau of the Census, *Statistical Abstract of the United States: 1990*, 110th ed. (Washington: Bureau of the Census, 1990).

4. J. Peter Stein, "The Never-Marrieds: Introduction," in *Single Life: Unmarried Adults in Social Context*, ed. J. Peter Stein (New York: St. Martin's Press, 1981).

5. "Living Alone and Loving It," *U.S. News and World Report*, August 1987, 52-60.

6. See, e.g., Stein, "The Never-Marrieds."

7. Bureau of the Census, *Statistical Abstract 1990*.

8. Novak, *Great American Man Shortage*.

9. Despite these differences, recent predictions are that 90 percent of individuals will marry in their lifetime.

10. Keith Bradsher, "For Every Five Young Women, Six Young Men," *New York Times*, 17 January 1990, section C1, 10.

11. Stein, "The Never-Marrieds."

12. Christine Doudna with Fern McBride, "Where Are the Men for the Women at the Top?" in *Single Life: Unmarried Adults in Social Context*, ed. J. Peter Stein, (New York: St. Martin's Press, 1981).

13. Cargan and Melko, *Singles: Myths and Realities*.

14. Barna Research Group, *Single Adults in America* (Glendale, Calif.: Barna Research Group, 1987), 77.

15. Barna Research Group, *Single Adults*, 40-43.

16. Stein, "The Never-Marrieds."

17. Barna Research, *Single Adults,* 79.

18. Harold Ivan Smith, *Singles Ask: Answers to Questions about Relationships and Sexual Issues* (Minneapolis: Augsburg, 1988), 68.

19. See our further discussion of this topic in chapter 10.

20. R.B. Thieme, Jr., *Right Man/Right Woman* (Houston: Vanity Press, n.d.).

21. Smith, *Singles Ask,* 80.

Chapter Ten: *Successfully Negotiating the Dating Game*

1. Raina Sacks, "The Dating Game," *In View,* May/June 1990, 16.

2. Megan Jenkins and Faye Dambrot, "The Attribution of Date Rape: Observer's Attitudes and Sexual Experiences and the Dating Situation," *Journal of Applied Psychology* 17 (October 1987): 875-95.

3. "Study Shows Church Kids Are Not Waiting," *Christianity Today,* 18 March 1988, 54-55.

4. Lewis Smedes, *Sex for Christians* (Grand Rapids: Eerdmans, 1976), 24-25.

5. Howard Frost, "Purity and Passion: A Biblical Approach To Mutually Edifying Relationships" *Priscilla Papers* 5 (Summer 1991): 10-13.

6. John Holzmann, *Dating with Integrity* (Brentwood, Tenn.: Wolgemuth and Hyatt, 1990).

Chapter Eleven: *Marriage: Old Dance, New Steps*

1. Morton Hunt, *The Natural History of Love* (New York: Alfred Knopf, 1959), 146-47; George Duby, *Medieval Marriage,* trans. Elborg Forster (Baltimore: John Hopkins University Press, 1978), 16-17.

2. "After all," said Martin Luther, "didn't Joshua command the sun to stand still, not the earth?" Here he was referring to Joshua 10, where God lengthened a period of daylight of about twenty-four hours in order for the Israelites to finish the destruction of their enemies.

3. Gundry, *Heirs Together,* 49-51.

4. Ibid., 57.

5. Ibid., 67-68.

6. Tavris and Wade, *The Longest War,* 269; U.S. Department of Labor, "Facts on Working Women," Bureau of Labor Statistics report 89-93, August 1989.

7. Susan Bianchi and Daphne Spain, *Wives Who Earn More Than Their Husbands,* Special Demographic Analysis CDS-80-9 (Washington: Department of Commerce, Bureau of the Census, 1983).

8. Carin Rubenstein, "The American Gender Evolution: Getting What We Want," *New Woman,* (November 1990), 62-65.

9. Balswick and Balswick, *The Family,* 260-62; *Statistical Abstracts of the United States: 1991,* 111th ed. (Washington: Bureau of the Census, 1991), 62.

10. William Lederer and Don Jackson, *The Mirages of Marriage* (New York: W.W. Norton, 1968), 39.

11. Richard Koestner, Carol Franz, and Joel Weinberger, "The Family Origins of Empathic Concern: A Twenty-Six-Year Longitudinal Study," *Journal of Personality and Social Psychology* 58 (1990): 709-17.

12. Carol Hymowitz, "Wives of Jobless Men Support Some Families—but at Heavy Cost." *Wall Street Journal,* 8 December 1982, section A1, 25.

13. Hurley, *Man and Woman in Biblical Perspective.*

14. Piper and Grudem, *Biblical Manhood and Womanhood.*

15. Foh, *Women and the Word of God.*

16. Bilezikian, *Beyond Sex Roles.*

17. Hull, *Equal to Serve.*

18. Wright, *A Cord of Three Strands.*

19. Howard Markman, et al., "Prevention of Marital Distress: A Longitudinal Investigation," *Journal of Counseling and Clinical Psychology* 56 (April 1988): 210-17.

20. Balswick and Balswick, *The Family,* 211.

21. Gundry, *Heirs Together,* 14.

22. John Gottman and Lowell Krokoff, "Marital Interaction and Satisfaction: A Longitudinal Study," *Journal of Consulting and Clinical Psychology* 57 (February 1989): 47-52.

23. Cf. Noatrius and N. Vanzetti, cited in Gottman and Krokoff, "Marital Interaction."

24. See Balswick and Balswick, *The Family;* Gundry, *Heirs Together;* James Fairfield, *When You Don't Agree* (Scottdale, Pa.: Herald Press, 1977); Lederer and Jackson, *The Mirages of Marriage.*

25. Rubin, *Intimate Strangers,* 77.

26. Ibid., 80.

27. Wright, *A Cord of Three Strands,* 113-14.

28. Rubin, *Intimate Strangers,* 86.

Chapter Twelve: *Toward the Future: Redeeming Man and Woman in Community and the Church*

1. Bradsher, "For Every Five Young Women."

2. Alvin Toffler, *Future Shock* (New York: Bantam, 1971).

3. Joseph Pleck, *The Myth of Masculinity.*

4. Felice N. Schwartz, "Management Women and the New Facts of Life," *Harvard Business Review* (January-February 1989): 65-76.

5. See, e.g., Sarah Hardesty and Nehama Jacobs, *Success and Betrayal: The Crisis of Women in Corporate America* (New York: Simon & Schuster, 1986); Amy Saltzman, "Trouble at the Top," *U.S. News and World Report,* 17 June 1991, 40-48.

6. Tavris and Wade, *The Longest War,* 5.

Index

addiction to relationship   94
adolescence   67, 70, 79, 98
Alsdurf, James and Phyllis   248
androgeny   73
Augsburger, David   43
balanced lives   255–56
Balswick, Jack and Judith   62, 85, 112, 134, 157, 248, 268
Barna Research Group   186
Benderly, Beryl Lieff   70, 85
Benson, David   124
biblical interpretations of femininity (traditional, neo-traditional, biblical feminist, secularist)   55–56
"big wheel"   117, 119, 127–28, 132
bike-riding metaphor   43
Bilezikian, Gilbert   30–31, 238
Block, Joel   120
body, emphasis on physical appearance   91, 105–6
buddyships   121
burnout   104, 138–41
Carli, Lina   180
Carr, Jacquelyn   157
childrearing   143–44, 147, 246
church, role of in gender relations   18
    being conformed to this world   20
commitment   176
communication in marriage   243–46
competition   120, 128, 169–73
complementarian   3
complementarity in relationships   33, 75
conflict resolution   173–76
cultural knowledge   67
Dalbey, Gordon   125, 134
dance/ballet metaphor   39, 226, 238–43
dating, meeting people for   204
    changes in style   205
    communication in   207–8, 214–15
Davis, Keith   180
decision-making styles   165–69
delaying marriage, reasons   183–84
dependency, problems of   93–94
discounting   100
double binds   123, 148–50
Doyle, James   145, 157

eating disorders   91, 106
effects of the Fall   33
empowerment   44, 99
equality of men and women before God   32
Evans, Stephen   73
Fairfield, James   248
fathers, relationships with sons   123–24, 127–28
    time with children   16, 143–44
female, dependence   92–96
    devaluing of qualities   95
    gender-role conflicts survey   107
    misunderstandings   92
    modern   89–92
    separation of work and family life   91
    socialization   91–93
    traditional   89–90
femininity-achievement conflict   98
Fields, Doug   201
finding a mate (models for)   220–21
Fischer, John   15
flexibility, implications of   42–44
    vs. fixation   42
    see also virtues, identity-flexible model
flexible gender identity, development of   44–47, 152–54
    see also identity-fixed and -flexible model
Foh, Susan   30–31, 238
gender-role differences, in psychological literature   161
    in Bible   31–37
    in church   35
    in society   36
gender-role maturity   56
    stages   57–59
gender roles, strain   145–46
    traditional relationships   82
gender roles, opening survey   23
gender roles, quiz   145
Gilligan, Carol   71, 98, 161
"give 'em hell"   117, 120, 128, 132–33
"glass ceiling"   171, 253
Goldberg, Herb   120
Gothard, Bill   55
Grudem, Wayne   30–31, 48, 238
Gundry, Patricia   30–31, 112, 157, 248
Hardesty, Sarah   112
Haynor, Steve   221
headship   34, 237–38
Hershey, Terry   224
Hoffman, Lois Wladis   112

Holzmann, John   224
Houck, Catherine   180
Hull, Gretchen Gaebelein   61, 238
Hurley, James   30–31, 238
identity-fixed and -flexible model, author   31, 38, 42, 51, 260–61
    see also virtues, identity -flexible model
identity-flexible model of marriage   246
identity-flexibility quotient   52–54
imago dei   32, 266
"imposter phenomenon"   101
interdependence   196–98
intimacy, male-male   117, 120–21
    male-female   121–23
Jacobs, Nehama   112
Kaiser, Walter   31
learned helplessness   79, 94–95
Lees, Shirley   48, 113
Levinson, Daniel   79, 120
Lynn, David   134
Maccoby, Eleanor and Jacklin, Carol   69
macho, and Christianity   119, 121, 125–26
    problems from being   75, 117-18
male, early socialization   123–24, 127–28
    fatherhood   123–25
    gender role conflicts survey   129–31
marriage, changes in   226–31
    moving from dating to   214–17
    scripts   17, 79
    types of relationships (traditional, transitional, egalitarian)   233–34
marriage squeeze   185
masochism   101–5
masochism scale   102–3
Mason, Mike   249
McDowell, Josh   225
McGinnis, Alan Loy   135, 180, 225
Mickelson, Berkeley and Alvera   30–31
Miller, Jean Baker   113
moment of resistance   98
"mommy track"   253
myths, of choice   68, 80, 255
    of gender constancy   68, 78
    of gender difference   69
    of gender stereotypes   75
    of invulnerability   75, 117-18
Piper, John   30–31, 48, 238
Rubin, Lillian   85, 126, 147, 249, 269
Scanzoni, Letha Dawson   113
Schaef, Anne Wilson   97

Schenkel, Susan   100, 181
Scott, Niki   181
self-esteem   93–94
self-nurturance   104–5
self-efficacy   104
sensitivity, and success   146–47
in dating   216–17
in marriage   254
sex roles   68
sexual struggle in dating   217–19
sharing credit/taking blame   99–101
singles in the church   186–88
Smedes, Lewis   218
Smith, David   120, 135
Smith, Harold   194, 201
spiritual aspects of life, primacy   37
in dating relationships   187–88, 219
Stafford, Tim   201, 249
stereotypes, benefits   77, 92
of men   117, 128, 136
of women   92, 95, 136–37
risks   77–78
Stout, Martha   113
"sturdy oak"   117, 120, 127–28, 132
submission   33
success, definitions of   146–47
and Christianity   142–43, 146
"Superwoman burnout"   138–42, 253
Temple, Todd   201
Toffler, Alvin   252
tolerance: see virtues, identity-flexible model
Tournier, Paul   51, 62, 85
Trobisch, Walter   51, 63, 202
Unger, Rhoda   68
van Leeuwen, Mary Stewart   63, 86, 113, 126, 135, 158, 269
virtues, identity-flexible model,
applied to dating relationships   205, 221–22
applied to friendship relationships   161, 179
as alternatives to stereotypes   74, 78, 84
as minimizing the stresses of modernity   153–54
definitions   50, 54–55
exercised in living as a single and with singles   195–99
in marriage   237, 246–47
in relationships with men   132–33
Ward, Patricia   114
"weirdness" in relationship   15
Wright, Linda Raney   38, 40, 238, 249
Yale-Harvard study   16